PLAY, GENDER, THERAPY

PSYCHOANALYTIC IDEAS AND APPLICATIONS SERIES
IPA Publications Committee

Gennaro Saragnano (Rome), Chair and General Editor; Leticia Glocer Fiorini (Buenos Aires), Consultant; Samuel Arbiser (Buenos Aires); Paulo Cesar Sandler (São Paulo); Christian Seulin (Lyon); Mary Kay O'Neil (Montreal); Gail S. Reed (New York); Catalina Bronstein (London); Rhoda Bawdekar (London), Ex-officio as Publications Officer; Paul Crake (London): IPA Executive Director (ex-officio)

Other titles in the Series include
(For a full listing, see our website www.karnacbooks.com)

Good Feelings: Psychoanalytic Reflections on Positive Emotions and Attitudes
    edited by Salman Akhtar
Psychosomatics Today: A Psychoanalytical Perspective
    edited by Marilia Aisenstein and Lisa Rappoport de Aisemberg
Illusions and Disillusions of Psychoanalytic Work
    André Green
Primitive Agony and Symbolization
    René Roussillon
In the Traces of Our Name: The Influence of Given Names in Life
    Juan Eduardo Tesone
Psychic Reality in Context: Perspectives on Psychoanalysis, Personal History, and Trauma
    Marion Michel Oliner
Shame and Humiliation: A Dialogue between Psychoanalytic and Systemic Approaches
    Carlos Guillermo Bigliani and Rodolfo Moguilansky
Theory of Psychoanalytical Practice: A Relational Process Approach
    Juan Tubert-Oklander
Art in Psychoanalysis: A Contemporary Approach to Creativiy and Analytic Practice
    edited by Gabriela Goldstein
The Female Body: Inside and Outside
    edited by Ingrid Moeslein-Teising and Frances Thomson-Salo
Death and Identity: Being and the Psycho-Sexual Drama
    Michel de M'Uzan
Unrepresented States and the Construction of Meaning: Clinical and Theoretical Contributions
    edited by Howard B. Levine and Gail S. Reed
Hostile and Malignant Prejudice: Psychoanalytic Approaches
    edited by Cyril Levitt
The Ethical Seduction of the Analytic Situation: The Feminine–Maternal Origins of Responsibility for the Other
    Viviane Chetrit-Vatine
Time for Change: Tracking Transformations in Psychoanalysis— The Three-Level Model
    edited by Marina Altmann de Litvan

PLAY, GENDER, THERAPY

Selected Papers of Eleanor Galenson

Edited by

Nellie L. Thompson

Psychoanalytic Ideas and Applications Series

LONDON AND NEW YORK

First published 2015 by
Karnac Books Ltd.

Published 2018 by Routledge
2 Park Square, Milton Park, Abingdon, Oxon OX14 4RN
711 Third Avenue, New York, NY 10017, USA

Routledge is an imprint of the Taylor & Francis Group, an informa business

Copyright © 2015 to Nellie L. Thompson for the edited collection and to the individual authors for their contributions

The rights of the contributors to be identified as the authors of this work have been asserted in accordance with §§ 77 and 78 of the Copyright Design and Patents Act 1988.

All rights reserved. No part of this book may be reprinted or reproduced or utilised in any form or by any electronic, mechanical, or other means, now known or hereafter invented, including photocopying and recording, or in any information storage or retrieval system, without permission in writing from the publishers.

Notice:
Product or corporate names may be trademarks or registered trademarks, and are used only for identification and explanation without intent to infringe.

British Library Cataloguing in Publication Data

A C.I.P. for this book is available from the British Library

ISBN 9781782200260 (pbk)

Edited, designed and produced by The Studio Publishing Services Ltd
www.publishingservicesuk.co.uk
e-mail: studio@publishingservicesuk.co.uk

CONTENTS

ACKNOWLEDGEMENTS ix

ABOUT THE EDITOR AND CONTRIBUTORS xiii

INTRODUCTION xv
  Nellie L. Thompson

PROLOGUE
Interview with Eleanor Galenson xxv
  Milton Senn

PROLOGUE
Our children, our future: li
a conversation with Eleanor Galenson
  Lucy LaFarge

PART I
SYMBOLISATION, THOUGHT, AND LANGUAGE

Introduction to Part I 3
  Patricia Nachman

CHAPTER ONE
A consideration of the nature of thought in childhood play   15
Eleanor Galenson

Discussion of Chapter One   35
Phyllis Greenacre

CHAPTER TWO
The impact of early sexual discovery on mood, defensive organisation, and symbolisation   47
Eleanor Galenson and Herman Roiphe

Discussion of Chapter Two   67
Phyllis Greenacre

CHAPTER THREE
The influence of hostile aggression on the development of expressive language   73
Eleanor Galenson

PART II
INFANTILE ORIGINS OF SEXUAL IDENTITY

Introduction to Part II   81
Lucy LaFarge

CHAPTER FOUR
Early genital activity and the castration complex   93
Herman Roiphe and Eleanor Galenson

CHAPTER FIVE
Object loss and early sexual development   107
Eleanor Galenson and Herman Roiphe

Discussion of Chapter Five   123
Albert Solnit

CHAPTER SIX
Observation of early infantile sexual and erotic development   129
Eleanor Galenson

CHAPTER SEVEN
Review of *The Infantile Origins of Sexual Identity*   143
    Elizabeth Lloyd Mayer

CHAPTER EIGHT
Review of *The Infantile Origins of Sexual Identity*   151
    Jerome D. Oremland

PART III
THE TRIPARTITE THERAPEUTIC MODEL

CHAPTER NINE
Treatment of psychological disorders of early childhood: 161
a tripartite therapeutic model
    Eleanor Galenson

CHAPTER TEN
Gender disturbance in a three-and-a-half-year-old boy   177
    Eleanor Galenson and Barbara Fields

CHAPTER ELEVEN
Psychoanalytic approach to psychotic disturbances in   191
very young children: a clinical report
    Eleanor Galenson

INDEX   211

ACKNOWLEDGEMENTS

Lucy LaFarge, "Our Children, Our Future: A Conversation with Eleanor Galenson", The American Psychoanalyst, 25: 11–13, 1991. Copyright © 1991 The American Psychoanalytic Association. Reprinted with permission of The American Psychoanalyst.

"A Consideration of the Nature of Thought in Childhood Play", Eleanor Galenson in J. B. McDevitt, & C. F. Settlage (Eds.), *Separation–Individuation: Essays in Honor of Margaret Mahler*. Copyright © 1971, International Universities Press. Reprinted with the permission of the Executors of the Estate of Eleanor Galenson.

Discussion by Phyllis Greenacre, "A Consideration of the Nature of Thought in Childhood Play", in J. B. McDevitt, & C. F. Settlage (Eds.), *Separation–Individuation: Essays in Honor of Margaret Mahler*. Copyright © 1971, International Universities Press. Reprinted with the permission of Eric Richter, Executor of the estate of the late Peter Richter, M.D.

"The Impact of Early Sexual Discovery on Mood, Defensive Organization and Symbolization", Eleanor Galenson and Herman Roiphe, *Psychoanalytic Study of the Child*, 26: 195–216. Copyright © 1972, Ruth S. Eissler, Anna Freud, Marianne Kris, and Seymour L.

Lustman. This material is reprinted with the permission of Yale University Press.

"The Influence of Hostile Aggression on the Development of Expressive Language", Eleanor Galenson, in T. B. Cohen, M. H. Etezady, & B. L. Pacella (Eds.), *The Vulnerable Child, Vol. 2*. Copyright © 1995. International Universities Press. Reprinted with the permission of the Executors of the Estate of Eleanor Galenson.

"Early Genital Activity and the Castration Complex", Herman Roiphe & Eleanor Galenson, *The Psychoanalytic Quarterly*, 41(3): 334–347. Copyright © 1972, by *The Psychoanalytic Quarterly*. This material is reproduced with permission of John Wiley & Sons, Inc.

"Object Loss and Early Sexual Development", Herman Roiphe & Eleanor Galenson, *The Psychoanalytic Quarterly*, 42(1): 73–90. Copyright © 1973 *The Psychoanalytic Quarterly*. This material is reproduced with permission of John Wiley & Sons, Inc.

Discussion by Albert Solnit of "Object Loss and Early Sexual Development" by Herman Roiphe and Eleanor Galenson is published with the permission of Benjamin Solnit, Executor of Estate of Albert Solnit, M. D.

"Observation of Early Infantile and Sexual Erotic Development", Eleanor Galenson. Reprinted from *Handbook of Sexology, Vol. 7. Childhood and Adolescent Sexuality*. E. M. Perry (Ed.), pp. 169–178, 1990. Copyright © 1990 Elsevier Publishers B. V. (Biomedical Division). Reprinted with the permission of Elsevier.

Elizabeth Lloyd Mayer, Book Review, *The Infantile Origins of Sexual Identity* by Herman Roiphe and Eleanor Galenson. International Universities Press, 1981. 301 pages. *The International Journal of Psychoanalysis*, 1983, 64(3), pp. 365–369. Copyright © 1983 The Institute of Psychoanalysis. Reproduced with permission of Blackwell Publishing Ltd.

Jerome Oremland, Book Review, *The Infantile Origins of Sexual Identity* by Herman Roiphe and Eleanor Galenson. International Universities

Press, 1981. 301 pages. *Journal of the American Psychoanalytic Association*, 33(3), pp. 678–684. Copyright © 1985 American Psychoanalytic Association. This material is reprinted with the permission of SAGE Publications.

"Treatment of psychological disorders of early childhood: a tripartite therapeutic model", by Eleanor Galenson. In S. Akhtar & H. Parens (Eds.), *Beyond the Symbiotic Orbit: Advances in Separation–Individuation Theory*. Copyright © 1991 The Analytic Press. Reprinted with the permission of Taylor and Francis Group, LLC.

"Gender Disturbance in a 3½ Year-Old Boy", Eleanor Galenson and Barbara Fields. In: S. Dowling, & A. Rothstein (Eds.), *The Significance of Infant Observational Research for Clinical Work with Children, Adolescents and Adults*, Workshop Series of the American Psychoanalytic Association, Monograph 5. Copyright © 1989, The American Psychoanalytic Association. International Universities Press. Permission to reprint this paper granted by the American Psychoanalytic Association.

"Psychoanalytic approach to psychotic disturbances in very young children: a clinical report", by Eleanor Galenson. *Hillside Journal of Clinical Psychiatry* 6(x), pp. 221–240. International Universities Press, 1984. Reprinted with the permission of the Executors of the Estate of Eleanor Galenson.

ABOUT THE EDITOR AND CONTRIBUTORS

Barbara Fields, MSW, is a child therapist in private practice in New York.

Phyllis Greenacre, MD (1894–1989), was a leading figure in the New York Psychoanalytic Society and Institute. A broad range of problems captured Greenacre's interest during her fifty-year career as a psychoanalyst: the reverberating impact of early trauma on psychic development; early ego and superego development, fetishism and perversion; the role of reconstruction in clinical technique and the dynamics of transference; and papers on creativity and creative individuals.

Lucy LaFarge, MD, is the editor for North America of *The International Journal of Psychoanalysis*. She is a clinical professor of psychiatry at Weill Cornell Medical College and a training and supervising analyst at the Columbia University Center for Psychoanalytic Training and Research. She has published numerous articles in the areas of analytic listening, concepts of narcissism, revenge, forgiveness, and applied psychoanalysis, and has a psychoanalytic practice in New York.

Elizabeth Lloyd Mayer, MD (1947–2005), was a Training and Supervising Analyst at the San Francisco Psychoanalytic Institute. The author of seminal papers on gender and the psychology of women, she also served on the Editorial Board of *Studies in Gender and Sexuality*.

Patricia A. Nachman, PhD, a member of New York Psychoanalytic Society and Institute, is a child and adult psychoanalyst in private practice in New York City. Dr Nachman is the former director of the Margaret Mahler Observational Research Nursery; for many years prior to that she was a senior research scientist in the Laboratory for

Developmental Processes headed by Dr Daniel Stern in the Department of Psychiatry, New York Hospital and Cornell Medical College.

Jerome Oremland, MD, has written extensively on creativity, Renaissance art and artists, transference and the role of dreams clinical psychoanalysis. He is the founder of the Center for Psychoanalytic Studies in San Francisco, and for a quarter of a century has been a professor at The International Institute for Psychoanalytic Research, Rome, Italy.

Herman Roiphe, MD (1924–2005), was a member of the New York Psychoanalytic Society and Institute. He became interested in investigating the emergence of the young child's sexual awareness and identity in the 1960s while working with Margaret Mahler at the Masters Children's Center in Greenwich Village. In 1968 he and Eleanor Galenson became co-directors of the Research Nursery, Albert Einstein Medical College, and began a twelve- year collaboration that resulted in their book, *The Infantile Origins of Sexual Identity* (1981).

Milton Senn, MD (1902–1990), a paediatrician with psychoanalytic training, served as Director of the Yale Child Study Center from 1948 to 1966. From 1975 to 1978 he conducted seventy-nine interviews for theAmerican Child Guidance Clinic and Child Psychiatry Movement Interview Collection, including interviews with Anna Freud, John Bowlby, Clare Winnicott, Peter Blos, Sr, and Margaret Mahler.

Albert Solnit, MD (1924–2002), was a Training and Supervising analyst at the Western New England Psychoanalytic Institute, who wrote extensively on child development and psychoanalysis. He was the Director of the Yale Child Study Center between 1966 to 1983, and for over thirty years served as the Managing Editor of *The Psychoanalytic Study of the Child*.

Nellie L. Thompson, PhD, is an historian and member of the New York Psychoanalytic Society and Institute, where she is the curator of the Archives and Special Collections of the A. A. Brill Library. She has published papers on early women psychoanalysts (Phyllis Greenacre, Helene Deutsch, Marie Bonaparte, Edith Jacobson), the contributions of émigré analysts to American psychoanalysis and the relations of D. W. Winnicott with American analysts. She is a member of the board of the Sigmund Freud Archives, and the editorial board of *American Imago*.

INTRODUCTION

Nellie L. Thompson

Eleanor Galenson had a remarkable career whose singular focus was her life-long interest in the maturational and psychosexual vicissitudes of infancy and early childhood. My aim in assembling this selection of her writings has been to highlight her approach to the study of the early years of life and, in particular, her contributions to understanding the developmental significance of the very young child's discovery of sexual difference, and the ways in which each child expresses this through play, symbolisation, and language.

Interviews that Galenson gave to Milton Senn and Lucy LaFarge provide a prologue to the volume. They introduce the reader to her voice, and portray the milieu within which she matured and worked as a paediatrician, researcher, and psychoanalyst. They also offer a narrative of her career from the early 1940s as a paediatrician interested in infants and young children, through her introduction to psychoanalysis, and on to her life-long absorption in the affective, psychosexual, and intellectual development of babies and young children. In them, Galenson recalls personal and professional relationships with colleagues that stretched over decades in collaborative research projects and observational and therapeutic nurseries. She also discusses individuals who enriched her thinking and research with young children. These include the philosopher Susanne Langer, the psychologist Jean Piaget, and the psychoanalysts Margaret Mahler and Phyllis Greenacre.

The papers in this volume are organised in three parts that illustrate different facets of Galenson's thinking and work: *symbolisation, thought, and language; the infantile origins of sexual identity;* and *the tripartite therapeutic model.* Parts I and II are introduced by Patricia Nachman and Lucy LaFarge, respectively, colleagues and friends of Galenson who are deeply familiar with her work. Nachman describes a conversation in which Galenson recounts a seemingly ordinary exchange she had just observed between a mother and her young son. As they discuss the vignette, its psychological richness and developmental significance emerges. This conversation beautifully illustrates Galenson's capacity to enter into the young child's unfolding experience, and the pleasure she took in reflecting on what she had observed.

LaFarge's Introduction to Part II situates the research findings and contributions of Galenson and Herman Roiphe within the prevailing psychoanalytic theory of the late 1960s and 1970s, when their papers were published. She offers an appreciation of their ground-breaking contributions, and notes that many of the questions they addressed remain unsettled today.

Part III begins with Galenson's paper describing the tripartite therapeutic model and its utility in clinical work with young children and their parents. Two additional papers illustrate the utility of this model in treating gender disturbance in a young boy, and its efficacy in treating psychotic children.

Several contemporary discussions convey the response of colleagues who engaged these papers from different perspectives. Phyllis Greenacre's discussion of Galenson's "A consideration of the nature of childhood play", and Galenson and Roiphe's "The impact of early sexual discovery on mood, defensive organization and symbolization" are included, as well as Albert Solnit's discussion of Roiphe and Galenson's "Object loss and early sexual development". When the last two papers were respectively presented at scientific meetings of the New York Psychoanalytic Society, on 26 October 1971 and 11 January 1972, material providing a detailed description of the setting and methodology of their ongoing research project was circulated in advance. (This material forms Chapter 3 in *The Infantile Origins of*

Sexual Identity.) Reviews by Elizabeth Lloyd Mayer and Jerome Oremland of *The Infantile Origins of Sexual Identity* illustrate its impact on psychoanalytic thinking concerning the emergence of sexual identity in very young children.

Eleanor Galenson's life and career

Eleanor Galenson was born in New York City on 28 October 1916 and died there on 15 January 2011. Her parents were first cousins. Her mother grew up in a village near Minsk, and her father in Rostov-on-Don. They both left Russia after participating in the 1905 Russian Revolution and, via different journeys, settled in New York. Her mother, Libby, had no formal education. After arriving in the US she worked as a lace maker and learned to read at night classes at the Rand School of Social Science, founded by members of the American Socialist Party. Her father, Louis, unusually for a Jewish child, attended a gymnasium in Russia. He initially travelled to Palestine, where he intended to settle, but was dissatisfied, and came to New York where he put himself through college selling postcards, and became an accountant.

Galenson often spoke of her close, warm relationship with her father, which was symbolised by the many dolls he gave her as presents. Although her relationship with her mother was difficult, her parents, like many immigrants, placed a high value on her education and that of her older brother Walter, who became a distinguished Harvard-trained economist. Despite the strains in their relationship, her mother fully supported Eleanor's ambition to become a paediatrician. Galenson often recalled her refrain, "women's work is not for you—no washing, cleaning, and ironing—concentrate on your studies and a career".

Galenson graduated from Barnard College in 1936. She was one of only seven women in her medical school class at Columbia University's College of Physicians and Surgeons, where quotas limited the number of Jewish students admitted to medical training. After graduating in 1940 she completed an internship at Bellevue Hospital, a residency in paediatrics at Mount Sinai Hospital, and a two-year fellowship from the Commonwealth Fund for training in psychiatry at the Payne Whitney Clinic at New York Hospital.

Galenson's interest in psychoanalysis was aroused while she was at Payne Whitney. She undertook psychoanalytic training at the New York Psychoanalytic Institute in 1947. She attributed this decision to hearing Phyllis Greenacre lecture at Payne Whitney on the adolescent sons of successful fathers:

> This was my first real contact with psychoanalysis. I don't even think I had read Freud at all, and I am not sure that I knew very much of what Dr. Greenacre was talking about, except for the fact that I knew I was in the presence of someone who had a very cogent and very exciting view of the whole question of the early determinacy of personality problems. [Greenacre] was the first woman for whom I felt unequivocal intellectual admiration ... There was an emotionality that she conveyed, a vividness. She had an enormous and special type of empathy that enabled her to present her material that way. From the very beginning, I knew that what she said was right. With Greenacre, I felt for the first time that here was someone who was putting into words the essence of what I felt. (Galenson, 1977)

While at Payne Whitney Galenson had married Aaron Himmelstein, a cardiac surgeon. During their honeymoon in Florida, Pearl Harbor was attacked. For the next four years they were separated by the Second World War. In the late 1940s they had two children, Paul and David, and settled into their respective careers. Himmelstein, then chief of cardiac surgery at Columbia Presbyterian Hospital, died tragically in 1959, ten days after being diagnosed with a brain tumour. Galenson found herself suddenly widowed with two young sons, eleven and nine years of age, to support. At her memorial service her son Paul noted that his mother did not betray any fear or doubt about her ability to independently raise her sons. He also observed that his mother made sure they "knew their own worth, made sure we could find our own way in the world, that we understood the needs of other people around us" (Himmelstein, personal communication).

Galenson's career as a paediatrician, child psychiatrist, and psychoanalyst was remarkably varied and visible. The variability is evident in her work in a range of settings: public health clinics, hospitals, private practice, and directorships of observational and therapeutic nurseries (e.g., Ruosso Therapeutic Nursery; Director, Deaf Infant Project, Lexington School for the Deaf; Co-Director, Research

Nursery, Albert Einstein Medical College). Visibility was afforded by her leadership in a wide range of research projects on infants and young children, and her many publications.

Galenson's appreciation of the complexities of infant research began during her initial research experience in 1962 as a research associate in the Child Development Project at the Albert Einstein College of Medicine, which was directed by the noted infant researcher Sybille Escalona. The findings of this project were reported in Escalona's *The Roots of Individuality* (1968). Galenson describes the experience of working with Escalona in her interview with Milton Senn.

In 1968 Galenson and Herman Roiphe became co-directors of the Research Nursery at Albert Einstein Medical College, beginning a twelve-year collaboration mapped in a series of papers published in the 1970s, and culminating in their seminal book, *The Infantile Origins of Sexual Identity* (Roiphe & Galenson, 1981). The crucial discovery of their long and rigorous project was that a new psychosexual phase emerges towards the end of the second year:

> ... we became convinced that we had been engaged in tracing the development of the sense of sexual identity from its vague beginnings during the earliest weeks and months to a definite conscious awareness of specific gender and erotic feelings and fantasies by the end of the second year. This definitive awareness has turn out to be a critical factor in ongoing psychological development and has therefore been designated as the beginning of a new psychosexual phase. (1981, p. x)

In answer to the question as to why, with few notable exceptions, researchers and observers have "overlooked these astonishing protean manifestations of early sexuality", Roiphe and Galenson cited Freud's observation on "the ubiquity of repression of infantile sexuality" among adults and, more pointedly, among adults as they relate to children.

Galenson's first psychoanalytic publications were two brief commentaries on papers presented by Masud Khan and Justin D. Call at the 23rd International Psycho-Analytical Congress in Stockholm in the summer of 1963. Khan's paper, "Ego distortion, cumulative trauma, and the role of reconstruction in the analytic situation" (1964), described the mother's role as that of a "protective shield" for her infant. Galenson found this description too restrictive. She argued that the relationship between the mother and infant is essentially that of a mutual adaptation, and rather than serving as a protective shield, the mother's "selection and attenuation of stimuli . . . serves more an as organizing process" for the infant (Galenson, 1964a, p. 279).

Call's "Newborn approach behavior and early ego development" (1964), postulated that the newborn infant's feeding at the breast or bottle represents "anticipatory behavior" signifying that the object "was identified, remembered, hallucinated, and actively sought". In other words, this "anticipatory behavior" is an expression of early ego functions. Galenson was not persuaded by Call's thesis and argued that this over-interpretation:

> . . . may lead to the danger of assuming that the presence and use of this sensimotor apparatus implies its use in a manner corresponding to or duplicating secondary process thinking with its corresponding behavior. *Such an assumption would impede our understanding of early psychic development* . . . (Galenson, 1964b, p. 295 italics added,)

In emphasising that the understanding of early psychic development can be impeded when the infant's behaviour is too quickly conceptualised as antecedent to a later developmental stage Galenson makes the larger point that the subtle communications between mother and infant are missed, along with their significance and contribution to the infant's psychic development.

Despite the reservations she had expressed about Call's thesis in his 1964 paper, in 1979, Galenson joined with him in founding The World Association of Infant Psychiatry (later renamed the World Association for Infant Mental Health). Its first congress in Lisbon, Portugal in 1980 sought to bring together infant researchers from around the world. The creation of this organisation illustrates Galenson's awareness that, although psychoanalytic theory had an important contribution to make to infant research, this complex new field required collaborators from many disciplines, and in Serge Lebovici's felicitous term, had to be "transdisciplinary".

Papers from the first two congresses were published in *Frontiers of Infant Psychiatry* (Call, Galenson, & Tyson, 1982, 1984). The Preface to Volume One reiterates the theme of complexity. The field of infant research embraces:

> . . . the processing and collating of data derived from a variety of sources; the issue of how to deal with varying levels of psychological complexity; questions of nosology as well as etiology; the relevance of

ethological and sociological data for understanding individual development and psychopathology; behavioral indications of the emerging sense of self-awareness; the various polarities and organizational patterns that characterize infancy; the hazards of prediction and the need for long-term in-depth case studies; and the resilience and activating capacities of the newborn. (p. xxv)

Galenson's intellectual and emotional engagement with psychoanalysis remained undiminished in her old age. This is illustrated by her passionate response to Lawrence Kubie's "The drive to become both sexes," that I brought to her to read in 2008. Kubie first presented this paper in 1954, but made no effort to publish it until 1972. It appeared in *The Psychoanalytic Quarterly* in 1974, a year after Kubie's death, and was reprinted in the journal as a "classic paper" in 2011 (Thompson, 2011). Galenson became an advocate for the paper and often gave it to friends and colleagues. This response reflects, I believe, her intuitive appreciation that the paper embodied themes that were personally meaningful to its author. She also felt that it provided her an opportunity to consider anew gender choice and the lifelong vicissitudes that accompany it (Galenson, 2009). Kubie's point of departure was the simple question of why the discovery of irrefutable reality of genital difference had such a powerful impact on young children, and continued to reverberate in ways both subtle and consequential throughout adulthood.

Like many who reach a venerable age, Galenson was often outspoken. She was particularly insistent that contemporary psychoanalysis had lost sight of the fact that adult analysis requires a deep and empathic understanding of infancy and early childhood, and of the role of the body in development. She found that many of Kubie's observations supported analytic interpretations that address infantile experiences expressed in dreams and associative material. His paper reinvigorated her clinical work and led her to feel "secure once more in utilizing my own analytic ideas derived from both my clinical and research experience with very young children" in work with adult patients (Galenson, 2009).

Kubie rewrote his paper many times over the years. The final published version includes an observation, autobiographical in origin that introduces a new element, the process of ageing, into the study of gender:

> ... the process of aging ... has sensitized me and made it possible for me to see more clearly the relationship of the drive to become both sexes to certain distortions which are introduced by the process of aging in myself, in friends, in relatives and above all, in patients. (Kubie, 1974, p. 356)

In accounting for this new perspective in Kubie's work, Galenson offered an interpretation that is at the same time an identification:

> Kubie had aged during the long gestation of his paper, finally publishing it in his 73rd year, and I am also aging, an aged analyst who is now 93, and perhaps I am returning to the question of gender as unfinished business from my earlier research with Herman Roiphe. (Galenson, 2009, p. 9)

Galenson does not describe what this "unfinished business" is from her earlier research nor did Kubie elucidate on his insight that his own ageing had introduced a new element in his thinking on the drive to become both sexes. Kubie's comment on ageing, however, captured Galenson's attention, leading her to point out that that ageing is a somatic bodily process, and somatic issues, beginning in infancy, have the capacity to resound more intensely and broadly throughout life. Ageing then often brings into sharper clinical focus unresolved anxieties and longings regarding one's gender identity. Galenson's observation unites the somatic experiences of the infant and the aged body as essential to understanding "the question of gender" and represents a final contribution to a question that engaged her curiosity and intellect to the end of her long life.

References

Call, J. (1964). Newborn approach behavior and early ego development. *International Journal of Psychoanalysis*, 45: 286–294.
Call, J., Galenson, E., & Tyson, R. (Eds.). (1982). *Frontiers of Infant Psychiatry, Vol. I*. New York: Basic Books.
Call, J., Galenson, E., & Tyson, R. (Eds.). (1984). *Frontiers of Infant Psychiatry, Vol. II*. New York: Basic Books.
Escalona, S. (1968). *The Roots of Individuality: Normal Patterns of Development in Infancy*. Chicago: Aldine.

Galenson, E. (1964a). Comment on Mr. Khan's paper. *International Journal of Psychoanalysis*, *45*: 279.

Galenson, E. (1964b). Comment on Dr. Call's paper. *International Journal of Psychoanalysis*, *45*: 294–295.

Galenson, E. (1977). Interview with M. Senn. In: *American Child Guidance Clinic and Child Psychiatry Movement Interview Collection, 1975–1978* (pp. 1–37). Bethesda, MD: United States Library of Medicine, National Institutes of Health.

Galenson, E. (2009). Unpublished. "Notes on Lawrence Kubie's 'The drive to become both sexes'."

Khan, M. (1964). Ego distortion, cumulative trauma, and the role of reconstruction in the analytic situation. *International Journal of Psychoanalysis*, *45*: 272–277.

Kubie, L. (1974). The drive to become both sexes. *The Psychoanalytic Quarterly*, *43*: 349–426 [reprinted in *The Psychoanalytic Quarterly*, *80*: 369–439, 2011].

Roiphe, H., & Galenson, E. (1981). *The Infantile Origins of Sexual Identity*. New York: International Universities Press.

Thompson, N. L. (2011). Introduction to Lawrence S. Kubie's "The drive to become both sexes". *The Psychoanalytic Quarterly*, *80*: 357–368.

PROLOGUE

Interview with Eleanor Galenson

Dr Milton J. E. Senn, 31 August 1977

Milton Senn: Dr Galenson (whom I will hereafter, in this interview, call Eleanor), I wonder if you would begin by talking about how you got into this field of mental health?

Eleanor Galenson: Well, it was actually a very fortuitous set of circumstances. I was, as you know, a psychiatric resident at Mt Sinai Hospital in 1942 to [19]43, having come up from Bellevue where I had been a general intern and then a paediatric intern. My husband, who has since died, was in the Army at that time, and Dr Murray Bass, who was my paediatric chief, was very much in favour of my getting some further experience in the emotional life of children. Dr Bass, through the man who became very important later on, Dr Milton Levine (whom you know, of course) urged me to apply to the Commonwealth Fellowship. This was really going to be a two-year period, after which I would return to paediatrics, and it had been all set that I would come in some capacity, probably to join with Dr Murray Bass and a man in cardiology. With that in mind, I came to New York Hospital and I would say that my first exposure, real exposure to good thinking in psychiatry came there through three key people: they were Dr Norvelle Lamar, whom we call "Boosy", who was my outpatient supervisor in what was then considered to be the treatment of a young child. These days we would not consider that child so young—it was an eight-year-old girl.

There was also Dr Katherine Woodward, who worked with mentally retarded children at Lenox Hill for a number of years, who also supervised me; but most of all, the key person, I think, in my change of direction was Dr Phyllis Greenacre, whom I heard speak for the first time when I was a Commonwealth Fellow at Payne Whitney Clinic at New York Hospital. She delivered a talk on the adolescent sons of successful fathers and some of their problems. That was my first real contact with psychoanalysis. I don't even think I had read Freud at all, and I am not sure that I knew very much what Dr Greenacre was talking about, except for the fact that I knew that I was in the presence of someone who had a very cogent and very exciting view of the whole question of the early determinance of personality problems. It was not a popular thing at that time to be analysed when you were a resident, or a fellow as I was. As a matter of fact, when I finally decided to undertake a personal analysis, Dr Greenacre, whom I approached, had no time and she referred me to somebody else. But I did not dare tell Dr Diethelm, who was then head of our department of psychiatry, because of his feeling that residents or fellows should not be in analysis, and as a matter of fact, he felt that it interfered with their psychiatric work.[1]

As you know, I left New York Hospital after the Commonwealth Fellowship was over and Dr Leona Baumgartner offered me a job in the City Health Department; she was then head of the Children's Division in the city (I can't remember the exact title) but they had a year's stipend for somebody to do something in the Department of Health. They didn't even know what they wanted to do with this stipend (it was a part-time job); Dr Sam Berenberg was part of the entourage, too. I then set a programme up for myself, after some discussion with Leona Baumgartner and Sam, visiting baby public health stations where mothers brought their babies for a periodic check-up, and it became evident that the only way that I could hope to do anything was to simply discuss with the public health nurses who were there, any questions that they might have. There was the occasional paediatrician—very occasional—but mostly these were the public health nurses who could ask me what I thought about this or that problem in relation to feeding, for example. I must say, in those days I had a lot more certainty about what I thought should be done than now, and I made some unhesitating pronouncements about what should be done.

Then they decided that it might be a good idea for the mothers and whatever paediatricians might be around, to come every time I was scheduled to come around, and with all the baby health stations in New York, Staten Island, and Brooklyn, which was the area of service to be covered, I didn't get around very often to these. But I set up these groups and I would come and they had questions, and we would simply have a sort of question and answer period during which one or another, mother or nurse, or paediatrician, would ask what I thought about child rearing. These were mostly young children; I would say, in those days, infants, up to the age of two and a half or three, and I shudder to think about some of the things I said without any doubts at all in my mind. I was very sorry to leave that job because I had gotten to enjoy it so. Leona Baumgartner thought that was a good idea; she tried to persuade the budget powers to continue this stipend but they would not, and so after about a year or two, I left the city employ.

I was invited then by the man who was then head of Child Psychiatry at Long Island University Hospital, Dr Howard Potter, to come into his Department of Child Psychiatry—I was supposed to be the liaison branch with paediatrics. I did that and I had a part-time appointment at New York Hospital at the same time. That was when you were there, Dr Senn, and when Henry Barnett and Lewis Fraad invited me to come and lecture or conference with their group. I would come there every week, I believe, and join in on the case conferences that they were having. At Long Island University Hospital, which is where Potter was, I simply never really found a place where I fitted in, or I should say, I did not know how to find a place for myself. Looking back on it, I had some very interesting paediatric opportunities. I was on the ward, there were individuals who were interested, but they were so busy doing their own paediatric thing that, after a while, I simply found myself not attached to any particular group and I left there.

Mt Sinai Hospital at that point, with Dr M. Ralph Kaufmann as its chief, was interested in attracting analytically oriented people. I should say, in the meantime what had been happening, along with this other professional part, was that I had decided to get into psychoanalytic training, although my first analyst was not a training analyst. I then applied for admission and I was admitted to the New York Psychoanalytic Institute, and I trained there from 1948 to 1953, when I graduated. I also began child analytic training there and really took everything that was offered at that time. They were not offering a final qualification as a child analyst at the time that I finished my courses. I was going on then with analytic training and I went to Mt Sinai with the idea of going into the Child Psychiatry Department. These were just after the war years and there were very exciting people there. Kaufmann built up a department that was very good in their adult division. I would say the child division never, in the time I was there, got off the grounds. For instance, they had a marvellous person in Dr Elizabeth Geleerd, who later on went on to do very good things; she lasted six months at Mt Sinai and then left because she felt that she could not really see a place for herself there.

MS: She was a psychiatrist?

EG: She was a psychoanalyst trained in Vienna, and then in England with Anna Freud for a while, and then she went to Topeka with that whole migrant group that was accepted out at Menninger's, and then she came to New York. She was then married to Dr Rudolph Loewenstein who was, you know, very prominent as an analyst for many years in New York.

I was spread rather thin, I guess; I was having my children—I had two sons—and I was in analytic training which I had finished rather slowly, and then at New York Hospital, just for a conference every now and then, and Mt Sinai where I never really did very much work. I went to their conferences, supervised the treatment of residents and fellows in the treatment of latency and adolescent children. Most of all, I kept on with a private practice which I began from the day I left Payne Whitney. I saw children, latency-age children, adolescents—that was my main practice in those years.

MS: Let's go back a minute to your Long Island University experience and Mt Sinai. Why do you think things didn't advance in the field of child psychiatry at those places? At Sinai, with Mo Kaufmann there, and aggressive and active and good staff, why did the children's field lag; what was going on there?

EG: Well, my best view of it is—and that is supported by some statements that Mo Kaufmann made in subsequent years—the feeling really was that child psychiatry was not a terribly serious specialty, that child psychiatry was not considered a very serious discipline by many of the people who—analysts though they were and many of them having taught that early childhood is so important for later development. The proof is in the pudding—the budget always came through adult psychiatry and, in my experience, even now in recent years, whenever cuts were made, they were made in child psychiatry. I never could get a really honest answer about it; it was always in the way of joking, "Oh, well, you know the kids, they are just kids", that kind of thing. Now, Potter, I think, tried very, very hard. My own personal memories of him—and I may be somewhat wrong—is that he was not a dynamic enough person that he didn't have the right ingredients to really get with his faculty or where the power was. Mo Kaufmann surely could have done it because anything he wanted, he could have gotten.

I was working in private practice at the same time, seeing children—never straying far from 96th Street because I was at 70 East 96th Street until I married my present husband some years ago. That is where I began and that is where I practiced all the years that I saw children and adults. My referrals—and I had a very, very active referral practice—came largely from paediatricians. These were paediatricians whom I had contacted at Mt Sinai while I was paediatric resident, and at New York Hospital, and it was a very interesting kind of referral because what they would say was, "Well, I trust you because you were a paediatrician and you knew something about it, and I will refer this to you".

I used to be so swamped, I would dread another phone call; but they would insist that I see the child myself, if only very briefly, and then refer them. Their feeling of confidence was certainly based on the fact that they knew me as a paediatrician; about psychiatrists they felt that they didn't really know any of them and they were strange people. So the rift between paediatrics and psychiatry was then a very serious problem and in many ways, I think, still is.

MS: Those were in the 1930s?

EG: Those were in the late Forties, and going on into the Fifties.

MS: To the present time?

EG: I believe that it goes on to the present time.

MS: What kind of problems did they refer to you in the Forties?

EG: Enuresis, school difficulties, "misbehaving" as they called it, behavioural problems in school. I had a lot of referrals from the various private schools around New York. It was the beginning of the learning difficulty era. For example, when Katrina deHirsch was just beginning her work she referred many patients for treatment . . .

MS: She was in speech pathology?

EG: . . . and learning difficulties.

MS: How did you feel about your results? Did you feel that you were accomplishing a change, that you were benefitting these children? Were the paediatricians satisfied?

EG: Well, it was a mixed group. I could honestly say that those children who were sent to me for creating trouble in school, either because they were too withdrawn or because they were misbehaving in one way or the other, that group, I think, were probably my star results, because I did get symptomatic improvement. I then began getting referrals from the schools themselves, the principal, or the assistant principal. Looking back on it, and even then, I think I knew that those children who were referred to me because of inhibitions in learning of one kind or another, children who were clearly intelligent but were non-achievers, I think that my results in that group were essentially far from good. There was another group that I used to treat about whom I later worried, the so-called psychosomatic group, the asthmatics, the ones who had gastro-intestinal complaints, etc. I had a series of children whose asthma was cured but who then became very serious behavioural problems of one or another kind. If their parents left them in treatment with me long enough, several of them became acting-out adolescents of a much more serious nature. On the other hand, many of those children were actually withdrawn from treatment when their parents began to experience hostile, aggressive acting-out at home that they could not handle.

MS: How do you explain the shift from one complex of symptoms to another?

EG: Well, I think that the regression was being expressed in the somatic and as I worked with that, it became directed to where it originally belonged, that is, towards the mother, primarily. The mother really preferred a child with whom she had been able to cope as a sick child and could not tolerate it—the overt aggression. My great mistake in those years was in relation to the influence of the parents. But in those days, I really did not take seriously enough the edict that it's the parents, one or the other, who are the cause of all of this and that; unless I could do something about changing their whole alignment with the child, it was like pouring water down a sieve. I do feel, though, that in spite of the fact that I was not able to modify a lot of these psychosomatic problems, something was accomplished.

When you are in practice for thirty years or so, as I have been, I began to have some of these people coming back to see me as adults. That has been fascinating. This last year I saw a young woman who had come to me on an anorexia problem at age ten or eleven years and had all kinds of other somatic complaints. I think what happened to her and to other child patients is that she found out there was some way of being approached psychologically, or getting psychological help. A number of those people came back to me in subsequent years and then I referred them for treatment as young adults. This particular young woman I have been able to follow because she has been to a colleague of mine, and I think is doing reasonably well.

MS: What was your approach in those early days? You saw the child once a week?

EG: No, I would see them two or three times a week.

MS: In play therapy?

EG: In play therapy.

MS: Did you deal with the parents at all?

EG: Yes. I would see the parents according to the standard that I had, about once a week.

MS: And what did you do with them?

EG: Well that was the problem; mostly listen to their complaints. I would try to give guidance to them about how to handle this child at home. Most of the time, with the best will in the world, these parents would listen to me but simply were not able to modify their own behaviour enough in their relationship with the child, so that I do not think very much happened.

MS: Did you do any changing of the milieu; working with the schools, changing things there for that particular child?

EG: Yes, now that was helpful in some instances, in some schools. I would say there were a few like Dalton; Ethical Culture and Walden were relatively unstructured and the child was sort of lost in that whole looseness. But they really did try to help and were indeed extremely helpful in maintaining the child in even a semi-structured environment, which did not happen anywhere else, so that during the time a child was in treatment they offered an environment within which that child could relate to teachers and peers. My first experience with an autistic child—it actually happened to be my first child patient—came to me through Dr Katharine Woodward, who ran a research project at Lenox Hill Hospital for years for psychotic and retarded children (she was really a remarkable lady from whom I recently heard—she is still alive). My first psychotic patient, whom I thought was very young in those years, came to me at the age of five and a half. He was the child of two mathematicians and he was one of these mathematical geniuses but unable to function at all in a public school in which he was. I had not yet read, at that time, the work that was just beginning to come out—Loretta Bender's work—until after I got this child. I knew I had some completely different kind of a child there and learned enormously from him; I kept in touch with that family and he is now leading a rather modified but at least self-supporting life outside of an institution as a worker for the Quakers to whom he found his way somehow. He is doing not too badly. At any rate, I knew I didn't know what he was about and I would say that that child, probably more than any of the others, made me question what we were doing, because he was so strange and so different.

These other children who had psychopathology that was more familiar to me, I took for granted and I felt sure that I would help them and that I was doing something. The psychosomatic group gave me pause to some extent, especially the asthmatic child I already mentioned whom I cured of his asthma very nicely and effectively within a year, to be replaced by a very dangerous acting-out behaviour. That child ended up, at the age of fourteen having attacked a woman in one of our centres and went in one of the Junior Penitentiary set-ups that they had. I would say that these failures, my clear failures that I had, made me question what I was doing in the rest of my psychiatric work.

MS: Where did psychoanalysis come in at that time in terms of helping you or giving you understanding, or whatever?

EG: I had attended Berta Bornstein's child analysis seminars which were absolutely marvellous in terms of their understanding of latency-age children and I had also controlled a case with her which we both agreed, after about two years, was not "analysable". But I don't think that I got any real help at that time from my child analysis work. I don't know why that was; I think the responsibility was equally divided between them and me. Dr Marianne Kris was leading a very interesting child analysis seminar which I attended for four years. Dr Mary O'Neil Hawkins' seminar on adolescence was brilliant. She was an off-beat person—and I think it was from her that I began to get some idea that child analysis just at that point did not have some of the answers that I was looking for.

MS: Could you share those insights that you now had about psychoanalysis—the disappointments I'll say—with your teachers? Were you of the mind that maybe you should not talk about this; maybe they might be hurt or insulted?

EG: The New York Psychoanalytic Institute then and now, unfortunately, is a rather awesome place where you really did not raise questions. It still remains a place where the distance between the faculty and the student is very great and you go through your courses and absorb what they teach you. I don't think that I appreciated these brilliant people who were teaching us then but I was not the only one.

Ernst Kris, Loewenstein, and Hartmann were theoretically far above the students' capacity at that time. I don't think I even understood most of what Hartmann was teaching. One did not question these concepts, and I think, I perhaps more than others because I was a very obedient student, did what I was expected to do—I read it, I gave it back and I didn't question very much. My questioning really did not begin for many, many years. You see, those were the years I was also busy bringing up my own children in New York. My husband had gone off to the war for five years before we had children, and then he came back and they were very busy years for us because he was establishing himself as a young and pioneering cardiovascular surgeon and physiologist with Dr André Coornand who later won the Nobel Prize in this field. So I can't quite blame myself for not having the time, energy, whatever, I don't know, to question what I was doing.

About fifteen years ago I was invited to join the faculty of the newly formed Department of Psychiatry at Albert Einstein Medical School by Dr Milton Rosenbaum and I came up there the second year of its existence. (They are now approaching their twentieth anniversary, so it probably was eighteen years ago when I went there.) I left Mt Sinai because this was a brand new, very exciting place and I was given the idea that child psychiatry was going to be very important there. Dr Lewis Fraad and Dr Henry Barnett were going to head paediatrics.

MS: Sibylle Escalona?[2]

EG: I had not yet met her when I went up there but I did meet her when I came up. I would say that was a turning point in my own career. I met Sibylle and we both agreed that most people who go into psychiatry know nothing about normal development and that they should be taught it, and that paediatricians also should be taught about normal development. Then we got together a joint venture which was really the beginning for me of what is now the most exciting part of my work or partly the most exciting part of my professional life. We taught a course for almost six years.

MS: Sibylle Escalona and you?

EG: Sibylle and I with two other people, Dr Harvey Corman, who has remained as a co-writer with Sibylle—and we had two other people who came to help us with the course, a man named Dr David Schechter from the William Alanson White Group (Corman is from the Columbia Psychoanalytic Group). Those were very exciting times. We set up a course that would meet once a week over the whole year and consisted of two parts; there would be a demonstration the first hour, and then there would be the second hour in which the whole group would get together to discuss what we had seen. We went from the neonatal period and ideally we were to reach adolescence by the end of the year but that was only rarely achieved.

MS: Who were the students?

EG: The students were multi-disciplinary; there were child fellows, paediatricians . . .

MS: Child development fellows?

EG: No, no, there were child psychiatry fellows, and there were paediatric interns and residents, social workers, psychology trainees. It was geared primarily for the child psychiatry fellows and the paediatric fellows.

MS: It was mandatory that those students take the course?

EG: Well, it was not mandatory but I would say that we were extremely popular, and I think we were extremely popular due to the influence of Fraad and Barnett who thought that this was a great thing.

MS: They were good supporters?

EG: Great supporters, quite. Why the child psychiatry fellows took our course, I am not quite sure. Sibylle at that time was a rare person, in a way: she was the chief of psychology there, she had great status and was thought a great deal of, and I would say that she was a great drawing card. So it was considered a great honour to be in her course and people attended that very regularly. The child psychiatry people attended most regularly, the paediatricians [had] Lewis Fraad to answer to if they did not attend. All those six years, they were really quite golden years. Sibylle, as you know, was very interested in infancy; she had come back from Topeka and she had done her longitudinal study, so we started out with neonates. She would bring in several neonates, and later she and I would interview young children and their parents. By the way, it was a maxim that we never varied from, that except for the neonates, no young child was ever interviewed without the mother being present. I think the first time we began to separate mother and child was somewhere in the early latency period. We had some very exciting times, because we also collected children's drawings, and we would have a show every year during which we would show progression from the early drawings on to the late ones.

MS: You saw these children with their mothers, and then what?

EG: We would see them once and then we would go to our discussion group. Our model was to try to show a normal child, as normal as we could get. We used our friends and we used our faculty children, and by and large, we had a normal variety of children. Then we would try to show the contrast the next time with a child who was disturbed.

MS: Of the same age?

EG: Of the same age. So we would show a normal and then a disturbed one. This was easy to do once we reached the three- and four-year-old group, since at that time early child psychopathology was really not recognised in the way we do these days. Many a time the child who was disturbed was taken from our own OPD, for example. Sibylle and I never had any problem at all when we wanted to show a child who was showing the effects of hospitalism, for example; we would walk on to the paediatric ward that morning and pick up a child. Now, this was at a time when this was probably one of the best paediatric wards around. Lew Fraad and Henry Barnett also knew we could pick up a child who was showing blatant and open effects of hospitalism. It was at a time when this was thought to be a good liaison programme between child psychiatry and paediatrics. There was a good liaison programme and yet one could find children with serious psychological problems, I am not just talking about mild reactions but very serious ones.

MS: You would find them where?

EG: On the paediatric service, just sitting there, ruminating, drooling.

MS: Were psychiatrist consultants to the Department of Pediatrics called in?

EG: Were they called in?

MS: ... and how did they help with these kinds of children?

EG: Well, occasionally they were called in but the most effective person was a man who has since left, named Michael Rothenberg—he is on the West Coast now. He "lived" on that Pediatric Service and his effectiveness was the result of his having become a familiar person to the paediatricians.

MS: Was he a paediatrician?

EG: He had been a paediatrician. He would spot these children himself, he was not called in to see them. In retrospect, you might think it was quite understandable, since the paediatricians were extremely busy and preoccupied with the life and death issues they were dealing with, I don't think that we should have, and I don't still think that we should disturb their defences against dealing with these deadly and life-endangering situations. I think we would have made them less effective paediatricians and I do not know that we still have an answer to that whole problem. I have some thoughts about it that I will tell you about—yet it was very discouraging to me at that time.

MS: It was at your Einstein days that you began to question dogma, question theory, even psychoanalytic theories and practices, felt free to express them. What were the other changes that took place in you at that time?

EG: I would say I really did not begin to question psychoanalytic dogma really until I began to have a research project of my own.

MS: When was that?

EG: That was twelve years ago. I will tell you a little bit about that. After a course with Sibylle Escalona—the course ended because we all got tired of giving it; it was an enormous expenditure of time and energy and truth to tell, we did not feel that we were affecting the people whom we taught enough. They, on the other hand, disagreed with us. We have since kept contact and many of them said that they were influenced by us to going into this field; for example, child psychiatry or becoming infant researchers themselves because of their exposure to us. But we did not feel that their handling of children had really become that different under our aegis, and maybe we were tired of just teaching with the tremendous output that we gave. And it may also have been that Sibylle, at that point, got her very large grant for a longitudinal study.

MS: Federal grant?

EG: Federal grant, NIMH grant, it was several million dollars to last for eight years, and she had asked me to be part of that project. We were to do two things: we were to standardise the Piaget-based infant scale, and having standardised those, those were to become part of our methodology in studying what originally would be eight infants and their mothers and their families, longitudinally, and this would be a normal developmental project to try to prove Sibylle's hypothesis; it was that with really short-term prediction, you could study a mother–child interaction and at the end, let's say of six months, say where that mother and child were not in their relationship with one another, and that would give you some idea of where they would be six months from now; the quality of the mother and the child would have changed each six months.

MS: According to the interaction?

EG: Yes . . . so that you were now dealing with a different set of givens and that would allow you to then make a prediction of what would happen six months hence, because long-term prediction, at that time, was already becoming rather disappointing. So we were to follow these eight people. We spent three years standardising the Piaget sensory motor scales which are now known as the Albert Einstein Sensory–Motor Scales. I would say that I learned an enormous amount about infants in that testing, but I think the scales are quite disappointing in what we hoped they would tell us.

MS: In terms of predictability?

EG: Yes. However, I don't think that they have been utilised enough and I am now trying them with deaf infants because I think that they may offer some additional material. But I think they were very disappointing in what we hoped they would bring.

Personally, I think this work freed me from the bondage of the psychoanalytic point of view. Not that I ever stopped using the psychoanalytic frame of reference, because I really do think that that has remained my point of view, but I realised that the answers were not there yet, had not yet been revealed, so to speak. The other thing it taught me was that Sibylle's way of working was not my way of working. The first five years—I was with that project five years—part-time, because I continued private psychoanalytic practice and child psychiatry all the time—not only did we standardise the Piaget scale, which was an interesting personal experience, but we also spent endless hours getting a manual together that was supposed to serve as our way of keeping track of what was going on in this mother–infant interaction. That manual is still in existence; it must have something like a thousand pages.

MS: In existence, and used where?

EG: Sibylle Escalona has it.

MS: Does she use it? Do other people use it?

EG: I don't think anyone else uses it.

MS: Why not?

EG: It was so cumbersome that it was unusable. In order to train observers to use this thing, you really had to train them to be infant specialists, because it could not be used as a checklist kind of thing. It turned out anyhow to be disappointing, except that it was sort of an indicator as to where you might be going. By the time you train people to use that manual, you train them as infant psychiatrists as well. I now feel that where the pay dirt is going to be is in the field of infant psychiatry.

At any rate, I quit the project when I found that we were spending three hours of an evening trying to define a single term and not coming to closure on the terms for weeks, and I knew that was not for me. I think that Sibylle suffers—and I respect her enormously, I don't think there is anyone who can take a child and make a clinical evaluation as she can, she knows children very well—but I think she suffers from a tremendous obsessional quality that has interfered with her work. Anyhow, I left there, and it so happened at Einstein at the time that Milt Rosenbaum had gone to Israel, leaving Dr Joseph Kramer as acting chairman, Joe Kramer needed somebody to help him run the Child Fellowship Program and asked me to come in as training director of the Child Psychiatry Fellowship.

My husband had died of a brain tumour and I found I wanted a change of some kind, and so I came into a three-quarter-time position at Einstein as director of training in child psychiatry. I was very ambitious and felt that what every child fellow should have was some training in normal child development. And so, it very fortuitously happened that Dr Herman Roiphe came along, having just left Dr Margaret Mahler's research project, and he had an idea, the merit of which I did not really know very much about. It was interesting: his idea was that sexual behaviour, development, and awareness began much earlier than any analyst had ever described. There had been sporadic reports in the literature about very early sexual awareness, and some awkward reactions to it, so-called castration reactions. Dr Lisbeth Sachs wrote one case up but felt that this was simply an early oedipal reaction. I saw some very young children in my private practice at that time—I kept on seeing children in my private practice—and I saw a few myself but I just could not account for it.

So, when Herman Roiphe came along with this idea, which nobody else was at all interested in, we decided to start a nursery together. I was very busy running the training programme and the first year that the nursery started I was involved in it only very tangentially. It began in the recreation room of a nearby housing project, which had to be swept out every morning after the adolescents had left it in chaos the night before. But we had the support of Joe Kramer, for one reason. He said, "Well, do whatever you want, you know something about early normal development, because you have been with Sibylle." You see, my work with Sibylle gave me that entrée.

MS: Was this a day care centre?

EG: No, we simply went to the people in the housing project; we went into the playground of the housing project and said, "We are looking for babies who are going to be about a year old in September and we simply want to study them. Would you like to join?" and we got about eight mothers and babies, to come in out of the rain, I think. It was a nice room and the winters were cold, and we simply offered them a place to come to.

MS: Every morning?

EG: Four mornings a week.

MS: All morning?

EG: Two hours.

MS: The mothers stayed with the children?

EG: Always. That was our original format. Herman Roiphe's hypothesis, which has since been published in *The Psychoanalytic Study of the Child*, under the name of "An early genital phase", (1968) was that somewhere around eighteen to twenty-four months of age, all babies discover the genital difference. Then in those babies who have suffered an untoward experience in the first year and a half of their lives—either because they had some somatic or body image disturbance, or because there had been some untoward mother–child interaction such as depression in the mother or prolonged separation from the mother when they reached this genital awareness, would show castration reaction. This was on the basis of one case that Roiphe had seen in Margaret Mahler's Nursery that he could not account for, and nobody else could as well as the few sporadic instances in the literature of early genital awareness. So we set this project up. That first year, it could not really be called research of any kind; it was simply getting acquainted with the fact that, indeed, it was fine that babies of the age of somewhere around eighteen months became very curious about the genitals of the others when they were diapered and at other times as well.

The next part of the story is again one of those accidents of fate. Joe Kramer had felt rather threatened by the fact that I had rather great ambitions about the training programme he had asked me to set up. It was going to be very much slanted towards early childhood, and for some reason, he decided that he wanted somebody else to come in as training director of child psychiatry. We had a rather unpleasant interlude then after which I was able to get funds because Joe Kramer had taken this job away from me. Funds, meagre though they were, supported this nursery project in the beginning.

Our next place was on the back stage in the local Catholic Girls High School, that was offered to us and that was the beginning of what turned out to be an almost twelve-year collaborative research project between Roiphe and myself. We achieved a kind of status within the department and when child psychiatry moved into a new building, we could then design our own nursery quarters. Dr Jack Wilder, who was then the acting chairman of the Department of Psychiatry, was very much in favour of all of this. He was not an analyst, by the way, but very pro-analytic in his point of view. What really saved the day was that most people there couldn't have cared less about the research we were doing.

MS: Who?

EG: The Department of Child Psychiatry. They thought we were very odd, I think. We had mothers and babies from the local housing project and we then attracted house staff families, mothers and babies, who would come to our nursery, In September they were about ten or eleven months old, and they stayed with us until the end of the academic year. We got these babies by going to the house staff quarters where we would talk to them or to the local playground around the hospital. We also set ourselves up as a training programme, where we offered residents in psychiatry an experience in normal child development. And again, I don't think it would have taken off, except for the fact that we assigned each resident to a mother–child patient and they followed that pair throughout the year with one supervisor who remained their preceptor throughout the year.

MS: What did they do with this mother–child?

EG: Well, that was, of course, the problem. We worked out a number of categories. They were not terribly scientific or methodical to begin with. They were the usual ones, I think, every child researcher used. First we would get their past history, then the ongoing material behaviour, including sleep behaviour, motor development, body image development, mother–father relationship, etc.

MS: How often would the residents see this family?

EG: They had to spend eight hours a week in this elective (we made it an elective, by the way), so that every resident was there only if he wished to be. It was very popular, so that by the time we had run it for three years, we had fifteen residents who worked with ten babies and mothers, which was really much too much, and we had to cut it down. Of the eight hours that was spent in this elective, at least two hours a week had to be spent in the nursery itself observing the baby and talking to the mother. They had to spend at least another hour recording what they had seen. We had a literature seminar each week concurrently, and they had an individual supervisory session with their preceptor.

MS: What kind of person was that supervisor?

EG: The supervisor was either Herman Roiphe or myself, or one of the young people whom we gradually trained, a cadre of people who worked with us.

MS: Psychiatrists?

EG: Child psychiatrists, although later on it became trainees from other disciplines such as psychologists and special educators, and we did have one or two people who came to us from other hospitals who, having been through their analytic training, wanted some experience in early child development. So they also substituted. The whole point of this programme was to steep these people in experience with the first two years of life, mainly beginning at about eight to ten months of age. Our point of view was this: if you could give them a thorough knowledge and grounding in what happens between a mother and a child—and the father (because they made home visits at least once every two weeks, hopefully when the father was there), you did not have the gamut of development but you could give them a feeling of what a child and mother were really like in that one developmental period. The reason it was interesting to me was, not only in relation to Roiphe's sexual development theory but in reaction to the development of symbolism as well, I had been asked to write a paper on play for the first meeting of the Association for Child Psychoanalysis. I had never written a paper before, really, and I worked like a fiend on that and came up with the whole question of the symbolic meaning of play. So it brought me into Piaget, into Suzanne Langer's work, into the whole linguistic area. It was the first time that I had really "gone abroad", so to speak.[3]

I wrote a paper which has since served me as the basis for work that has gone on into the whole question of the development of the symbolic function, and that was the other area of the focus of our work. Therefore, in the course of observing children's play, what we then asked these residents to do was to observe certain categories which we called "derivative play". For example, there were certain kinds of play that were clearly based upon some of [Erik] Erikson's model and Lili Peller's work in play, that is derivative of various instinctual phases and somatic experiences.[4] There was the anal, and urinary, and final genital derivative play which became clear to us in many details during the first three or four years that we had been working in it. We could then give the residents clear examples of what we meant by anal derivative play, for instance. For example, a child who suddenly became very interested in the question of control, games would then involve turning light switches on and off, or playing with a toy where one has to push something in a tunnel and it comes out the other end. There was urinary derivative play—we were very lucky that we built the bathroom immediately adjacent to our nursery so that the toddlers and their mothers not only had free access but the toddler insisted that they get into that bathroom and there is where we observed the anal, urinary, and then genital material that Mahler did not. She has since acknowledged this, because their bathroom was way off somewhere, and the mothers went off to diaper their babies where nobody was around to watch them. Our babies would clamber on the doors of the bathroom and had to get inside.

MS: This research then modified your notions about your psychoanalytic theory as well as human behaviour?

EG: The psychoanalytic literature had long ago favoured the idea that there was the anal phase, and then the later regular genital phallic phase, but we were able to see anal behaviour and the influence of the anal zone awareness on practically every aspect of the child's life, including his play. This was a living illustration of anal phase development.

MS: How were your mentors in psychoanalysis receptive or not receptive to your coming up with evidence that showed that the earlier psychoanalytic theories should be modified?

EG: Well, that remains a sore point. I would say that maybe we expected more rapid acquiescence than anyone should. However, there have been some people who have been extremely interested, and influenced in their thinking by some of our findings and little by little it is creeping more and more into the analytic literature. Finally, Margaret Mahler discussed a paper of ours given at the New York Psychoanalytic Institute ["Some suggested revisions concerning early female development" February 11, 1975 (Galenson & Roiphe, 1976) and she admitted in that, because their material had been directed towards studying object relations rather than instinctual phases development, they had really not gotten that material initially, or rather had not taken cognisance of it. But as they went back over their records, they could find it recorded nonetheless.

MS: Where do you think child analysis is now? Where do you think child psychoanalysis is going as a therapy, as a technique to benefit children who are emotionally disturbed?

EG: I think they are missing the boat to some extent. First of all, there are very few child analysts who are convinced that you can analyse a child under five. There are, maybe a group of ten, twelve people in the country who actually are working with three year olds. On the other hand, as you know, there are some most important people in the trend towards early infancy work. Al Solnit, Louis Sander, a man on the West Coast, Justin Call, who is really quite important in this field, E. James

Anthony is very much involved in all of this, Judith Kestenberg, Margaret Mahler herself, of course, and then [Anni] Bergman and [Fred] Pine who come along in their work with Mahler. These are all analysts but the main body of child analysts, even in the Association of Child Psychoanalysis, still don't have a major interest in the field of infancy or early childhood. So what has happened is that I find myself, as do a number of people who are working with early childhood, joining forces with yet another group, many of whom are paediatricians, Berry Brazelton, Klaus, and Kennell in Western Reserve, a man named Daniel Stern at New York Hospital who has done some very interesting work about microanalysis of mother–infant interaction.

By the way, I should tell you this. After our normal research had been going for about three years, I started a therapeutic nursery there for children three years and under, in the course of which we had thirty-six autistic children coming our way over the course of six years. Our treatment model was mostly modelled after Margaret Mahler's tripartite model, mother always being there, and part of the therapeutic work. People of every discipline worked in our nursery, special education psychology, social work, anyone who was interested in early childhood. Some trainees came from child psychiatry. We had a couple of paediatricians in training and we simply trained them to work with these very, very disturbed young children and their mothers. It was a combined therapeutic effort, a training effort and also a research effort. I am still convinced that a therapeutic nursery like that will die on its feet unless it has a research orientation. The people who treat such sick children have to give so much to both the mothers and the children, the work is so debilitating, that it has to be fortified by what I have always seen as my particular contribution to that set-up, the reading seminars that always were part of our work, and the weekly conferences, that have always been part of both the normal research nursery and the therapeutic nursery. It was always my job to try to conceptualise and to see where we were theoretically. I found rather late in life—and where it came from, I don't know—that I had a certain understanding of the whole preverbal era which made me feel quite definite and sure of myself making inferences from behaviour back to what I thought was going on in terms of the psychological development of the child.

MS: Where do you think that insight came from?

EG: Well, I discussed it, of course, at length in the two analyses that I have had, personal analyses that helped me a great deal. I don't think I got as much from my first analyst; I think he learned more from me about early childhood than I from him but he was very interested in my work and he was also a good friend of Phyllis Greenacre. Greenacre has been for me one of the most fruitful people in the analytic field, in terms of her papers and in terms of talking over all of my work with her, and she supported these early ideas that seemed crazy to a lot of other people. My first analyst probably encouraged me to go into the field of infant research because, in a way, I was working out what I think was a very important personal problem of mine. As I look back on it, I was one of those failure-to-thrive infants who somehow lived. According to my mother's description of my background, I was supposed to die before I was a year old and I somehow, miraculously lived, in spite of the fact that I wasn't eating. And I knew that in my first analysis, I never got an understanding of what that was all about and what certain quirks in me were all about. Somehow or other, I became convinced and I have compared notes with Margaret Mahler who has a similar background in terms of her early physical pathology as a child, that we were trying to work out something that we did not understand in our own lives and that gave us an entrée into this field.

MS: Where do you think child analysis is now, particularly thinking of all the children who are disturbed, emotionally disturbed, needing help? What are we going to do about that in psychoanalysis?

EG: I think that the best we can do is to work out . . . well, let me tell you what my present point of view is. I have a feeling of despair about offering what I consider decent treatment to the bulk of the sick children that are out there. I think what we have to do is to work out effective ideas or some knowledge of what the basic problem is that goes wrong between mother and child in that first year of life. I have been very affected by the work of Lewis Sander up in Boston (not out in Denver), of Brazelton, and of a group of people whom I respect whose work now begins to show, Stern among others, that something goes wrong in the meshing of mother and child in the first six months.

For example, my own idea about the cause of childhood autism is really quite different than some other people's, in that I feel it's either the mother who cannot respond because of her own inner problems, depression, whatever, or a real deficit in the child's capability to seek response. We had a lot of mothers whom I would call depressed mothers, but you don't find that they have been depressed until you get to know them very well, and that often means three years later. Then they tell you how depressed they were, wanting to kill that child, for example. Or, there is the child who, for its own constitutional reasons, does not have enough sending power, he cannot draw the mother to him, and can't demand enough from that mother to make her pay attention.

I think the bulk of our work should be put into training people to work with very, very young babies and their mothers, and by young I mean from birth on. Workers should be drawn from every discipline. I don't care where they come from. Detection and intervention, I think, is most effective when done before the first two years of life are over, hopefully before the first year is over. That is where I think our efforts should go.

MS: Intervention by anybody that can help: paediatricians, nurses, psychiatrists?

EG: Right. And for the first time, the Academy of Pediatrics has asked the Academy of Child Psychiatry to come in on a joint venture in which we are setting up institutes where both paediatricians and child psychiatrists will hear about work done during the infancy period.

MS: What kind of institute? These are transient annual meetings or permanent organisations?

EG: Well, the first institute is going to be in February 1978 out in Newport Beach on the West Coast. We are going to have the second one three months later in New York, and the third one is planned for a year later. This is the function of a newly formed committee of the Academy of Child Psychiatry called The Committee on the Psychiatric Dimensions of Infancy. I am its second chairman; the first chairman was Justin Call. The idea is that we will hopefully get back to where we started—to the paediatricians.

MS: Who are the attendants in these institutes? Practioners in paediatrics and psychiatry? They are to commune with each other and teach each other?

EG: We are going to have experts presenting their material, the best in the field. Then we are going to have workshops after that. We are going to have both paediatricians presenting material and child psychiatrists presenting material. Most analysts are still not all that involved.

MS: Thank you very much. I think this is an interesting, rounded out picture of where you have been and how you evolved your ideas and how your practice has changed. Thank you very much.

EG: You are welcome and I am very, very glad to do it. I hope I have not been too lengthy, but it has been quite an experience to discuss the past years.

Notes

1. Oskar Diethelm, M.D. (1897–1993) was the chairman of the Department of Psychiatry at Cornell University Medical College and Psychiatrist-in-Chief of the Payne Whitney Clinic between 1936 and 1962. A protégé of Adolph Meyer at Johns Hopkins's Henry Phipps Clinic, Diethelm shared his mentor's ambivalence towards psychoanalysis.
2. Sibylle Escalona (1915–1995), born in Berlin, came to the US in 1935. She spent eight years doing research and clinical work with infants and young children at the Menninger Foundation, Topeka, Kansas, where David Rapaport was the Director of Research, a position Escalona eventually assumed. In 1956 she moved to the Albert Einstein College of Medicine. In an interview she recounted the breadth and depth of infant research in the 1940s and 1950s, as well as the research findings of her two books: *Prediction and Outcome* (Escalona & Heider, 1959), and *The Roots of Individuality* (1968) (Escalona, 1983). Winnicott highly praised her work (Thompson, 2013).
3. Galenson's paper, "The nature of thought in childhood play" is the first paper in this volume.
4. Galenson here is referring to Erikson's 1937 paper, "Configurations in play—clinical notes" where he described gender differences in the spatial configurations of children's play. That is, boys built towers and girls constructed enclosures. Lili Peller, an émigré child analyst who wrote extensively on play and language. See: "Phases of ego development and play" (Peller, 1954).

References

Erikson, E. (1937). Configurations in play—clinical notes. *The Psychoanalytic Quarterly, 6*: 139–214.

Escalona, S. (1968). *The Roots of Individuality: Normal Patterns of Development in Infancy*. Chicago: Aldine.

Escalona, S. (1983). The Reminiscences of Sibylle Escalona. *Infant Development Project*. Columbia Center for Oral History. New York: Columbia University.

Escalona, S., & Heider, G. M. (1959). *Prediction and Outcome: A Study in Child Development*. New York: Basic Books.

Galenson, E., & Roiphe, H. (1976). Some suggested revisions concerning early female development. *Female Psychology, Supplement, Journal of the American Psychoanalytic Association, 28*: 29–57.

Peller, L. E. (1954). Libidinal phases, ego development and play. *The Psychoanalytic Study of the Child, 9*: 178–198.

Roiphe, H. (1968). On an early genital phase: with an addendum on genesis. *The Psychoanalytic Study of the Child, 23*: 348–365.

Thompson, N. L. (2013). Winnicott and American analysts. In: J. Abram (Ed.), *Donald Winnicott Today*, (pp. 386–417). London: Routledge.

PROLOGUE

Our children, our future: a conversation with Eleanor Galenson

Lucy LaFarge

Lucy LaFarge: How did you first become interested in psychoanalysis?

Eleanor Galanson: My first real interest was stirred by a talk that Phyllis Greenacre gave at the Payne-Whitney Clinic on the children of successful fathers. I was very impressed with what she had understood, which was far more than I had ever heard, and I talked to her immediately after that meeting. I was in the process of thinking that I should probably get into psychoanalysis and possibly on into psychoanalytic training. At that time, I was at Payne-Whitney as a Commonwealth fellow. I had originally planned to go back into paediatrics after two years, but I knew as soon as I began psychiatry that I was in the right place.

I obtained analytic training in two phases. First was my personal analysis—a very preliminary, one-year stint with Eugene Pumpian-Mindlin. It was an odd way to begin because, although he eventually became a full-fledged analyst, at that time he had little or no analytic training himself. That contact with Pumpian-Mindlin was important. He was very bright, and although the treatment was unorthodox it had the makings of an analysis.

A training analysis followed. I wanted to go into analysis with Greenacre, but she had no time. Eventually I was steered to Bela

Heksch. What I remember best from that analysis was how important it had been for me that my father had had what was supposed to be a coronary when I was seven or eight. It was diagnosed by an eminent cardiac specialist, and my father was told that he would be dead within the year. However, he continued to work and to have pericardial pain. He had what would now be called cardiac neurosis. After two years, he was told that his heart was okay. He had episodes of what I now know was acute anxiety.

LL: Do you think that the presence of a real strain trauma in your life was one of the reasons why you became interested in the observation of actual children rather than only the backward projection of childhood experience?

EG: That experience was undoubtedly central. I still remember all the details—how it felt, hanging out the window waiting for him to come home. But there was another experience that I remember being told about rather than remembering directly: I was a failure-to-thrive child from age two months to two years. That was a bona fide illness. I remember being told of a famous statement made by an uncle of mine. He told my mother that there were a lot of graves over in the cemetery, and if I died there would be another. I think this anorexia had a lifelong effect, since it was such a real and intense experience.

My own very early experiences probably contributed to the strong response I had to Greenacre. She was the first woman for whom I felt unequivocal intellectual admiration. It's hard to separate what she said from the way in which she said it. She was an extremely effective speaker. There was an emotionality that she conveyed, a vividness. She had an enormous and special type of empathy that enabled her to present her material that way. Recently, when I was attending an analytic case presentation, I could not really understand the material until I stopped listening to the words and started listening to the "music." That was the quality that Greenacre gave out. It was what made her charismatic as a lecturer. But from the very beginning, I knew that what she said was right. I had never put my own early experiences into any usable form. With Greenacre, I felt for the first time that here was someone who was putting into words the essence of what I felt.

LL: How did you begin your own creative work?

EG: I began to work creatively rather late. I was pregnant during both the first and third years of my analytic training. Almost all my emotional interest and attention was focused on my children. I was very preoccupied, and I don't think I understood very much about analysis until later years, although my mentors did not pick up any weakness in my grasp of theory.

I owe my first serious attempt at analytic writing to my good friend Jacob Arlow. I had been invited to discuss a paper on a panel. Afterward, Jack came up to me and said, "I always thought you were beautiful, but I never thought you could think so well". I had a lot of respect for Jack. I decided to write and wrote my first paper on play. I was using play, as all of us were, in treating children. Seeing nine children a day was a very intensive experience, and I had become comfortable with the medium of play and with talking about it. Play was not a strange land for me. My real problem was in trying to conceptualise the meaning of play.

LL: How did you become involved in the study of female development?

EG: Just at the time when I began to plan the nursery that I would run at Einstein, Herman Roiphe showed me a paper that was later published about a little girl in her second year when he had been studying in Mahler's nursery (Roiphe, 1968). The child had displayed a very early castration reaction. I was interested. I had already written the paper on play and was interested in language development. I had done some work with Victor Rosen on delayed language development in psychotic children. These interests had led me to concentrate on the second year of life. Then Herman told me about the little girl. In this child with an early castration reaction, he had also observed an associated change in language development, although that was not what we later discovered during our joint research about the deletion of sex-linked words under the impact of the early castration reactions. Our mutual interest in the second year led to a collaboration. From the very beginning, in the research nursery funded by the Department of Psychiatry at Albert Einstein, we had two hypotheses, one having to do with sexual development and the other having to do with the development of language, thought, and play.

LL: Were you surprised by your findings about sexuality?

EG: I was surprised by the consistency, by the broad spread of the effect in both boys and girls, of their awareness of sexuality, its effect on every area including language development. It took fifteen years to collect and go over our data. The data were collected by the residents, using twenty-five different categories of behaviour. It was my job to examine the flow sheets and try to determine the commonalities.

As I went through the data on the sixty-five children, I found surprising similarities. We began to realise that we were dealing with across-the-board findings such as the band-aids the girls requested, their stealing pencils, their playing horsey, their masturbatory activity. I was very interested in structural similarities between seemingly different behaviours, such as a ball dropped into a hole as being similar structurally to defecation.

Then we began studying children before their discovery of genital difference and found that we were able to date the onset of urinary and anal awareness by observing derivative behaviours. For example, urinary-derivative behaviour consisted of a child's playing with faucets and pouring instead of drinking at the table. These structural similarities provide a way of thinking about play. Every area of these children's lives seemed to be influenced by the early genital psychosexual phase they were going through. It helped to know Mahler's (1963) view about how children try to find in the outside world what they are experiencing within their own bodies.

LL: To form your hypotheses about infantile sexuality, then, you had to form a series of hypotheses about play and its relation to drive development that had not been formulated before.

EG: These hypotheses about play had been formulated in part. Mahler had come up with the idea of the child's externalisation of inner experience. Then, from another direction, that of the linguists, came the idea of structural similarities. I simply put that idea together with Mahler's idea to find a way of categorising play. This combination was enormously helpful. In this way, we were able to study psychosexual development through behaviour, language, and play.

LL: How have your findings concerning early female development affected your work with adult women?

EG: While I was working with children, I was also seeing adult patients. A number of women were graduate students in whom I saw the equivalent of the little girl's experience during her phase of pre-oedipal acute castration anxiety. In my adult female patients' examination anxiety, intellect now stood for the phallus. The castration anxiety was clearly connected with anxiety about separation and anxiety about bodily intactness as well. This linkage was consistent with my own personal experience.

Another thing I became aware of in our research was the great importance of the father's validation of the girls' femininity. I saw that often a girl's receiving a doll or a doll carriage when she was at the height of her pre-oedipal anxiety was crucial in her turning very strongly and erotically toward the father. He was the one who acknowledged her femininity. She sought him out, and he responded, and then came her increasing interest in dolls. My father was extremely loving and gave me dolls, dolls, dolls, and from early on I liked to make doll's clothes. My pleasure in that experience contributed both to my later interest in observing children and to the satisfaction that I found in being a mother. Having children was something that I never doubted I wanted to do from my earliest years.

My father was very affectionate toward me, and that affection protected me from much of the competition with my brother and my mother, which would have defeated me. I was never considered a beauty by my mother, but somehow or other I got the idea—from my father, I think—that I could get up before an assembly at school and recite poetry with pride. I remember the great satisfaction I had in having an audience. The audience may be your father. It should be your mother, but if not, it is your father. Also, part of my confidence came from the fact that, for whatever reason, I've always had a good sense of my own body. I danced from very early on, ice skated, and was very athletic. Maybe I became an athlete in order to be accepted by my brother. My body has always served as a source of pleasure. My intellect was more of a problem. I didn't have much confidence in my intellectual abilities. I knew, though, that I was good at many things. For example, though my brother was quite hypochondriacal, I was counter-phobic and daring. My brother's hypochondriasis probably also led to my choice of a medical career.

LL: That accounted for your deciding to become a doctor?

EG: My choice of vocation came from two other sources: my father's tacit support of my taking care of the dolls he had given me; and my cousin, John Garlock, was an outstanding physician, much admired by my mother. He was the first Jewish resident at New York Hospital and later became head of surgery at Mt Sinai. The summer after my father was proclaimed all right, my brother broke his leg while playing football and was operated on by John. My brother was in a cast for the next six months. That period was a nightmare and changed the character of my family. They were preoccupied with medicine and thought of John as a genius. I think my going to medical school was probably in part because being a doctor was so special to my family.

LL: You said earlier that one of your main interests when you began your research nursery was in language development. Where has that taken you?

EG: I have studied interferences with language development over and over again. I can remember talking to my good friend Justin Call long ago about our peculiar early finding that girls drop male–female labels while in the throes of early castration reactions. We are still puzzled by that finding. In our study of deaf children, we found that they are delayed in urinary- and anal-phase development as well as in language development. I think—not everyone agrees with me—that their delay in language development is a function, not only of their impaired hearing, but also of the distortion of the mother–child relationship, a distortion that takes place very early in these children.

LL: These are deaf children of hearing mothers, or of deaf mothers, or of either?

EG: Of either. The delay is worse when the mothers are deaf. Their behaviour with the children is very deviant. In their own development, they had the same problems their children are having. The mothers hold their children always facing the world, never facing themselves, even when giving them the bottle. Their rationalisation is that since the children cannot hear, they should be able to see the world. The rationalisation covers up the fact that these mothers either do not have the need or do not have the capacity for intimate contact with their children. Their relationship is never a comfortable, truly symbiotic one. The child remains distant. When you work with deaf children, you have to substitute for the maternal object.

Another of our findings was that neither deaf mothers nor their deaf children play with toys. My early work with play helped me to understand those deaf children who could not progress even to the stage of using a toy as a concrete symbol for semisymbolic play because the relationship with the mother was of such poor quality and self and object were not well distinguished. We engaged the children in regressive activity. We fed them bottles, held them, rocked them—provided them with tactile, kinesthetic, primitive kinds of experiences they had never had.

LL: Why were those experiences impaired in addition to the auditory ones?

EG: The mother–child relationship depends very much on feedback in all modalities. Some of the children we worked with were not recognised as hearing impaired until they were six or seven months old, when they stopped babbling. While some of the mothers had instinctively used visual cues, most mothers had not. One mother held the child in front of the mirror, for example, and her child had a fair amount of spontaneous language development. Such observations brought me to the conclusion—not everyone agrees with me—that unless there is a neurological impairment, language delay is secondary to object relations pathology. To treat these children, you work with the object relations pathology. The children go through the delayed development of urinary and anal awareness—sometimes out of sync with other aspects of their development—and when anal derivative play appears, language emerges spontaneously. Also, both hostile and non-hostile aggression emerges at the same time. From being passive children, they begin to hit out and assert themselves.

LL: Recently you have been working with very young gender-disordered boys. What have you been finding?

EG: It has become evident that there are several different kinds of gender disturbances, which range from very benign to very malignant. There is no doubt that a child with a serious gender disturbance that is manifest by the end of the second year has a history of disturbance that began much earlier, during the first year of life. There is a quality of concreteness in the thinking of these children and in their general behaviour. They don't play in the ordinary way. They enact plays, for example, probably because their anxiety about disidentifying with the mother results in an unstable maternal attachment. The boys cannot disidentify with mother and retain their phallicity at the same time. Instead they surrender their phallic quality and remain caught in an overly intense symbiotic relationship with the mother.

The relationship has an unusual quality to it. The boy seems to get the mother's thinking and fantasies by osmosis. How he becomes tuned into the mother's wishes is very hard to explain. He imitates the mother's actions and facial expressions to an incredible extent yet does not seem to truly internalise her emotionally. He is the mimic of later life. The difficulty in his individuation, in the development of his own self-representations is a very serious one, because he has a problem not only with genital representation but with the total self and object representation. The genital problem is only the final aspect of the total problem.

These boys adopt all the feminine accoutrements—the mother's pearls or beads or bags, anything that smells of her. The attachment is based on very primitive qualities—taste, kinesthetic sense—all the perceptual modalities. The boys develop an armamentarium of fetishistic objects that serves to protect them against intense separation anxiety. Why do they have such great separation anxiety? Probably the major reason is that they are sitting on a dangerous load of very primitive hostile aggression that threatens the maternal object relationship. Their fantasies, the figures they draw based on their fantasies, are all of monsters or sharks that could devour mother. Lots of blood and gore. The boys have to defend themselves against this oral aggression as best they can. Their defence takes the form of an infantile fetishistic attachment to the mother. The way to deal with these children in therapy is to help them and their parents to recognise and tolerate their anger at the mother, which has to emerge in very small quantities or they go into panic states. The children's anxiety and rage is very great, and the mothers need to be helped to tolerate it.

LL: You work with the mothers as well.

EG: Always. Either the mother or the father is in the therapy room at every session, and the parents are seen separately in addition. There is no doubt that the mothers of these children are dealing with their own very deeply repressed aggression. It comes out mostly in the form of "I am afraid of what will happen to my child" or "I am afraid of my father's rages". The mothers often have a history of important depressions. For example, one mother told me, "I went back to work early after he was born because it was important to my career". It turns out that the mother had fantasies of strangling the child and went back to work to escape from her infanticidal wishes. These were barely conscious at the time and were recollected at a much later period after treatment of the boy had been underway for two and a half years.

LL: What might be remembered later as the child's reaction to the separation with the mother going back to work would actually be related to the mother's earlier reaction toward the child.

EG: Yes. Also, you have to look at the relationship of the mother to *her* mother to get the real flavour. The mother of the gender-disturbed child is often bound in a sadomasochistic relationship with her own mother; she has never felt that her mother approved of her. The son is somehow supposed to make up to the grandmother for the mother's shortcomings. Such mothers have to make the boy into a female because they have come to connect hostile aggression with maleness. In their families of origin, the parental relationship was such that the girl (the mother of the gender-disordered son) never went on to form a satisfactory relationship with her father. It's a three-generation issue.

LL: Much has been written recently about burnout in psychoanalysis. You have been creative for a long time. How do you account for your continuing creativity?

EG: I never tire of going to our nursery and watching children. I focus on one child, and at the end of ten minutes I am very deeply engrossed in that child and curious about the meaning of that child's behavior. I seem to be able—I don't know why—to screen out other things that are going on and concentrate on that child. Children know that. That's what makes one a good therapist for young children: to be able to communicate to the child that you have eyes and ears only for that child and for no one else.

In connection with my adult patients, this morning I was talking to a colleague who has seen a few of my adult patients for medication. He told me that they all love me. "Boy, they hang on to you," he said. I think the secret is not just that they are dependent people, but that I find most people very interesting. Yes, I'm tired after a week's work with the accumulation of paying attention, but I never get tired while I'm *paying* attention, trying to figure them out.

References

Mahler, M. (1963). Thoughts about development and individuation. *The Psychoanalytic Study of the Child, 18*: 307–324.

Roiphe, H. (1968). On an early genital phase: with an addendum on genesis. *The Psychoanalytic Study of the Child, 23*: 348–365.

PART I

SYMBOLISATION, THOUGHT, AND LANGUAGE

Introduction to Part I

Patricia Nachman

Every few weeks, without fail, I would receive a phone call from Eleanor Galenson. Her voice filled with excitement, she would begin to tell me about a baby she had observed that day. For her, each child she saw in her clinical practice communicated discoveries that never ceased to capture her attention and ignite her mind.

Two weeks before Eleanor's death, I received a phone call about a twenty-three-month old toddler. As she talked about this child she touched upon some of the factors that were central to her thinking about the use of symbolic thought in very young children. Her interest in the origins of symbolic representation stemmed from years of observation as she noted those children who readily made the shift from action to thought as compared to those who had much more difficulty.

In her quest to understand the origins and development of symbolism she was open to discoveries in other fields that might shed light on the questions she was pondering. She turned to authors outside of the psychoanalytic literature and focused on work from the fields of psychology and psycholinguistics and eagerly read Susanne K. Langer, Jean Piaget, Heinz Werner, Jerry Bruner, and Lev Vygotsky, and invited a psycholinguist, John Dore, to her weekly clinical meetings. After absorbing an understanding of how academics outside of the field of psychoanalysis conceptualised pre-symbolic thought, she began to compare the psychoanalytic concept of primary process thinking with the psycholinguist's understanding of pre-linguistic thought.

During our phone conversation Eleanor proceeded with an enthusiasm that I had heard many times before. On this day she was telling me about Jake. Jake was sitting with his mother at a table drawing when Dr Galenson started to observe them. With enormous energy and much gusto he scribbled heavy dark lines back and forth on a piece of paper with a "jumbo" crayon. "What are you drawing?" his mother asked. Jake did not answer. He was absorbed in his drawing and continued to scribble vigorously. Suddenly, he stopped drawing and with a sigh looked up and said, "Mommy, my penis hurts when I draw". His mother hesitated for a moment, smiled, and then suggested that he play with something else. Jake ran across the room and picked up a toy broom and instead of sweeping with it he began to vigorously poke at a pile of toys that were on the floor. His mother quickly admonished him, "be careful . . . brooms are for sweeping". Jake hesitated for a moment, swiped at the toys one or two more times, picked up a car and stated to play with it by rolling it back and forth with an occasional crash into another toy—all the while clutching the broom with his other hand.

Looking back on this scene it is easy to see why Eleanor was so struck by what she saw in this everyday vignette between a mother and her child. It illustrates a number of issues pertinent to the affective and interpersonal context in which symbolisation is born as well as some of the psychodynamic and biological factors that she believed were strong influences in the development of the symbolic function. Basic to these precursor components is the close relationship between biological needs and their psychic representations, which ultimately will have a major impact on the content of symbolisation. Thus the earliest symbolic representations will be of the body with the descriptive properties of the symbol taking on the physical qualities of the body.

Eleanor and I both commented on her good fortune to be present during the brief moment in Jake's development when the link between the body and its representation is still part of conscious awareness. Or in Susanne Langer's terms, where there is no separation between the signifier and the signified. We knew that, within short time, Jake would no longer *directly* equate the jumbo crayon with his penis but instead would hold the crayon in mind as a symbolic and most likely an unconscious representation of his penis.

Our conversation returned to a place where we had been many times before—the central role of the body in symbol formation. Eleanor's thinking was always anchored to the affirmation of Freud's postulate that the ego is first of all a body ego. She deeply believed that the means by which one experiences and formulates aspects of external reality are built up through experiences of one's own body.

It is not surprising then to find that erotogenic zones became the main focus of her research. Bodily needs in relation to libidinal phase development gave this cornerstone of psychoanalytic theory a central place in all of her work. She believed that through play the child expresses its fantasies and its wishes and that the child's play gave expression to the natural experiences that were activated during the maturational development of the psychosexual zones. Jake provided a good example of this emergent process. Looking back on this scene we can identify many antecedents of Jake's "symbolising activities"— whether in gesture, play or language. He verbalised the word penis and in action and in play continued to be aware of his penis though it was now in the process of being represented by the crayon as well as the broom and cars. Jake turned to poking some toys with the broom, never letting go of it even as he shifted his interest to mildly aggressive play with cars. Eleanor commented to me how Jake's awareness of his penis was infused in the *form* of his play. "I believe that whatever he does at this time will in some way represent his penis—there must be new sensations that he has not experienced before that is making him so aware of this part of his anatomy in his current mode of play", she said with the conviction of someone who had observed this form of play in young children many times before.

The importance of perceptual, motor, and cognitive development for symbolisation can never be excluded from consideration and although these elements were often not focused on in her written work they were very much a part of her thinking. For example, Jake had now been upright for several months. Eleanor pointed out, as she had many times before, that along with this achievement he was now able to see his penis, observe his urine stream, and experience new sensations of which we could only guess at although in this instance Jake told us very readily that he was experiencing a sensation that hurt. It is of interest to note that Eleanor had worked with Sibylle Escalona, a noted infant researcher, testing children on the Piaget Object Permanence Developmental Scales. She was familiar with the changes in child cognitive maturation and with developmental timetables and the influence such changes exert on other emerging processes—and that only very gradually is cognition separated from sensory experience. We talked about Jake's outstanding motor, perceptual, and cognitive development and how these emerging capacities seemed to be flourishing in concert including his capacity for symbolisation. Our conversation detoured for a moment as Eleanor turned to a topic that she was passionate about—the disadvantages children have when they are developmentally compromised or environmentally deprived.

These thoughts brought us to a topic that was the central in all of her work. In this instance how the relationship between the parents and child impacted on the child's development and capacity for symbolisation. Here we can observe the careful attention Eleanor gave to the *interpersonal setting* within which the first symbolic acts occur and thus influence the development of further symbolisation. Returning to Jake and his mother, Eleanor noted how very well attuned they were to each other and asked if I had noticed that when Jake said his penis hurt while drawing his mother told him to "stop drawing". For a while we debated the mother's response to Jake because one could argue that she was playing into his fears by telling him to stop playing. "Perhaps she should have guided him more on the side of reality", I offered. "No", Eleanor uttered emphatically, "this mother knew exactly where he was at". At this moment in his life the crayon in his hand made a direct line in his mind to his penis and the sensations that followed, and although Jake's mother may not have been able to articulate his level of symbolic development, intuitively she understood that he was having these sensations and that it was better to validate them, rather than instruct for him that drawing does not make penises hurt. We talked about how well attuned this mother was with her child, and agreed that in three or four months, her suggestion to do something else instead of drawing when Jake complained about his penis hurting would most likely not have been appropriate. We commented once again on how finely attuned mothers (parents) need to be to developmental shifts at the moment they are occurring; and, how this example helped us to examine the process of displacement from the original zonal site to outside objects that are then utilised as concrete semi-symbolic representatives of the bodily experience; a displacement that is an essential element in the symbolic process.

Eleanor noted how in this mother–child interaction Jake was able to look up at his mother, and share with her that he had an ache. We read into his gesture his implicit trust in his mother and his feeling that she might be able to be helpful to him. His leaving the drawing table quite agreeably suggested that he thought her advice was good. We also noted that when she admonished him about how he was playing with the broom he stopped what he was doing and chose something else to play with on his own, even though he showed some resistance by holding on to the broom and making mild crashes with a toy car he picked up. Thus, he was able to protest by letting his mother know that he did not like the limit she placed on his aggressive play with the broom. To us this appeared to be a child who was libidinally connected in a positive way to his mother, but was also expressing some phallic aggression and protest, while at the same time was able to modify his behaviour according to his mother's wishes. We speculated that there was a favourable balance between libido and aggression in this pair and that the positive quality of the mother–child relationship would help to maximally promote Jake's development and, more specifically, his capacity for symbolisation.

The papers Eleanor wrote on symbolisation crystallised these thoughts in a more formal manner. In "A consideration of the nature of thought in childhood play" (1971) she examined the mental organisation or structure of children's play especially for the light it may shed on the nature and genesis of thought, the understanding of the development of the symbolic function and the precursors to the process of sublimation.

This paper draws on the literature from a variety of fields outside of psychoanalysis including developmental psychology, cognitive psychology, and psycholinguistics. The contributions of Werner and Kaplan, Mahler, Vygotsky, Piaget, and Langer and their theoretical formulations and clinical material, serve as the foundation upon which this paper rests. The work of these authors supported Eleanor's view that the earliest stages of thought initially evolve from experiences with the body, its parts, and the bodily processes. But it was Langer's work (1942) that had the greatest impact on her thinking because it provided detailed formulations concerning the nature of pre-linguistic thought. According to Langer, the keynote of pre-linguistic thinking is the communication of *feeling* through modes of activity and motion. Phyllis Greenacre (1959) expanded upon this idea by pointing out that play arises as a way of channelling the intensities of feeling and action patterns; she proposed that play functions as a means of energy discharge. Play also carries with it a degree of plasticity so that there is room for individual variation a notion that was later aligned with the capacity for creativity and sublimation. In the simplest state play is a powerful mode of communication for the very young child. Eleanor was keen to understand more about the structure of children's play patterns particularly for the light it might shed on the nature of pre-symbolic thinking.

Langer's work on the development of symbolism in music and visual art provided the substantive foundation she was searching for. Langer believed that visual forms are as capable of articulation and complex combinations as words, but that visual forms are altogether different from the laws of syntax that govern language. Langer called this "pre-representational symbolism" and illustrated it in relation to music and visual art.

These ideas helped to support Eleanor's view that pre-linguistic infants were capable of thought long before language evolves, and that such thought is more in keeping with the qualities associated music and art than the qualities characteristic of discursive language. These symbols as in art and visual forms are global and changeable, structured in the child's world of sensation, feeling, bodily rhythms, shape, and time, and most importantly, an awareness of repetitive elements, similar in configuration, that are registered by the infant. Thus play utilises the overflow of energy and allows for the continuity of experience and strengthens representational gestalts. Langer and Greenacre's conceptualisations added compelling support for Eleanor's view that symbolism originates from a somatic foundation.

What then does Eleanor Galenson conclude about the nature of thought in children's play? Drawing on a clinical example she described how the sequences of play lead back to early bodily experiences that appear to have contributed to the particular variety of symbolic representation. She also concurs with other authors that pre-representational thinking is endowed with a quality that makes it capable of connotation and is employed to articulate emotional and sensuous experience that has similarities to music and art. But Eleanor contributes an additional consideration to these ideas. She posits that the organisation of thought is not only a matter of sensation and bodily experience but the choice of symbolised objects depends on the drives and the development of the currently active psychosexual erogenous zones. She concluded her paper by advocating for further systematic studies of the sequences and variations of symbolic representations as very young children advance through the stages of psychosexual development.

In "The impact of early sexual discovery on mood, defensive organization, and symbolization" (Galenson & Roiphe, 1971) Eleanor Galenson elaborates thinking about the infant's sense of its own body, drawing on the example of a child who has a somatic problem and its impact on several areas of her subsequent development as she becomes aware of the genital difference between boys and girls.

This paper refers to earlier work of Herman Roiphe's (1968) that documented the existence of a phase, earlier than had previously been thought, from about sixteen to twenty-four months when very young children discover the anatomical difference between boys and girls. Roiphe proposed that this sexual interest is a normal developmental period but that it also is a period when the discovery of the sexual difference can have an intense impact on a child and particularly on those children who have had unduly harsh early experiences (e.g., physical disturbances of the body or poor or absent mothering). These children tend to show early castration reactions and the development of early ego functioning is more problematic. The paper gives detailed descriptions of the behavioural patterns that underlie their conclusions.

The observations are of one little girl from the age of twelve to twenty-two months, were used to illustrate Roiphe and Galenson's hypothesis that children who experience, during their first year, such insults as a major physical defect, severe illness, surgical intervention, orthopaedic corrections, or emotional neglect by the mothering figure will suffer severe anxiety at the discovery of the sexual difference that will be observable in the primitive symbolism of their play.

Ruth had a congenital defect for which a corrective device was worn from the third to the twelfth month of her life. Her mother's extreme anxiety made it impossible for her to respond adequately to Ruth and what she was experiencing leading to a disturbance in Ruth's developing relationship with her mother. The resulting disturbance in body schematisation and the mother–child relationship distorted and delayed Ruth's separation individuation process and interfered with the establishment of an optimally stable mental representation of self and mother. Once she was free of the corrective device and could enjoy developed free locomotion, there was a spurt in individuation and in symbolic development along with the emergence of symbolic play and an enlarged verbal capacity. But her anxiety continued to be intense at around nineteen and twenty months with the onset of her genital curiosity and her observation of the genital difference. She regressed back to earlier biting and mouthing behaviour and she became disturbed by broken toys. The toilet handle, knobs, cars, and a variety of protruding objects became objects she repeatedly fingered and vigorously held on to. At the same time there were changes in her mood, along with anger at her mother, a loss of self-esteem and a marked inhibited and depressive reaction. At follow-up at thirty-one months of age Ruth's earlier difficulties in the areas of self esteem, object relations, and other aspects of ego functioning such as non-verbal and verbal symbolisation were still in evidence; the castration anxiety of her second year of life remained in evidence. Galenson used this clinical example primarily to illustrate the fundamental impact of the body as the original source of symbolic thought, and the effect of these early representations on the disposition to anxiety, and the resulting defensive operations, affects, and mood, and the quality of the capacity for symbolisation.

While the previous paper emphasised the body and the effect of bodily illness or injury on the evolving ego functions of defence, mood, and thought, in *Influences on the Development of the Symbolic Function* (Galenson, 1984) Galenson emphasised the influence of object relations on the onset, nature, configuration, and structure of symbolic play as it comingled with the influence of the unfolding of psychosexual organisation. It is well known that deficits in object relations exert a profound effect upon the infant's investment in toys and play of all kinds, but often the cases that were cited were extreme examples of deprivation. In response Galenson paid attention to the differences in play and symbolisation of children from less extreme conditions and accordingly fine-tuned the variations in the quality of play and symbolisation she observed. She pointed out how differences in parental style and attitudes play a part in the choice of symbols and play activity, noting how very different mothers were in their enjoyment of play, how they used inanimate objects, and how comfortable they were using fantasy or expressing feelings.

However, while all of these factors are important, Galenson concludes her paper by stating emphatically that it is the general quality of maternal responsiveness to the infant that most facilitates or inhibits psychological development. The mother's capacity to correctly acknowledge and validate the nature of her infant's affective state and her acting contingently with it, enables the infant to discriminate affective states which, in turn, plays a vital role in the development of thought and symbolic function. Difficulties in the parent–child relationship or failure in maternal contingent unresponsiveness to the infant's process for thought and early symbolic steps jeopardise the infant's capacity to transform mental representations into more complex and various symbolic systems.

It is fitting to include in this chapter Galenson's paper on "The influence of hostile aggression on the development of expressive language" (1995) because it emphasises the importance she placed on drive theory in her understanding of the mother–child relationship. In this paper she emphasises the dynamic factors and the contribution of the drives and their modification as to how ego development proceeds. Accordingly, the libidinal–aggressive drive imbalance in the case she presents appears to interfere with the developing symbolic function, specifically in regard to expressive language.

In trying to understand more about the unconscious and its symbolic representations, with remarkable energy and perseverance, Eleanor focused on the second and third year of life. The period when early symbol formation is still a very intimate reflection of the drive components and their biological connection to the erotogenic zones. She was virtually alone, along with Roiphe, in recording those pre-symbolic forms of representation that are natural to the thinking of very young pre-oedipal children.

Eleanor's work has helped us to see that the second and third year of life is a particularly fruitful arena for the study of symbolisation in that it offers numerous examples of pre-symbolic activities that shed light on the process as a whole. By looking at the ontogenesis of symbolisation she examined in *status nascendi* the early development of transitional objects, play, and language. In terms of the clinical situation and the early detection of psychological difficulties, she strongly believed that clinical adult and child practitioners benefited from a deeper understanding of the development of both normal and pathological symbolic functioning.

Finally, Eleanor felt that an examination of the roots of the symbolic process may bring us closer to understanding its most complex form, the creative process in the artist. We tend to lose touch with the somatic foundation and normal fluidity that occurs in preverbal symbol formation and therefore in early thought processes. We have been surprisingly blind to the temporal dynamics of rhythm, force, and balance, which provide the temporal backbone that gives a feeling of coherence to early mental life. Eleanor's work, informed by the contributions of Greenacre and Langer, hints at this in her descriptions of preverbal thought, but the ideas that absorbed her attention are just now beginning to be more fully understood and explicated in current day research.

Eleanor was a pioneer in the endeavour to understand the mind of the young child and up until her last day she was excited and enthusiastic about sharing and comparing her thoughts and observations. She had the rare ability to capture the nature of the subjective experiences of very young children in a way that was plausible and dynamically meaningful. At times I would admonish her about the inferential leaps she was making but she quickly defended herself by saying that we would remain clinically sterile unless one was willing to make such leaps particularly about the subjective life of the infant. "After all", she said, "one needs the freedom to follow their intuition and allow 'creative' moments to unfold—at least preliminarily". I often thought to myself during our conversations that despite our seriousness and determination to understand more and more, that we too were in touch with the mind set and developmental wellspring of play—we brought to this endeavour lots of energy, we tried to make sense of things, and we both enjoyed it so very much.

References

Galenson, E. (1971). A consideration of the nature of thought in childhood play. In: J. B. McDevitt and C. F. Settlage (Eds.), *Separation–Individuation: Essays in Honor of Margaret Mahler* (pp. 41–74). Madison, CT: International Universities Press.

Galenson, E. (1984). Influences on the development of the symbolic function. In: J. D. Call, E. Galenson & R. Tyson (Eds.), *Frontiers in Infant*

Psychiatry (Vol. I) (pp. 30–37). New York: Basic Books.

Galenson, E. (1995). The influence of hostile aggression on the development of expressive language. In: T. B. Cohen, M. H. Etezady, & B. L. Pacella (Eds.), *The Vulnerable Child, Vol. 2* (pp. 51–57). Madison, CT: International Universities Press.

Galenson, E., & Roiphe, H. (1971). The impact of early sexual discovery on mood, defensive organization, and symbolization. *The Psychoanalytic Study of the Child*, 26: 195–216.

Greenacre, P. (1959). Play in relation to creative imagination. *The Psychoanalytic Study of the Child*, 14: 61–80.

Langer, S. K. (1942). *Philosophy in a New Key*. Cambridge, MA: Harvard University Press.

Roiphe, H. (1968). On an early genital phase: with an addendum on genesis. *The Psychoanalytic Study of the Child*, 23: 348–365.

CHAPTER ONE

A consideration of the nature of thought in childhood play

Eleanor Galenson

Play, that ubiquitous and unique form of childhood behaviour, has been studied extensively by representatives of a variety of disciplines, including psychoanalysis and psychology. Considerations of the content of play, as well as of its function, have been prominent in the writings of Erikson (1950), Freud (1900a, 1920g), Peller (1954), Waelder (1933), and many others. Another aspect of play, its inherent or underlying mental organisation or structure, has received less attention and is worthwhile examining: (1) for the light it might shed on the nature and genesis of thought, (2) for further understanding of the development of the symbolic function, and (3) in relation to possible precursors of the process of sublimation.

Since a solitary ego function has been chosen for study, it will be helpful to establish the framework within which it will be considered. Mahler's (1952, 1963; Mahler & Elkisch, 1959) monumental work in delineating patterns of normal and pathological development during the first few years of life has provided a solid body of data concerning the earlier symbiotic period and the phase of separation–individuation. She has stressed the central role of bodily experience as follows (1963): "In conceptualizing the genesis of the eventual 'sense of identity' I tend to regard demarcation of the body image from the image of the object, the mother, as the core of the process" (p. 309). Mahler has illustrated repeatedly that this demarcation is inextricably intertwined with the vicissitudes of developing object relations and ego functions.

It is against this general background of Mahler's fundamental contributions that we shall examine certain aspects of the particular ego function subsumed under the general category of play. Specific aspects of her work on the emotional and motor spheres that are particularly relevant for cognitive development will be referred to subsequently.

Examination of the structural or organisational properties of play requires, to begin with, a description of the basic components of play. The *sine qua non* of all young children's play is a *behaviour* or *action* of some kind. The presence of verbalisation is, in contrast, a highly variable component, and there is a wide range from totally silent play to intensively conversational sequences. The complexity of play behaviour does not vary primarily with the degree of verbalisation. Some non-verbal play is quite intricate, and verbalisation may accompany extremely simple play action.

Both the verbal and non-verbal components of most play are behaviours that are assumedly expressive of an underlying thought process or fantasy, as well as whatever affect may be involved. Our purpose is to explore some aspects of the underlying mental processes in some non-verbal play, to raise questions concerning distortions or changes in thinking under varying conditions, and to trace the developmental face of these early mental processes as they lead toward either normal or pathological thinking and behaviour in adults. I propose the existence of two alternative developmental lines, one leading from childhood play toward creative work and sublimation, and one eventuating in acting-out behaviour.

In approaching the problem of the nature of the thought processes involved in the verbal and non-verbal components of play, we are immediately confronted with the basic issue of verbal *vs.* non-verbal thought. Many who have been concerned with the nature of thought in general have considered language and conscious thought as essentially unitary. Freud (1900a) linked preconscious processes with the mnemic system of linguistic symbols (p. 574), and wrote about the connection between thought and verbalisation as follows:

> Thought processes are in themselves without quality, except for the pleasurable and unpleasurable excitations that accompany them, and

that in view of their possible disturbing effect upon thinking, must be kept within bounds. In order that thought-processes may acquire quality, they are associated in human beings with verbal memories, whose residues of quality are sufficient to draw the attention of consciousness to them and to endow the process of thinking with a new mobile cathexis from consciousness. (p. 617)

Unconscious thought, according to Freud, had to pass through a stage of verbalisation, via the preconscious. However, in "An outline of psychoanalysis", Freud (1940a[1938]) hinted at his dissatisfaction with this obligatory identity of conscious thought and language:

The inside of the ego, which comprises above all the thought-processes, has the quality of being preconscious. This is characteristic of the ego and belongs to it alone. It would not be correct, however, to think that connection with the mnemic residues of speech is a necessary precondition of the preconscious state. On the contrary, that state is independent of a connection with them, though the presence of that connection makes it safe to infer the preconscious nature of a process. (p. 162)

According to this statement, the presence of speech is a clue to the preconscious nature of a thought process, but the connection with a verbal memory trace is not obligatory.

Greenacre (1952) made reference to the existence and the possible genesis of non-verbal thought:

Anyone who works much with severe neurotics becomes aware how much their communication is in terms of body language—whether of involuntary body tensions, gestures, transitory somatic changes, as well as acting out. All of these forms of communication, even when they appear within the analytic situation, are peculiarly difficult to analyze and may be obstacles to analysis, probably because they essentially belong to a *preverbal form of thinking* and represent an actual earlier difficulty in making this transition in the life of the child. (p. 231, my italics)

Greenacre seems to imply that the persistence of such preverbal thinking is pathological, but suggests that there is indeed a normal early phase of non-verbal thinking.

Vygotsky (1934) deals extensively with the question of the nature of thought processes. He begins by differentiating inner from vocal speech, and traces the development of inner speech of the adult to what Piaget (1923) termed the "egocentric" speech of the child. Vygotsky (1934) considers that inner speech represents the individual's "thinking for himself" (p. 18) rather than in connection with other people:

> Inner speech is not the interior aspect of external speech—it is a function in itself. It still remains speech, i.e., thought connected with words. But while in external speech thought is embodied in words, in inner speech words die as they bring forth thought. Inner speech is to a large extent thinking in pure meanings. It is a dynamic, shifting, unstable thing, fluttering between word and thought, the two more or less stable, more or less firmly delineated components of verbal thought. Its true nature and place can be understood only after examining the next plane of verbal thought, the one still more inward than inner speech. That plane is thought itself. As we have said, every thought creates a connection, fulfils a function, solves a problem—the flow of thought is not accompanied by a simultaneous unfolding of speech. The two processes are not identical, and there is no rigid correspondence between the units of thought and speech.
>
> Thought has its own structure, and the transition from it to speech is no easy matter. Thought, unlike speech, does not consist of separate units. When I wish to communicate the thought that today I saw a barefoot boy in a blue shirt running down the street, I do not see every item separately: the boy, the shirt, its blue colour, his running, the absence of shoes. I conceive of all this in one thought, but I put it into separate words. A speaker often takes several minutes to disclose one thought. In his mind the whole thought is present at once, but in speech it has to be developed successively. (p. 149)

In these descriptions of thought, inner speech, and outer speech, Vygotsky emphasises several characteristics of thought that are different from those of "inner" speech: namely, its lack of unitary structure and temporal arrangement, its dynamic aspects, and its inconstant tie to words. These characteristics of inner thought are difficult to articulate, precisely because language is not always the medium best suited for their expression. It is to this very problem that Langer (1942) addresses herself in *Philosophy in a New Key*, in which she deals with the nature and development of symbolism in music and visual art, as well as general problems of symbolism and thought. Langer (1942) disagrees with many linguists and philosophers in that she assumes a "genuine semantic beyond the limits of discursive language" (p. 86). She is convinced that the field of semantics is wider than that of language, but believes that this field is obstructed by two main tenets of current epistemology: "(1) That language is the only means of articulating thought, and (2) that everything which is not speakable thought is feeling" (p. 27). Langer takes issue with the restrictiveness of the theory that admits only discursive symbolism as a bearer of ideas, and that regards "thought" in this restricted sense as our only intellectual activity, beginning and ending with language.

> ... I do believe that in this physical, space-time world of our experience there are things which do not fit the grammatical schema of expression. But they are not necessarily blind, inconceivable mystical affairs; they are simply matters which require to be conceived through some symbolistic schema other than discursive language. (p. 88)

Langer has developed her ideas of what this other symbolistic schema is. She believes that visual forms are as capable of articulation and of complex combination as words, but that the laws governing this sort of articulation are altogether different from the laws of syntax that govern language. The most radical difference is that visual forms are not discursive; that is, they do not represent their constituents successively but simultaneously, a statement that is already familiar from Vygotsky's description of thought. Langer calls this non-discursive symbolism "presentational symbolism", and illustrates it in relation to music and visual art. Unlike words, the meaning of each symbolic element in presentational symbolism can be understood only through the meaning of the whole and through its relations within the total structure. This view ties in with Vygotsky's description of thought processes as lacking separate units.

Langer enumerates three characteristic features of true language or discourse: (1) the presence of a vocabulary, the elements of which are words with fixed meanings, and a syntax; (2) the possibility of defining one word by combinations of other words, or dictionary construction; and (3) the existence of alternative words for the same meaning, that is, translatability. In contrast to language, visual and musical symbolism possesses no vocabulary, in that there are no independent units with fixed meanings apart from the contextual meaning. Further, it is impossible to define musical or visual symbols in terms of other symbols; nor can they be translated into other terms. Langer (1942) summarises the difference between the two types of symbolism:

> The meanings given through language are successively understood, and gathered into a whole by the process called discourse; the meanings of all other symbolic elements that compose a larger, articulate symbol are understood only through the meaning of the whole, through their relations within the total structure. Their very functioning as symbols depends on the fact that they are involved in a simultaneous, integral presentation. This kind of semantic may be called "presentational symbolism" to characterise its essential distinction from discursive symbolism or "language proper" (p. 97).

Langer maintains that musical symbolism has all the earmarks of true symbolism but one. While it is capable of connotation and is used to articulate emotional and sensuous experiences, it never has a fixed meaning. She calls this artistic form an unconsummated symbol (Langer, 1942): "Articulation is its life but not assertion: expressiveness, not expression" (p. 240). Finally, Langer (1942) considers the matter of truth and falsity, positive and negative:

> Artistic truth, so called, is the truth of a symbol to the forms of feeling—nameless forms, but recognisable when they appear in sensuous replica. Such truth, being bound to certain logical forms of expression, has logical peculiarities that distinguish it from propositional truth; since presentational symbols have no negatives, there is no operation whereby their truth-value is reversed, *no contradiction*. Hence the possibility of expressing opposites simultaneously. (p. 262)

Langer alludes to two aspects of presentational symbolism that also characterise primary-process thinking, namely lack of negation and the use of symbols, the meaning of which is not fixed. These same features are found in non-verbal play as well. A child who places her doll in a toy bed is carrying out an act that has a meaning dependent solely upon its context. While the addition of words to the doll play might bring in the element of negation, the purely non-verbal behaviour of removing the doll from the bed is merely another act, with its own meaning, again dependent upon its context. The onlooker may infer a negative meaning when the second action is placed in reference to the first, but the symbolism of the action itself does not imply negation. The relationship between presentational symbolism and primary-process thinking is an intriguing one, particularly since it is clearly relevant to the type of symbolism that will be described subsequently in relation to childhood play.

The seminal nature of Langer's ideas finds expression in Furth's (1966) book on *Thinking Without Language*. In examining people with severe and at times total language deficiency, he discovered that such deficiency may be present without an equally general deficit in thinking. There are, indeed, two interesting differences between the test material of deaf subjects and of normal people. First, their percepts are organised according to Gestalt principles, and show a greater reliance on preverbal modes of perceptual organisation. Second, the deaf subjects are slower in their ability to discover new aspects of the material, but they show quite normal capacity to comprehend and use logical symbols. Although the differences deserve further study, the similarities of the deaf to the hearing in that their capacity for logical thought and for symbolisation is intact, is an important finding. Furth concludes that language as a symbol system is objectively different from thinking, basing this partly on his research with the deaf.

More recently, Vernon (1967) published material of somewhat the same nature. He reviewed thirty-two research studies in which no language measures of thought processes were analysed in children and adults with language impairment caused by deafness, either congenital or acquired. His data confirm that, even when no words are available, conceptual thought exists and is measurable by tests that do not use language criteria.

Piaget (1923, 1936, 1937, 1945) has made some crucial contributions to the understanding of the development of thought, language, and play. From his observations of the play of normal children, he derived his formulations on mental functioning in the first two years of life, which he called "sensorimotor intelligence". He described the type of mental organisation underlying behaviour in this period. Wolff (1967) compares Piaget's theoretical assumptions and conclusions with those of psychoanalytic theory. He points out that Piaget regards action and ideation as a continuum in that he views the earliest forms of thought as the sensorimotor actions themselves. In contrast to psychoanalytic theory, Piaget's concept of intelligence is predicated on the proposition that action patterns devoid of imagery gradually give rise to representational thought. The beginning of mental imagery is the change that is characteristic of the sixth of Piaget's sensorimotor stages of thought development. In Piaget's (1936) words, "invention through deduction or mental combination . . . characterises systematic intelligence" (p. 331). He states further:

> . . . the present behavior patterns do not appear to operate by groping or apprenticeship, but by sudden invention; that is to say, that instead of being controlled at each of the stages and *a posteriori* by the facts themselves, the searching is controlled *a priori* by mental combination. Before trying them, the child foresees which maneuvers will fail and which will succeed. (p. 340)

The new hallmark of the sixth stage of sensorimotor development is the achievement of solid, dependable mental representation of action patterns that can be intentionally rearranged in thought without manifest action. This is the important transitional step from physical action to representational thought, problem solving that is not accompanied by simultaneous motor activity. Piaget provides an illustration of this new type of problem solving, in which bodily action is no longer necessary, in an experiment. In order to retrieve an object that has disappeared into a cylinder, the child who is as yet below the sixth stage of spatial problem solving must follow the route taken by the object through the cylinder with his own body. He must act out the route taken in the displacement of the object. The fundamentally new achievement that characterises Piaget's sixth stage is the child's ability to come to the same spatial conclusion without having to carry out the action with his body. Apparently he can now visualise the various possible pathways, for he looks in the end of the tunnel through which a ball has been pushed by a stick and can go to the opposite end to find it without having to move his body along the route taken. For this type of problem solving, Piaget postulates that internal mental representation of the pathway taken by the ball must be achieved. Having perceived the ball entering the tunnel, the child can restructure reality mentally by providing himself with the image of the route the ball takes so that he can then find it at the other end without having to follow the pathway with his own bodily action.

This new developmental phase, in which there is mental experimentation that is then translated into action, appears at a time when language as a symbolic expression is often still very rudimentary. It is precisely this chronological sequence of mental problem solving without the prerequisite of language development that is relevant to the problem of non-verbal thought and its development in relation to the symbolic function.

Piaget's views on the development of the symbolic function are reviewed with considerable clarity by Furth (1967). He notes that Piaget subsumes a wide range of children's activities under matters relating to the symbolic function—imitation, imagination, play, dreams, and language—of which language is viewed as only one among several others. The first true symbol according to Piaget is imitation in the absence of the model, an act that he calls deferred imitation. For example, sweeping the floor as mother has done would constitute representation of the absent object as known. This deferred imitation, a symbolic act, is linked developmentally with the internal image. In contrast to the act of deferred imitation, the internal image, whether kinesthetic, visual, or of some other modality, is limited to internal experiencing, and although functionally similar to the act of deferred imitation, it is freer and more readily available since it is not tied to gross muscle movement. The internal mental imitation cannot be directly observed by another person, and has to be inferred from the child's spatial orientation, drawing, and memory performances, or from his play behaviour. Piaget considers that this thinking, which is derived from deferred imitative action, is a mental activity, but one that is outside of awareness. Only the products of such thinking may become conscious—products or symbols that may take the form of drawings, play, or words. Thus play is a symbolic activity, a product of symbolic thinking, and an important step in the development of the symbolic function.

The period of development following the sensorimotor stage (from about one and a half years of age) and prior to the beginning of "operational intelligence" (at about six to eight years of age) has been called by Piaget the period of "symbolic thinking". It is characterised by the presence of symbolic play, rather than the earlier forms of play, for which other writers, such as Waelder (1933) used the descriptive terms of "sensorimotor" or "functional" play. Play behaviour such as throwing, jumping, skipping, etc., was differentiated from play in which assimilation of some reality experience seems to be the central issue. Functional play begins early and may persist into adulthood, side by side with symbolic play.

It is open to question whether such functional play should not also be considered as symbolic. Illumination in this area comes from several sources: Langer (1942), in discussing the rhythmicity and other dynamic aspects of musical symbolism, suggests that this might correspond to bodily rhythms, and therefore constitute symbolism of a special type. Mahler and Elkisch (1959), discussing psychotic mechanisms in children, deal extensively with the abnormal "equation of the inner impulse and the outside phenomena of machines" (p. 227). The study of such pathological states led to Mahler's (1963) work concerning the normal developmental task of the integration of bodily sensations, a process that takes place with the help of the mother's constant emotional participation during the phase of separation–individuation. This integrative task in relation to bodily sensations seems particularly relevant to so-called functional play in childhood and to the later forms of such play in adults.

In regard to symbolic thinking between one and a half years and six to eight years, Piaget (1936) considers that the characteristic type of thought is half-way between the extreme of no representational thinking (the earlier sensorimotor period of action) and the formal thinking of the six- to eight-year-old. Symbolic play begins in the early phases of this period, before the development of language as a useful and symbolically meaningful expression. Such play appears sporadically in some babies as early as fourteen months of age, and increase in frequency during the second year of life. Since representation of an absent object is involved in this symbolic play, it is particularly relevant to the study of thought development, for it is in just such play that Piaget postulates an underlying form of mental organisation to which the term "thought" may be applied for the first time, and to which Piaget gives the name "symbolic thought". Such symbolic thought, whether conscious or unconscious, remains highly characteristic of the mental organisation of children throughout the early years, even long after language has developed.

The earliest symbolic games are only partially so. Piaget (1945) describes play behaviour such as pretending to drink out of a box, or lying down on the floor and pretending to go to sleep. The symbolic aspect consists of using a box instead of a cup, and lying down on the floor instead of in bed. Yet there is no symbolism involved in the child's action of drinking or lying down, in that he is actually carrying out one of his own usual acts. His action is not symbolic, although the objects or situations he uses are substitutes for the real. Piaget conceptualises these games as the child's efforts to rethink past experience in the only manner available to him at the time, namely through bodily actions.

The next step in the development of symbolic play and symbolic thought is the projection of the child's own actions on to new objects. When he puts his toy bear to bed instead of lying down on the floor himself, his own behaviour is generalised to new objects, and the symbolic act of going to bed is completely disassociated from his own action. The symbolic act thus acquires greater mobility and wider applicability, an important progressive move toward its use as an instrument of free thought. However, the symbolic act is not yet entirely freed, since the symbolic units (both the action of putting to sleep and the bear used) are imitations of the original act and object, and have attributes in common with them. A bear has form and shape, as has the child's body, and the act of putting to sleep is part of both the real and the play experience. So these games continue to develop in symbolic complexity.

The final fate of such play is of great interest. One line of development of the symbolic function is directed toward its final form in language, in which the symbol shares no obvious attributes with the object. Langer (1942) has this pertinent description of the symbolic form characteristic of language:

> All language has a form which requires us to string out our ideas even though their objects rest one within the other: as pieces of clothing that are actually worn one over the other have to be strung side by side on the clothesline. This property of verbal symbolism is known as *discursiveness*; by reason of it, only thoughts which can be arranged in this peculiar order can be spoken at all; any idea which does not lend itself to this "projection" is ineffable, incommunicable by means of words. (pp. 81–82)

Another attribute of language was mentioned previously, namely that of fixed meaning that is socially shared and capable of definition by other words.

In contrast to words, which are the symbols of language, the symbols of play are individual ones created by each child for his own use. Although such symbols may be shared intermittently with one or several people, they often remain entirely idiosyncratic. Objects are used to "accommodate to" or conform to the child's inner image in a manner that is strikingly reminiscent of Langer's nondiscursive or presentational symbolism. Many objects used in play meet an additional criterion of Langer's presentational symbolism in that they are capable of connotation, although not fixed or assigned; they are unconsummated symbols. For example, a block may be used as a truck, but suddenly becomes part of a house when placed in a certain spatial relationship to other blocks, or part of a tower when placed in still another spatial dimension. A stick is now a gun, but may soon become a pencil, and finally a fishing rod in another context. In view of these similarities between the symbolism of music and visual art on the one hand, and that of symbolic games on the other, I propose the existence of another developmental line parallel to that of language—namely, from symbolic games toward creative work. I would consider such work as a product of sublimation deriving from the early games in contrast to direct expression of impulse in the form of certain acting-out behaviour to be discussed below.

Evidence for such generic continuity could be adduced by demonstrating structural similarities in these seemingly different forms of thought and behaviour. But then we are faced with the definition of what one means by structural or organisational properties. Erikson (1950) attempts such a definition in his application of his concept of instinctual modes to play behaviour. For example, pushing a stick into a hole resembles taking a bolus of food into the mouth in that there is a container in which something is placed. Wolff (1967) utilises Erikson's approach, pointing out that Erikson's modes refer to the formal properties of physiological functions rather than to physiological functions as such, and that the configurational, or space-organising properties that characterise these modes are derived from body functions but extend later to become styles of thought and social interaction. Wolff refers also to the ideas of Werner and Kaplan (1963) concerning certain characteristics of early psychic function that they have called "vectorial properties".

There is one fundamental characteristic of such patterns that must be stressed here because of its extreme significance in the later exploitation of these patterns in the service of depiction; we refer to the *dynamic-vectorial* nature of these patterns. By this we mean that the sensorimotor patterns possess qualities that defy a merely physical analysis of the movements of the specific bodily parts; they have such qualities as direction, force, balance, rhythm, and enclosingness. Such performances as these seem to have considerable relevance to later symbol formation. They reflect the fact that there is an early experience of dynamic similarities obtaining between entities—here body parts that are materially different (pp. 86–87).

These "vectorial properties," or organising principles, are surely pertinent both to the structure of play and to the artistic creation of adults.

The relation of play to the work of the artist is discussed by Greenacre (1959). Commenting on the role of play, she states: "That is, I suspect, one of the main functions of play in connection with creative imagination. It aids in delivering the unconscious fantasy and harmonising it with the external world" (p. 76). Greenacre takes up the matter of the type of symbolism involved:

> The service of play in the artist in introducing more executive work in materializing the creative product does not depend on clear visual or auditory imagery even when it is carried on in fantasy and not played out overtly. It involves the whole spectrum of sensory modalities and corresponding responses, e.g., visceral as well as outer-body-rind relations such as tactile and kinesthetic stimulations and responses. (p. 79)

Some artistic individuals, it would appear, have access to a wider range of symbols than others do, whether by virtue of innate endowment or environmental influences. Similarly, we observe the variation in diversity, originality, and other qualities in the symbolic play of children. Many factors that influence play are already well known, for example, new situations, new people, changes in body state, etc. However, a systematic study of such variations might reveal hitherto unsuspected patterning in regard to such aspects as spatial characteristics, rhythmicity, variety of symbols used, etc.

One of the difficulties of such a systematic study is the matter of finding a method of categorising and recording the phenomena under consideration. Language is hardly a suitable vehicle for non-verbal thought, and the translation of private thought images into word would surely lead to distortions in the nature of structure and content tending toward conformity to those conventionally agreed upon. The development of such a methodology might be considerably facilitated through the study of the distorted play of disturbed children as well as the study of normal play. The following case material provides illustrations of this structural or organisational frame of reference in relation to several behavioural sequences taken from direct observational material.[1]

Illustrations

An eighteen-month-old girl, Ann, was invited to "play with" the interviewer, while her mother sat at one end of a room in which various types of doll furniture, blocks, cars, etc. were resting on a table placed at some distance from the mother. Ann systematically removed most of the toys from the table, placing them in a small semicircle at her mother's feet. She then sat on the floor, looked up at the interviewer for a moment or two, and then just as systematically moved the small pile of toys from the "inner circle" at her mother's feet to a point about equidistant between mother and interviewer. And finally, she placed a doll in the interviewer's lap!

This vignette, familiar to many from their first contact with an infant who is interested in, but still wary of strangers, seems to be a partially symbolic acting out, via the spatial arrangement of the toys, of the bodily withdrawal and rapprochement sequence in the relationship with the mother. The toy is a partial symbol for the body. Actual contact with the stranger as the final step is suggestive of an even more specific symbolisation, now using doll for self.

Children in the second half of the second year of life are occupied with just these matters of separation of self from object, and with developing body schematisation. Of particular interest to us in our research nursery has been anal, urinary, and genital schematisation. We see behavioural evidence of bodily sensations and direct body exploration on the one hand, and symbolic or representational use of dolls and furniture on the other. More difficult to identify are the intermediary steps; those derivatives of body sensation or self-exploration that are removed from the original impulse or body part, or affect, but not represented by a fixed or socially agreed upon substitute. These derivatives share many attributes of presentational symbolism as described by Langer (1942): namely no independent units with fixed meanings apart from the contextual meanings; no dictionary construction; they cannot be translated into other symbols; and their meaning is understood only in the context of the total structure.

It is precisely the open-endedness and the lack of rigidity of such symbols that make them so important for sublimation toward creative work or, under other circumstances, directed toward acting-out behaviour. We have tried to study these derivatives of bodily sensations and affects by identifying certain formal characteristics or vectorial properties, and certain patterns of behaviour have emerged.

> Ruth, aged eighteen months, has recently begun to distinguish her urinary and bowel products both by gesture and naming. This has been accompanied by intense visual and manual inspection of her genital area, and visual inspection of several male infants of her own age while they were being changed. She likes to play with a little toy toilet, and she seats herself on a potty chair without actually using it for its intended purpose. All of this is accompanied by increased stranger anxiety and self-biting, as well as biting her favourite toy bear's ear and foot. This child had an important partial motor restriction during her first year of life which, we believe, has led to intensification of her reaction to genital sensations and her awareness of genital differences.
>
> Ruth exhibits several groups of behaviours, each group sharing certain formal characteristic attributes. She points at and presses her own umbilicus in response to her mother's prompting. Then she presses her doll's umbilicus, and soon she presses all bells and buttons and insists on grasping and pushing at car handles and other protrusions. We have reason to suspect that her mother's original displacement upward—that is, genital to umbilicus—has become Ruth's route as well, and a number of symbols for the avoided genital have emerged.
>
> Ruth shows another group of behaviours involving openings and enclosures in her play with the "shape box"—a box with lid openings of various shapes through which appropriately shaped objects are to be pushed—that is reminiscent of the anal opening and its functioning. Ruth enjoys this box very much. She varies its use by pushing the forms in the reverse direction, upward through the holes. Yet another variation consists of her holding the oblong form in a slow, deliberately teasing fashion above each of the wrong openings as she glances toward the observer, before she finally drops it through the correct opening. Closely resembling this concern with enclosures is Ruth's repetitive removal of all the toys from a shelf to the floor, and just as deliberate replacement of them to their former position. The emptying and filling aspect is clear, as well as the matter of control over the objects.
>
> Ruth has begun to "draw". Her first efforts were scribbles from side to side, and some discouraging attempts to imitate her mother. Then she had a difficult week, during which her irritability increased, along with her self-biting and clinging to a favourite toy dog. This was the climax of her increasing awareness of genital differences. She subsequently began to

work hard at trying to draw a straight line beginning at the bottom of the paper and extending upward. Four days later, she began to bend the line, and finally drew a circle.

In all these instances, the spatial configurations (as in the shape-box group) are the common formal properties that unify the various experiences, that are quite different in other respects. These formal or dynamic properties derive from the body experience in the first instance, and are then found in other situations and with other objects that become linked through their common dynamic similarity. Ruth seems to find many opportunities through which she experiences these similarities, and perhaps this indicates the wide repertoire through which her earlier bodily experiences will find expression.

> Sandy has a different repertoire. His first year of life was characterised by frequent diarrhoea and constipation, and by a highly sensuous, predominately tactile and kinesthetic relationship with his mother. He expresses himself by pushing—children, adults, chairs, baby carriages—and by banging on things. Sandy has a much less diversified range of activities than Ruth for the expression of bodily sensations and impulses, and his activities are particularly close to the original form of the impulse or sensation.

These two children show quite different patterns in their non-verbal behaviour. They differ in their sex and their early bodily experiences, as well as in the nature of the mother–child relationships. Will their styles of thought and sublimatory development be related to these early patterns, and can one make any predictions on the basis of these patterns? How can such non-verbal, body-grounded experiences become part of analytic work? The following may suggest some possibilities.

> A long analysis with a highly narcissistic woman, who was intensely preoccupied with erotic fantasies and sexual acting out, had been only modestly fruitful and became stalemated. Her rages alternated with isolation of affect, leaving her feeling anxious, distant, and empty. Her repeated attempts to commit herself to people as well as to various types of work were of limited duration and incomplete. A change was ushered in when I asked about her thoughts and feelings during defecation (my work with young children having alerted me to such material). She could describe none at all, both to her surprise and mine. It soon became apparent that very early denial of perception and affect in connection with the loss of faeces into the toilet, as she had probably dealt with object loss even earlier, had remained the predominant model for dealing with separations and

losses of all kinds and with her massive castration anxiety. Her peculiar way of dealing with body events, based on disturbed individuation of self from object, has subsequently served as our model in the analysis of her airplane phobia, her response to criticism, her distorted object relations, her rage reactions, to name but a few instances. For the first time in the analysis, real working through occurred, in contrast to prior attempts at reconstruction of object loss.

I have described sequences of play behaviour from the point of view of their structural organisation, emphasising how this leads back, in each instance, to earlier bodily experiences that appear to have contributed to the particular variety of symbolic representation. I believe that the later fate of symbolic play depends to a considerable degree upon these early bodily experiences, as well as upon the original endowment. Which circumstances influence the line of development toward sublimation, particularly involving creative work, and which circumstances lead to acting out? With Greenacre (1959), I surmise that the artist has access to wider than average variety and richness in his symbolisation, but whether largely through endowment or through specific environmental influences remains as yet undocumented by direct observational material.

In contrast to the symbolic richness of the artist's work and the wide variety in the play of normal children, there is clinical evidence that the symbolic play of disturbed children tends to be narrower in variety, richness, and originality. There is also a greater proportion of direct expression of impulse via bodily movements. I propose that such impoverishment in early symbolic play results in restriction in the routes available for the expression of bodily sensations and the mental processes connected with them, a restriction that may eventuate in pathological acting out and other morbid behaviour.

We anticipate that systematic study of the sequence and variations in symbolic capacity, as evidenced in symbolic play patterning, will enlarge our understanding of factors that tend to enhance or to inhibit the process of sublimation.

Summary

The play behaviour of young children is viewed as a behavioural manifestation of non-verbal thinking. Issues of relevance to the understanding of the development of thought in general and of the symbolic function in particular are discussed, and a line of development is proposed, leading from early non-verbal thought as manifested in play, either toward sublimation, particularly artistic creativity, or toward acting-out behaviour in adulthood.

The complex interrelationship between the organisation of thought on the one hand, and drives and affect development, on the other, is a matter of fundamental importance. The possibility is suggested of studying this interrelationship in the play behaviour of young children, with particular regard to the organisational patterns of play and to variations in this patterning under conditions of stress and pathological development.

Note

1. Derived in part from the Normal Research Nursery of the Department of Child Psychiatry, Albert Einstein College of Medicine.

References

Erikson, E. (1950). *Childhood and Society*. New York: Norton, 1963.
Freud, S. (1900a). *The Interpretation of Dreams*. S.E., 4–5. London: Hogarth.
Freud, S. (1920g). *Beyond the Pleasure Principle*. S.E., 18: 3–64. London: Hogarth.
Freud, S. (1940a[1938]). *An outline of psychoanalysis*. S.E., 23: 141–207. London: Hogarth.
Furth, H. G. (1966). *Thinking Without Language. Psychological Implications of Deafness*. New York: Free Press.
Furth, H. G. (1967). Concerning Piaget's views on thinking and symbol Formation. *Child Development*, 38: 819–826.
Greenacre, P. (1952). *Trauma, Growth and Personality*. New York: International Universities Press, 1969.
Greenacre, P. (1959). Play in relation to creative imagination. *The Psychoanalytic Study of the Child*, 14: 61–80.
Langer, S. K. (1942). *Philosophy in a New Key*. Cambridge, MA: Harvard University Press.
Mahler, M. (1952). On child psychosis and schizophrenia: autistic and symbiotic infantile psychosis. *The Psychoanalytic Study of the Child*, 7: 286–305.

Mahler, M. (1963). Thoughts about development and individuation. *The Psychoanalytic Study of the Child, 18*: 307–324.

Mahler, M., & Elkisch, P. (1959). On infantile precursors of the "influencing machine". *The Psychoanalytic Study of the Child, 14*: 219–235.

Peller, L. E. (1954). Libidinal phases, ego development and play. *The Psychoanalytic Study of the Child, 9*: 178–198.

Piaget, J. (1923). *The Language and Thought of the Child*. London: Routledge & Kegan Paul, 1948.

Piaget, J. (1936). *The Origins of Intelligence in Children*. New York: International Universities Press, 1952.

Piaget, J. (1937). *The Construction of Reality in the Child*. New York: Basic Books, 1954.

Piaget, J. (1945). *Play, Dreams and Imitation in Childhood*. New York: Norton, 1951.

Vernon, M. (1967). Relationship of language to the thinking process. *Archives of General Psychiatry, 16*: 325–333.

Vygotsky, L. S. (1934). *Thought and Language*. New York: MIT Press, 1962.

Waelder, R. (1933). The psychoanalytic theory of play. *The Psychoanalytic Quarterly, 2*: 208–224.

Werner, H., & Kaplan, B. (1963). *Symbol Formation*. New York: Wiley.

Wolff, P. H. (1967). Cognitive considerations for a psychoanalytic theory of language acquisition. In: *Motives and Thought: Psychoanalytic Essays in Honor of David Rapaport* (pp. 299–343). *Psychological Issues Monograph 18/19*. New York: International Universities Press.

Discussion of Chapter One

Phyllis Greenacre

In her paper, "A consideration of the nature of thought in childhood play" (1971), Galenson proposes to examine the mental organisation or structure of children's play, especially for the light it may shed on the nature and genesis of thought, and further for the understanding of the development of the symbolic function and the possible precursors of the process of sublimation. She focuses on questions of the thought process as indicated by the fantasies evident in both verbalised and non-verbal play. She would follow their developmental fate as it leads to creative work or to recreative games and hobbies in adult life, or less favourably to acting-out propensities in which fantasy is expressed primarily in action, and verbalisation, although available, plays a secondary role.

The Max Muller edict of 1887, "no thought without words" (Muller, 1888) had a powerful influence in its day and has, I suspect, persisted in the attitudes of psychoanalysts, many of whom still say that anything that has occurred preverbally cannot be dealt with by analysis. Yet I think I would be even more emphatic now about the need to pay attention to non-verbal communication during the analytic hour than I have been in years past. The psychoanalytic situation stresses the importance of speech in contrast to action. The analysand's position on the couch, by subtle suggestion, limits the extent of active movement, and the suggestion is furthered by the direction to the analysand to speak whatever thoughts and feelings he becomes aware of during the hour. Yet the movements on the couch, postures, mannerisms, changes in tone and intensity of voice, flushing, sweating, and special states of body tension are all part of the expression of feeling and may represent explicit communications.[1] They are non-verbal, and sometimes derived from preverbal responses, as well as from experiences that had not or could not be verbalised at the time they occurred and are preserved in a non-verbal state. One must realise, certainly, that speech is not acquired in a stage that clicks into place with as much of a "this is it" triumph, as often appears in the infant's attainment of walking. To be sure, there are spurts of acquisition of talking, but on the whole it is staggered in its accomplishment, extending over a considerable period of time during which the non-verbal and verbal elements mingle variously. The experienced analyst approximates the attitude recommended by Lewis (1951) in studying the development of speech in children: "In a sense one must be a naturalistic observer at heart to be an empathetic observer of young children".

It is the persistence of these non-verbal components in the analysand's communications during the analytic hour that makes me realise the limitation of teaching through tape recordings of sessions. There may be preverbal communications that are accessory to the spoken ones, rather than being substituted for them. Also, audio tapes cannot adequately reflect what goes on reciprocally in the mind of the analyst and plays a part in the whole interchange. The replaying of the tape calls on the observer for *his* reactions rather than those of the analyst.

Play by definition involves motion or action and usually implies spontaneity and pleasure. The idea of imitation is also connoted just as with the word "act". (Incidentally, when we think of playing and acting we at once come to the suggestion of the importance of vision, of which I will say more later.) Imitation is one of the main ingredients of the play of the mimic and the equipment of the actor. It is a development of more complexity than early play activity that serves the function of discharge. It may also be the beginning of humour.

But if we look at play and try to examine its interaction with ideation and word formation, we may hark back to biological considerations.

Play clearly appears in animals who do not talk, though they may have other means of communication (Thomson, 1927). He states that one of the basic criteria of play is that it is not immediately useful and it is not work, although it may be strenuous and lead to exhaustion. It is, however, not mere exercise, but perhaps it exercises best. It has no deliberate end, yet it is indispensable if the animal is to attain the full use of its powers. It is not necessarily social, nor competitive, though rivalry may give it zest. (If competition is the primary end, then the playful activity becomes work.) Its keynote is anticipation of modes of activity characteristic of adult life (Groos, 1898).

We can deduce that play has some maturational pressure that may contribute to its mainstream, but that it also involves sensorimotor responses in reaction to the environment. Thomson (1927) further remarks that play is not common among birds and at best only incipient in invertebrates. He questions why it appears in the life history of so few creatures. There must be a biological advantage in play, yet one that only certain species have been able to secure.

The idea that play arises from an overflow of energy may have some truth. The baby pleasurably blowing bubbles seems to be engaging in some unnecessary, undirected mouth play that is a needless expenditure of energy but a satisfying one. A little later, when the infant discovers his hands, he treats them as playthings granted to him from the outside. He follows them with his eyes in a way similar to visual play with mobiles. Toys and tools, we recall, are fundamentally fashioned after body parts, of which they serve as prosthetic elaborations.

The healthy developing infant is endowed with more energy than is needed in the basic process of bodily growth and the maintenance of physical homeostasis. This extra energy can be available in response to external stimulations of varying number and intensity. Thus the play activity that utilises this energy may be channelled both by the biologically determined maturational patterns exerting endogenous pressures and by the way in which these patterns are affected: impeded, reinforced, or given new outlets by environmental stimuli.

But play, because it is not all set and immediately goal-directed, and because there is a margin of energy available, gives an opportunity for testing new variations of activity before the screening process of the struggle for existence has become too fine a mesh. It affords room for new departures especially valuable in animals whose adult life demands plasticity and resourcefulness. Here, one is reminded of otters, of whom Maxwell (1960) remarks that otters are extremely bad at doing nothing. Their play is almost endless.

Play, if we are to differentiate it from games, is spontaneous and allows idiosyncrasies and experimentation. It seems, however, that play cannot occur by maturation alone; it requires some liberating stimulus from the environment. However, play is susceptible to the impingement of a variety of stimuli, and is not totally restricted in response to those that fit neatly, positively or negatively, into the incipient maturational patterns. This degree of plasticity in response to external stimulation secures a certain freedom for individual variation (perhaps the earliest forerunner of initiative) before habit formation sets in. To summarise these considerations—the biological significance of play is partly its function as a safety valve for overflowing energy, as an expression of imitativeness, and as a correlate of agreeable feelings. But mainly, play is an irresponsible apprenticeship for adult activities and an opportunity for testing new departures, especially in habit. It is not directly useful, but has a prospective value in educating efficiency (Thomson, 1927).

What is the relation of play to the beginning of thought?

Thought seems to mean the ability to retain and to utilise inner images that have arisen from sensorimotor experiences similar in configuration—as well as experienced at different times and under different conditions. These elements are emphasised by Langer (1942), although she states them in non-biological terms. The introduction of an appreciation of time as an element connecting related experiences, making them a line of continuity of experience rather than a series of separated dots, may be associated with awareness not only of repetitive elements but of those variations in imprecisely related experiences that give the fringe of exciting stimulations to play. Sense of time gives backbone to the representational gestalt. How much a creature benefits from such variations in early experiences, in contrast to being bound by mere repetition, seems to me to be an indication of the very dawning of thought and the earliest precursor of imagination.

To speculate a bit, it seems that there just have been in eons past some vast change in the world's ecology that caused human births to appear premature (in relation to external conditions) in that the young were helpless and not nearly able to take care of themselves, that only those infants could survive who could in some way hang on to their mothers postnatally in order to make up for their developmental inadequacies. At the same time, there must have been conditions that permitted the mother, in turn, to hold on to these infants and to nurture them until they became independent. This is in contrast to subhuman animals, many of which (at some distance from the human) seem really to be miniature adults at birth, for example, the guinea pig. In the human infant, individuation was delayed, but a greater and more complex relationship with the mother was established.

But to me, the most important result would be that this prolonged postnatal body relationship (Mahler's symbiotic stage) would involve a complexity of communication between the mother and infant from the beginning, as the mother puts her adult abilities at the infant's disposal and the infant in turn absorbs these into his own maturational patterns. Such communication starts with an exchange of chiefly cutaneous and kinesthetic sensorimotor responses, to which those of the reciprocal mouth–breast relationship are soon added, as well as an interchange through visual contact. These visual and oral activities of the infant furnish some degree of early focusing and contribute to the inception of the gradual organisation of body awareness which is to progress rapidly along fairly set maturational patterns during the first year of life. All this is against a variable background of rhythm and sound. Further, vision enlarges the area of awareness both of the infant's own body and of the content of the environment.

It is evident that the mother's contribution to this primitive symbiotic state must be fluctuating and complex in comparison to the infant's side of the relationship. It inevitably furnishes a great number of *variables* within the framework of the *constancy* of the basic maternal body gestalt, which we know to be requisite for the infant's developmental progress. Gross or sudden changes in the maternal gestalt are reacted to with signs of infantile distress or withdrawal. But lesser changes may furnish accessory stimulation for responses over and above what is necessary for the maturational stage. These are, I believe, the earliest forerunners of play in that, like play, they are not dependent entirely on maturational pressure, are not immediately useful, but give opportunity for testing new variations of activity not obligatory for the barest struggle for existence. Since symbiosis prevails at this stage, the effect is that of a reflection of maternal expressions and body tensions, which suggests imitation but is more immediate and more nearly automatic. I have referred to this earlier as the "mirroring reaction" of the infant (Greenacre, 1941).

The variations in the mother's bodily behaviour may then furnish liberating stimuli that come from outside the infant but, in accordance with the strength of the introjective–projective mechanism, seem to be experienced also as belonging to the infant himself. It appears further that these are reproduced less within the obligatory core of the special maturational phase, and more as fringe benefits related to it, not necessarily leading to any definite goal. To give an example, in the earliest days of postnatal life, the infant may be affected by slight or minimal activities of the mother's body, if she is a mother who holds her baby and cuddles him much. What "goes on" in the mother appears in myriad minor ways and includes not only the impact of body tensions and visible changes in her appearance, but some reactions to the sensory awareness of the rhythms of her respiration and possibly even of her heartbeat, as well as to the larger rhythms of her walking, speech, singing, etc. Some deposit from these reactions must be left with the infant as his increasing maturation permits corresponding separation from her. It is possible that these almost subliminal absorptions from maternal body activity add stimulation to the infant's motor activities and are distributed in different ways throughout his own body responses.

As individuation progresses, this maternal contribution is integrated into the infant's internal functioning while reactions to more externally experienced maternal activities take on a more definitely imitative or complementive character. In due time, such reactions are no longer dependent on the presence of the original liberating stimuli. They may be elicited also by similar or related stimuli, and they may attain individual uniqueness and spontaneity. By this time, simple reality testing (of the second-look type) is also established. This may indicate the dawn of memory as an autonomous function above the level of the organic memory of conditioning. It is but a step here from the rapidly growing infant's registering the modified and still modifiable quasi borrowed activity patterns to his making them his own, separate from the mother's. They will gain further increment from his experimental testing of the ever-expanding area of new stimulations from the widening environment. At this time the play of curiosity and experiment is in orbit, leading to rudimentary speech sounds and representations in posture and behaviour that furnish the material for symbolic realisation and communication.

What is the relation of this to thought process and to speech?

The attainment of walking and the acquisition of speech occur in approximately the same era, that is, toward the end of the first year and the beginning of the second. Although there are differences in the time of achievement in different infants and sometimes discrepancies between the two in the same infant, they approach simultaneity sufficiently to raise questions of possible common or interrelated influences contributing to both. Walking and talking are definite constituents in the process of separation of infant from mother, which is demanded by the growth and increasing strength of the infant. They both express and promote such a separation and implement its further development. Both have gone through stages of incipience, partial accomplishment, and approach a final capacity for independent performance. It is the stage of incipience that has emerged from a period of play activity.

But all of this is probably not realised until there is a fair degree of integration of the body self accompanied by some internalised body image. Walking must contribute greatly to body–self awareness as well as to perception of relative size and the realisation of sequence and continuity of experiences. This in turn would tend to create simple impressions of cause and effect. At the same time, the possibility of direct exploration with all the senses is greatly increased. Anyone who has watched the exhilarated sensory explorations of a child of fourteen months or so will become aware of the playful testing that is going on in response to the vast and stimulating unfolding of the environment's resources. Speech, however, is an economising function of great value chiefly in the service of expression and communication.

Speech, it seems to me, develops in stages, each of which is preceded by a period of playfulness, whether this be the blowing of bubbles, the varied testing movements of the tongue, clucking noises, smacking of the lips, or imitations of the sounds of others, human, animal, or even from inanimate sources. I refer here to the child's attempts at imitating such sounds as the noises of steam engines, whistling of a tea kettle, or the gushing of water—sounds that may furnish later onomatopoeic contributions to words, especially to those unique verbal concoctions that are so endearing in the young. There is a progression of preverbal vocal symbols that are both expressive and communicative but have not yet gained the precision, condensation, complexity, and range of speech. Their use is associated with symbolic gestures and body movements.

What starts as play may merge into communication as it is seen and understood by the adult onlooker, whose responsiveness substantiates it. The repetition of these sounds, at first in play and then in the service of useful communication, directed and not merely at random, is an indication of the establishment of early thought processes that precede more sophisticated language. The finer development of language grows both out of the progressively integrated maturational needs and the stimuli due to the infant's increasing mobility in space. Explicit communication through sound may supplant communication through mutual vision. It seems probable that the development of thought is in progress at this time, gestated in play activity, born from the need for more differentiated communication, and facilitated by the responses of recognition from the human environment.

It may be significant that speech begins and is then elaborated during periods of special spurts of development of strength of the body sphincters. The muscles of the mouth, pharynx, and larynx that play such a part in speech have rather complex sphincter like activities. Clinically, we know that the infant's speech may be much affected by the vicissitudes of sphincter control in other parts of the body. It is my suggestion that there may still be such a degree of plasticity in the body organisation forming the basis of the self image that synchronous and similar body developments of early childhood affect each other through avenues of easy displacement. There is thus a kind of somatic foundation for symbolism. One must also take account of the interplay between the influences of the sphincter achievements and the libidinal phase development so important in the patterning of increasing object relationships.

There is an analogous situation in the achievement of walking. This is reached during a period of phenomenal growth in body size, with especial growth of the long bones and their accessory musculature. There is an increased general body playfulness with greater pressure of physical separation from the mother. The addition of the lively play of romping with both parents may produce delight by the vigour lent to the infant in the trial separateness of being bounced on the mother's lap or tossed in the air by the father. This probably facilitates total body surface and kinaesthetic awareness with differentiation and accentuation of rhythms. It affects spatial and relative size appreciation, increases the range and quality of perception, and gradually admits sequence and primitive time values. This would seem to forecast the beginning of secondary-process thinking.

There are two other aspects of Dr Galenson's paper that I shall discuss briefly: the relation of speech to acting out, and the relation of the development of thought and play to creativity. I believe that the deepest important roots of acting out are to be found in disturbances in the period in which action as a way of communication is being supplemented and supplanted by speech. There may be an actual impairment in the execution of speech, but more often the disturbance is due to the degradation of the function of speech that is not given its full dignity with acceptance of its utility. This frequently results from the mother's unwillingness to permit the infant his separateness. The interplay by mutual visual communication is retained, with increasing scoptophilia and exhibitionism in the child. There is a fixation at the playful period preceding attainment of talking. Speech becomes an infantile adornment and then, as the tension of discrepancies in development increases, speech may assume too much the role of an expressive outlet for frustration—a part of general behaviour, rather than a specialised means of gaining a one-to-one response on a rational basis.

With regard to the relation of the development of both thought and play to creativity, there is much more to be said than space limitations permit. In a paper (1957) on "The childhood of the artist" I stated my observations and belief that certain characteristics are inborn in the potentially gifted child and may either flower or be stunted by the exigencies in the later development of his personal life. Most important of these special qualities is the increased sensitivity of the sensorimotor equipment permitting earlier and greater intensity and range of responsiveness to external stimulations, including patterns of form and rhythm. Such an infant is not restricted in responsiveness to what is directly provided by the symbiotic relation to the actual mother, the primary object, but includes to an unusual degree peripheral object forms that resemble her or parts of her body. Such peripheral subjects, or "*collective alternates*" (Greenacre, 1957), are libidinally invested but are also the objects of non-hostile aggression. They form the seeds of the love affair with the world that, with all its hazardous disappointments, is the fate of the creative individual.

I have already described the way in which, during the symbiotic phase, there is a constantly changing play of maternal body activities that are not directly related to the infant's leading needs, but go on as part of the mother's own demands, peripheral or accessory to her relationship to the infant. As the infant grows, the environmental area extends beyond the mother and the variety of stimulation increases. This is especially pronounced in the potentially gifted infant with his earlier and more widely developing perceptiveness. Those gratuitous stimulations not immediately absorbed in the direction of the developing libidinal phase serve as extra liberating excitations, leading to expressive responses in infantile play. Such expression may be absorbed in the infant's general activity, and attain no special significance if discharge has been the leading or only function. But it may furnish material for the earliest experimentation, permitting variations in the details of expression of maturational patterns, and be the forerunner of initiative. In the potentially gifted infant with vigorous maturational pressures and specially sensitive responsiveness, there is both an increase in the need for play and the appearance of multiple symbolic forms based on the collective alternates. There is a peculiar richness even in this early stage of development, that is preverbal, or partially verbal at best.

Note:

1. This is also discussed in connection with Winnicott's suggestion that the analyst may act as a transitional object to the analysand (Greenacre, 1969).

References

Galenson, E. (1971). A consideration of the nature of thought in childhood play. In: J. B. McDevitt & C. F. Settlage (Eds.), *Separation–Individuation: Essays in Honor of Margaret Mahler* (pp. 41–74). Madison, CT: International Universities Press.

Greenacre, P. (1941). The predisposition to anxiety. *The Psychoanalytic Quarterly, 10*: 66–96; 610–637.
Greenacre, P. (1957). The childhood of the artist: libidinal phase development and giftedness. *The Psychoanalytic Study of the Child, 12*: 27–72.
Greenacre, P. (1969). The fetish and the transitional object. *The Psychoanalytic Study of the Child, 24*: 144–164.
Groos, K. (1898). *Play of Animals*. New York: Appleton.
Langer, S. K. (1942). *Philosophy in a New Key*. Cambridge, MA: Harvard University Press.
Lewis, M. M. (1951). *Infant Speech, a Study of the Beginnings of Language* (2nd edn). New York: Humanities.
Maxwell, G. (1960). *Ring of Bright Water*. New York: Dutton.
Muller, F. M. (1888). Identity of language and thought. In: *Three Introductory Lectures: Signs of Thought*. Chicago: Chicago Open Court.
Thomson, J. A. (1927). *The Mind of Animals*. London: Newnes.

CHAPTER TWO

The impact of early sexual discovery on mood, defensive organisation, and symbolisation

Eleanor Galenson and Herman Roiphe

The girl whose early development will be described in this paper is one of a group of infants who have been studied in a research nursery established at The Albert Einstein College of Medicine. We have been engaged in an investigation of genital development during the second year of life and the interrelationship of this genital development with other areas of personality formation. We deliberately included in our infant group a number of infants who experienced certain somatic disturbances during their first year of life. In Ruth, an infant with such an early somatic problem, we were able to observe the impact of her awareness of the genital difference in relation to several areas of her subsequent development—the establishment of a basic mood, her particular type of defensive organisation, her level of play behaviour and symbolisation, and the quality of her developing object relations.

The contributions of Greenacre and Mahler to very early development, their theoretical formulations and clinical material, have served as the foundation upon which our own work has rested. We have selected, from the larger body of their work, a few specific statements that we consider particularly relevant to the infant we are describing.

Greenacre (1953) alluded to the effect of certain disruptive influences occurring during the first eighteen months or so of life. She distinguished two groups: infants who suffered from early physical disturbances, and infants who experienced disturbances in the mother–child relationship. Greenacre stressed the interference with the developing sense of the infant's own body, the effect upon the emerging ego, and the possible consequences for later sexual development. Many of her later publications further amplified this early proposition.

Mahler (1966) described the particular vulnerability of the child during the period from about fourteen to sixteen months of age, a period characterised by ambivalence toward the parents and hostile dependence on them. These seem to call forth both the early pathological defence mechanism of splitting the good and bad mother images and the mechanism of turning aggression against the self.

Mahler (1966) mentioned two developmental events that take place at this age period:

> I must emphasize the importance of the double trauma of toilet training and of the discovery (at a much earlier age than we have thought) of the anatomical sexual difference as contributory factors in the genesis of the propensity of girls to depressive moods.... [The depressive reaction] has been observed in girls definitely more often than in boys. Their anger toward and disappointment with the mother for not having given them the penis could be traced convincingly in several cases". (p. 164)

We shall discuss these seminal observations in relation to the influence of such developmental events upon the establishment of mood and defensive organisation.

Some details of this early period of normal sexual interest and activity as well as certain distortions in development were described by Roiphe (1968). He proposed that this sexual interest is a normal developmental sequence that occurs sometime between the ages of sixteen and twenty-four months. Roiphe also singled out a group of children who show castration reactions or distorted development during this period of early genital discovery, provided that they earlier had had experiences that resulted either in an unstable body schema or in an unstable mental representation of the maternal object. Such experiences included physical disturbances or poor or absent mothering.

Our research was designed to investigate and document the existence of this early phase of sexual interest and activity proposed by Roiphe. We assume that this phase begins sometime between the ages of sixteen and twenty-four months and is characterised by certain primary behaviours, including frank masturbation and the expression of intense curiosity about the anatomical differences between the sexes, both in relation to other children and adults. Moreover, we planned to consider other changes in behaviour, particularly the child's play and behaviour toward the mother, which occur within the temporal context of this phase and that may be affected by this early sexual activity.

In addition to objectively verifying the occurrence of these behaviours, we proposed to document the existence of a set of mutilation anxiety reactions occurring in children who experienced, during their first year of life, a major birth defect, severe illness, surgical intervention, orthopaedic corrections and immobilisations, loss of a parent, or depression or other gross emotional neglect by the mothering figure. The mutilation reactions were expected to occur in such predisposed children when they arrive at the phase of early genital awareness. They would be characterised, in boys, by verbal expression of the fear of losing the penis, and, in girls, that they already have lost the penis. Other evidences of this reaction were expected to consist of a variety of fears and aversions, hypochondria, regression in toilet training, and abrupt changes in eating or sleeping patterns.

A final hypothesis of our research design concerned the existence of a genetic continuity between some forms of early play and the non-verbal type of symbolism that characterises musical and other artistic forms. In an earlier paper, Galenson (1971) proposed this genetic continuity, and described a type of data analysis that might be particularly suitable for demonstrating this development of complex non-verbal symbols from the primitive symbolism of the infant.

Methodology

The psychoanalytic proposition that the direction and force of instinctual pressures, the nature of mother–child relationship, and body schematisation exert moulding and distorting effects upon one another is by now a basic frame of reference for direct infant observational research carried out by psychoanalysts. It has been extremely difficult, however, to document the facts and details of this reciprocal interdependence from the data of direct infant observation. These data consist of a variety of observable behaviours—motoric, affective, play—from which we deduce the status of underlying drive development, object ties, body schematisation, and the developing mental representation of self and object. Since the infant still lacks speech, the task of interpreting these data is enormously difficult.

In the earlier paper concerned with precisely this dilemma of understanding infant behaviour characteristic of this essentially preverbal era, Galenson attempted to demonstrate the genetic continuity between early play and later artistic non-verbal symbolism by calling attention to certain structural similarities between these seemingly very different forms of behaviour and thought. Werner and Kaplan's (1963) work on symbolism offered considerable support for this point of view. These authors compare the dynamic–vectorial nature of patterns of early psychic functioning with the qualities of direction, force, balance, rhythm, and enclosingness that are easily distinguishable in the early patterns of sensorimotor development. Werner and Kaplan propose that these dynamic–vectorial properties have relevance for later symbol formation, in that these qualities "reflect the fact that there is an early experience of dynamic similarities obtaining between entities—here body parts—that are materially different" (p. 86).

Galenson proposed that this "structural" or "dynamic–vectorial" type of analysis could be useful in studying the behaviour of young infants in order to identify the original body zone from which a particular bit of observed behaviour was derived. For example, thumb sucking is a zonal activity that has a characteristic pattern of rhythm, quality, form, etc. This oral pattern should aid in identifying behaviours that are currently located elsewhere, but were originally oral in nature. The current site might be the own body of the child, his mother's body, or inanimate objects. The point is that such derivatives of body sensation or self-exploration, although displaced from the original zone, are not represented or symbolised by a fixed or socially agreed-upon symbol, the word, and perhaps never will be. It is interesting that these early forms of infant play share many attributes with the symbolism of musical and visual art forms, in that there are no independent units with fixed meanings, apart from the contextual meaning; there is no dictionary construction; they cannot be translated into other symbols; and their meaning is understood only through relations within the total structure. Galenson proposed, therefore, that there is a genetic connection between early body-derived play and the symbolism of the creative arts.

Structural analysis based upon the foregoing propositions has been a basic part of our methodological approach. We follow the process of displacement from the original zonal site to another body area. The next step is externalisation to outside objects that are then utilised as concrete semi-symbolic representatives of the bodily experience. It is through this link with the original zonal area that we hope to document, from the data of direct infant observation, the assumption that play, as all other infant behaviour, is patterned by the instinctual drives. In addition, we hope to follow the development of some of these open-ended and very plastic early symbols of infant play as they become more complex. We suspect that in certain infants the early symbols will be integrated and utilised for the non-verbal symbolism of artistic forms, whereas other infants will show a greater proclivity for acting out the earlier symbolic play.

In the case material that follows, some structural or pattern analyses of clusters of infant behaviour will be included, to demonstrate this aspect of our research methodology.

The setting

Our data are collected in the nursery, which was established in 1967, according to the model at The Master's Children Center developed by Mahler (1963; see also Pine & Furer, 1963). A large room, with a small kitchen and bathroom immediately adjoining it, is furnished at one end with an informal grouping of sofas for the mothers, while small tables and chairs, open toy shelves provided with toys appropriate for this age group, two rocking horses, a large-sized doll's bed and several doll carriages occupy the remainder of the room. A changing table is set against the wall next to the bathroom, and a one-way screen that is used for video-taping occupies part of the wall immediately adjacent to the toy area. Infants have free access to both the bathroom and kitchen. Our research population is a self-selected upper-middle-class group. Nine mothers attend with their infants four mornings each week, for a two-hour session from September, when the infants are between twelve and fifteen months of age, to June of each year. Although our nursery is offered as a kind of indoor playground, the parents are informed that we are engaged in research concerning normal development during the second year of life. The mothers are expected to take care of their own children, although our two nursery teachers act as additional supervisors.

Each mother–child pair is assigned to a pair of observers consisting of a senior staff member and a junior member, either a psychiatric resident or child psychiatry fellow who has elected to work in the nursery during the entire year. Each observer attends at least one session each week, while several senior observers attend two or more. Developmental data concerning the first year of life are gathered at the beginning of each nursery year (although more recently we are visiting prospective babies at home during their first year of life, prior to entrance in our programme, and obtain this early material at that time). Ongoing data are gathered in the following manner: the observer questions the mother about the child's behaviour at home during the preceding week, making certain that a group of behavioural categories selected in advance are covered. The observer spends the remainder of the nursery session directly observing the child. A ten-minute period is recorded directly in the form of a narrative record, while the rest is dictated after the session as an impressionistic account. All material is reproduced and circulated to the two observers as well as the two directors.

The data for each mother–child pair are summarised every two months, again according to preselected categories, and these summaries are then presented for staff discussions at the weekly staff conference. Formulations of the material already gathered, as well as predictions concerning future development are developed out of these presentations. Although follow-ups have been obtained on only a portion of our research population thus far, systematic follow-up is now included in our research design.

Ruth's early development

The data that follow were collected over a period of ten months starting when Ruth was twelve months old, while she and her mother attended our nursery during four mornings each week.

The first year

Developmental details of Ruth's first year of life were difficult to elicit from her mother, who had been anxiously preoccupied with the future fate of a congenital defect in Ruth. A corrective device, applied in the perineal area, was worn by Ruth from the third through the twelfth month of life. (Details of this defect and the corrective measures applied cannot be offered here for reasons of confidentiality.) Following a normal pregnancy and delivery, Ruth had been bottle-fed until age six months, when she began to spit out solids. Her mother, feeling this signalled a need for self-sufficiency in the whole feeding area, responded by allowing Ruth to feed herself and by abruptly withdrawing all bottle feeding. No particular sequelae were noted by the mother, although there was a large variety of oral behaviours, including mouthing and licking of objects and tongue protrusion and pulling when Ruth entered our nursery during her twelfth month. The less-than-optimum recognition of Ruth's cues, as evidenced in the abrupt, probably traumatic weaning, proved to be characteristic of this mother's relationship with her child, and lent a particular quality to the developing object ties.

The device applied for correction of the congenital deformity was worn at all times, except during bathing and changing; it placed a mild restriction upon leg motion, but had only slightly delayed motoric development. Ruth stood with support at seven months, crawled at eight months, and walked with support at fourteen months, and without support at sixteen months. Ruth had made a remarkable accommodation to the corrective device as she crawled about most efficiently.

Yet in spite of a fairly smooth development in the motoric, perceptual, and other areas, her developing object relations were of a peculiar nature. From her sixth month on, Ruth had suffered intense "stranger anxiety", the most striking elements of which were her visual hyper-vigilance and her clinging to her mother's body. At about the same time she had developed a fear of the noise of a vacuum cleaner, of lying down in the tub for hair washing, and of her periodic physical examination for her congenital deformity. All but the fear of strangers and the fear of her paediatrician had disappeared when she entered our nursery at age twelve months. Her stranger anxiety was still so intense that it took several days before her staff observer could approach without eliciting intense distress, even as Ruth sat on her mother's lap. We learned from her mother that Ruth's way of mastering her separation anxiety was to fall asleep immediately when left with a neighbour for baby-sitting.

We feel that the persistent separation and stranger anxiety derived from several sources: first, the periodic removal of the corrective device was perceived as an intermittent loss of a body part; second, the partial motor restriction added to the difficulties of her developing body schematisation and limited aggressive motor discharge; and third, the mother's anxious concern about the body deformity and its future fate along with her less than adequate mothering resulted in some disturbance in Ruth's developing object relationships. In short, Ruth was experiencing more than the ordinary difficulty in the establishment of the mental representation of the maternal object and of the self, the symptomatic expression of which was her intense separation and stranger anxiety that continued well beyond the average period. Therefore, according to Roiphe's (1968) hypothesis, Ruth would be expected to demonstrate a major distortion in development when she arrives at the period of genital discovery.

Ruth's fourteenth to sixteenth months

From about fourteen months of age Ruth began to practice many varieties of "object-disappearance" games, including the usual peek-a-book, mirror peek-a-boo, repetitive toilet flushing, and repetitive use of the mail-box toy (in which forms are dropped through cut-out slats and then retrieved).

In her relationships with people, modest frustration evoked mild temper tantrums, as well as focused hostility directed to other persons or herself. She would, for example, scratch, bite, and tease her mother and her favourite staff member, or bite her own fingers. Focused affectionate behaviour also appeared as Ruth kissed and hugged people, dolls, and other objects. In relation to certain aspects of ego functioning, we witnessed an interesting spurt in her use of symbolic speech. Ruth acquired names for her parents and dolls that she soon used even in the absence of these objects. Semi-symbolic play also began to appear when she placed dolls in bed, on the play toilet, etc. Ruth attained this level of symbolic play at sixteen months, at least two months later than many of her peers.

From the group of behaviours just described, we infer that more distinct and stable mental self as well as object representations were becoming established. As self and object differentiation proceeded, object-directed aggressive and affectionate behaviour emerged, as well as a certain amount of self-directed aggression in the form of self-biting. (We have come to regard the balance between self- and object-directed aggression as a crucial determinant for later development.) The spurt in symbolic functioning as evidenced both in speech and in semi-symbolic play appeared to accompany the increasing self and object differentiation.

The increasing individuation was, however, accompanied by manifest anxiety, as indicated by an intensification of oral behaviour. This included eating, as well as her earlier forms of thumb and object sucking, and tongue licking, pulling, and protrusion. Furthermore, Ruth's engaging in any new activity was contingent on a specific condition—the maintenance of direct visual contact with her mother at all times, which her peers of sixteen months no longer needed. Yet, in spite of these evidences of more than usual anxiety, her chronically "anxious" searching look, with eyes slightly narrowed and gaze soon averted, now gradually gave way to a more open, bright expression, often with a trace of playful teasing. We infer from this that some greater stability of the mental self and object representations had been achieved.

Body exploration

We were particularly interested in following those behaviours dealing with the identification of body parts. At fourteen months, Ruth could name her own facial features and appendages, as well as those of her parents. She had been exposed to her mother's naked body from the beginning, but it was not until her fourteenth month, at the same time as focused hostile aggression and affection emerged, that she began to stare intently at her mother's breasts and pubic hair, as yet without attempting to touch them. It should be mentioned that her father, unlike her mother, had avoided undressing in Ruth's presence from her sixth month onward.

At about fourteen and a half months, the umbilicus became the focus of Ruth's attention as part of a highly exciting, reciprocal umbilicus-touching game with her mother. Soon afterward, interest in anal functioning became evident as Ruth insisted upon being in the bathroom during her mother's toileting procedures, a common occurrence in all the families we have studied. She pointed to and developed a distinctive name for the stool in the toilet, and flushed the toilet repetitively both at home and in the nursery. All of this took place in the absence of any effort at toilet training by the mother. At sixteen months, when she had just begun independent walking, Ruth gestured that she wanted to see her stool in the soiled diaper that had just been removed from her. She then proceeded to sit on the potty chair in the nursery while clothed. Shortly thereafter she acquired a distinctive word for urination, a step following the usual developmental progression from anal to urinary zone.

These behaviours indicated to us that there was increasingly stable mental representation of her own body. New themes appeared in her play activities. She stacked blocks to build high towers, piled toys into carriages and other receptacles, repetitively emptied drawers and shelves of their contents and then refilled them, performing all this in an orderly and deliberate manner, in contrast to her previous "throwing style". She insisted that her toys remain just where she had put them, and now was able to take toys away from her peers and defend her own possessions.

The new organisational level of her play was, we inferred, related to the ongoing anal and urinary schematisation in that the anal and urinary areas and functions were evidently achieving more solid mental representation. Anal traits of possessiveness as well as some degree of elementary organisation, demonstrated in Ruth's orderly arrangement of concrete objects and her interest in their spatial relationships, seemed to reflect the new level of personality organisation.

The enormous surge in almost all areas of development that had begun at fourteen months reached a climax during Ruth's seventeenth month, just one month after she had finally attained unaided locomotion. She could now maintain distance from her mother as she engaged in social interchange; and her oral activities subsided remarkably; she held her own cup alone for the first time. Her sleep, which had been disturbed for several months, became peaceful, and she developed an attachment to a transitional object in the form of a "fuzzy dog" which was her constant night-time companion. For the first time since the initial development of stranger anxiety during her sixteenth month, Ruth now greeted strangers without a trace of her former apprehension. This remarkable qualitative change in the nature of her object relations indicated to us that there was increasing reliability of the mental object representation, as a result of which her separation anxiety almost completely disappeared.

In the midst of the new-found pleasure and freedom of her early seventeenth month, evidence of Ruth's first focused genital interest was observed in the nursery and simultaneously reported by her mother. Her occasional fleeting gesture toward the genital area during changing in the preceding month or so was now, at seventeen and a half months, replaced by intentional genital handling during every changing as she inserted two fingers between her labia. She crouched down and peered up between her widespread legs; undressed dolls, calling some of them "boy" for the first time; examined their perineal areas; and smilingly used the family word that had been offered her for both genital and anal areas (again, a common practice in the families we have studied). She tried to lift and peer beneath her mother's skirt and that of her favourite staff member. Her interest in the reciprocal umbilicus game dwindled, but the changing of other nursery children, which Ruth had previously ignored, now became of great interest to her. She hovered about the toilet, pushed the potty seat about the nursery, and shadowed her mother whenever she entered the bathroom. From this behaviour, we confirmed that mental representation of the genital area and of the anatomical genital difference was being established as we had had earlier evidence that she had been aware of urinary and anal functions and sensations.

Intensification of genital awareness and mutilation reaction between eighteen-and-a-quarter and nineteen months

Some three weeks after the onset of her genital curiosity, that is at eighteen-and-a-quarter months of age, subtle but pervasive changes in mood, in the nature of her object relationships, and in other aspects of ego functioning began to appear. On one occasion Ruth was watching with her usual interest the changing of a boy in the nursery. Fully clothed, she then sat down on a potty chair, holding a long xylophone stick perpendicularly against her perineal area, and displaying an odd look of uneasiness on her face. The toilet flush handle became of increasing interest to her as she fondled and licked it whenever she was near it. We could follow the pathway of displacement from the visual percept of the offending male genital itself to a variety of sites away from the body (by utilising the structural type of analysis previously described), as Ruth insistently and repetitively fingered knobs, car handles, and a variety of to her protruding objects, which she now named "flush", a word previously reserved exclusively for the toilet handle.

Under the impact of her increasing anxiety about the observed sexual difference, distortion in verbal symbolisation had occurred. The single attribute of phallic shape now united otherwise dissimilar objects under the common symbolic word "flush". She was visibly disturbed by all broken toys, refusing to use broken crayons that had previously been entirely acceptable. We felt this behaviour indicated that these toys had become invested with the significance of the two body zones with which she was now most concerned, the genital and anal, and a defect in the concrete external inanimate object that was thus invested could no longer be tolerated. It appeared that these two areas of ego functioning, play and speech, had suffered distortion through the increasing use of denial as she tried to cope with mounting anxiety. In the same manner, the toilet handle that through displacement had come to represent the offending male genital now evoked so much anxiety that its symbolic word designation was no longer maintained in a discrete form. Instead, the word "flush" was generalised to other phallic-like objects. Thus, this particular word symbol lost some of the specificity it had previously attained.

We have witnessed many instances of such invasions of ego functioning in connection with instinctual development and ongoing body schematisation. Although these states are usually temporary, there is, of course, the possibility of a subtle and permanent influence on precisely those areas of ego functioning that are in the process of rapid development during the latter half of the second year of life: namely, developing symbolisation both in the verbal and in the non-verbal areas. Visual symbolisation in particular undergoes developmental elaboration at this age. One would therefore expect that stressful events occurring during this critical development period would leave permanent traces in the visual–perceptive area of functioning. Moreover, in this particular child, the development of visual perception was probably even more complex than is usual in view of the visual fixation that had been so impressive in her earlier stranger anxiety.

Ruth now engaged in new visual activities. She ran to look at any baby being changed in the nursery, immediately thereafter glanced down at her own perineal area, and spoke her word for urination, indicating that the visual inspection involved a direct comparison. She became an intent window gazer in the nursery, and was overheard murmuring "Daddy" on several occasions as she stared out at an empty street, seemingly occupied with fantasy. Her obvious concern with the genital differences exerted pressure on her parents, who now allowed her to witness her father's urination on several occasions. She was fascinated by the sight.

Her intense visual sexual curiosity seemed to combine with the sensations of genital arousal that she experienced as she witnessed changings and urinations. From this constellation an interesting group of phenomena emerged. Whenever she found someone looking at her, she blushed a deep red colour and tried to hide her face. Simultaneously, she developed a new interest in all forms of fire, such as her father's matches, her grandfather's barbecue, and fire engines. She repeated the words "hot" and "fire" in all these situations, and looked at the "hot" events with obvious fascination and clear signs of erotic excitement.

First, as to her "fiery" interest: Ruth had experienced genital sensations of localised arousal and warmth as she masturbated, sensations now retrospectively connected with her earlier oral perceptions of warmth. (Ruth's first word had been "hot", a warning used by her mother against burning her mouth with hot food.) In addition to the internal associative link, there was an external one in that the local genital warmth found an equivalent perceptual quality in the fires she observed and whose warmth she felt; and these fires in turn became linked with fire engines. All fiery events were thus equated with genital arousal, leading to the emergence of a new symbol: fire stood for sexual arousal! The connections between looking, sexual arousal, interest in fires, and the word "hot" had become established.

These interesting phenomena of blushing and hiding her face on being looked at appear to relate to the matter of the developing sense of identity. Greenacre (1958) has emphasised the crucial role of the face and genitals, in contrast to other body areas, in establishing individual recognition of the own body self. Ruth's facial inspection had earlier been an important aspect of what we inferred to be her primitive attempts at self-object differentiation. As she now tackled this same task on a more complex level, she avidly inspected genitals and objects to which genital displacement had taken place. It must be emphasised, however, that her earlier experiences had contributed a less than optimally firm body basis.

The corrective device worn against the perineal area during the first year had surely aroused genital sensations, resulting in greater than average instability of genital schematisation. Now, at one-and-a-half years, her new and acute awareness of genital arousal, and the confusing comparisons of her own genitals with those of others, constituted a new threat to the already distorted genital schematisation. We speculate, therefore, that displacement occurred from genital area to the face, which had been the site of the earlier efforts at identity establishment. Having become aroused as she visually inspected her father's genitals, she now became aroused when she was visually inspected herself. Genital blushing and facial blushing were, for the time being, simultaneous phenomena, although we assumed that the genital aspect would soon become inhibited and eventually repressed. (The ready displacement from genital to face, as well as the extensive employment of introjective-projective mechanisms are, of course, characteristic of psychic functioning during this developmental period.)

Toward the end of her eighteenth month, Ruth's comparisons and inspections of the genital area began to decrease; simultaneously, a slow deterioration in her mood set in. The cheerfulness of her seventeenth month was replaced by irritability and decreasing frustration tolerance, but this time the aggression was not directed against the mother, as it had been at fifteen months. Instead, she teased and provoked other adults and again began to bite her own fingers in a renewed emergence of self-directed aggression. The earlier fear of strangers and the clinging to her mother returned in ever increasing intensity.

The use of displacement following an earlier developmental pathway

The mechanism of gradual displacement was evident as Ruth's attention turned upward from the offending genital zone to her former interest in her umbilicus. She repeatedly pushed her finger into it, lifted the clothing of our nursery dolls, and pointed at and named a non-existent umbilicus, using the word "button", which was not the name her parents had used to designate this area. Many inanimate protuberances also became "buttons" in the same type of symbolic distortion we had observed during the period when she had first scrutinised the anatomical genital differences. As part of this effort to deny the genital difference by affirming the ubiquitous umbilicus in its place, Ruth tried to pin a safety pin on the abdomen of her favourite Teddy.

Crisis at nineteenth-and-a-half months

During one of her usual nursery sessions, Ruth bit ferociously on her own fingers, and then chewed on the ear of a toy bear after she had witnessed the changing of an infant girl. She had chewed and macerated a similar toy bear's ear at home a few days previously. On yet another morning, she was being supported in the arms of her staff observer for a better view of an infant boy's changing, which she had rushed to observe. Suddenly she averted her gaze, pulled off first one of the observer's earrings, and then the other, and gestured her wish to be put down on the floor. Running into the adjacent bathroom, she tore off toilet paper, dropped it into the toilet, and then tried to flush it away as she simultaneously licked at the flush handle.

All these behaviours indicate a wish to dispose of protrusions. Avoidance and displacement mechanisms were increasingly in evidence as her gaze avoided the perineal areas of dolls whose abdomens she diligently examined for the "button". She was more and more distressed by broken or imperfect toys, pointing at their defects and actually using the word "broken". And a new fear of falling objects, particularly if they caused spattering or splashing, emphasised her awareness of the urinary aspect of the male genital. Temper tantrums returned, her sleep was once again disturbed, and the "toy dog" transitional object, which had been her obligatory night-time companion, now became a daytime necessity as well. In addition, a new obligatory object made its appearance in the form of a doll that Ruth called "boy". She insisted that this doll, which resembled her other usual girl dolls in every way, be seated next to her at all meals, and that "he" receive a mouthful of food each time she fed herself.

In attempting to understand the meaning of these new developments, we assumed that Ruth had arrived at only marginal stability in the maternal object representation, compromised during her early months by the sudden weaning, the less than optimum mother–child relationship, and the limitation of aggressive motor discharge in consequence of the corrective device she wore. Now her awareness of the genital difference and the additional burden of anger and disappointment at her genital state resulted in a split in the maternal image, with projection of the bad object. Recrudescence of the fear of strangers indicated a renewed fear of object loss that followed the weakening of the maternal object representation through splitting. Simultaneously, a split in the mental self-representation seemed to have occurred, with the obligatory toy dog and the doll "boy" representing split-off portions of Ruth's mental self image.

As this critical period continued, inhibition of genital curiosity was soon reflected in a narrowing of her recently enlarged area of general curiosity. Ruth turned from her recent rich doll play to play with toys that involved the solution of tasks related to spatial relationships as well as anal functioning. The use of such toys had been the most prominent aspect of her early play. Now she again began to stack blocks, pile toys on top of one another within all kinds of receptacles, and use the "shape box" repetitively. This restriction of general curiosity paralleled the growing inhibition of Ruth's interest in toileting. She lost interest in the toilet and conspicuously avoided all references to the genital, anal, and urinary functions and areas. In sharp contrast, her interest in the toilet flush handle itself intensified, and she now used the word "flush" to designate the entire toilet, the opening and closing of doors, the electric light switch, and the brake of her carriage. All of these objects and situations shared the element of control rather than that of phallic shape, which had characterised her earlier symbolic distortion.

Her favourite inanimate companions were no longer the toy dog, but a number of dolls that she carried along without using them in play, one of which she named "baby". It seemed that Ruth had begun to use the concrete doll to take the place of the longed-for phallus. Her use of the name "baby" for this doll-phallus signals the establishment of a very early phallus-baby equation.

The turning point

Ruth's worsening sleep disturbance reached its peak during her father's unusual absence from home over a period of several nights. She wept bitterly as she called for her mother, repeating her distinctive words for urination and defecation. She was inconsolable throughout the night. The following morning she deposited a stool in her newly acquired potty chair for the first time, after which she stood up, gazed at the stool in amazement, and promptly urinated on the floor.

This acute reaction to the father's absence must be viewed against the background of the severe early stranger and separation anxiety that had waned and now had returned again. With the temporary loss of the father, the fear of maternal loss was rekindled, and Ruth's defecation in the potty on this fateful morning seemed to represent a final surrender to her mother's wishes as she parted with the stool-phallus.

As if in vague recognition of the meaning of Ruth's gift of her stool, her frantic parents decided to purchase on that day a carriage and baby doll that she had been requesting for some time. With the carriage at her bedside and the doll in her arms, Ruth had her first quiet night in several weeks. Her last audible word as she fell asleep was "flush"!

Ruth's use of dolls at this critical time suggests that they now served in part as infantile fetishistic objects in an effort to repair her sense of the defective genital. We have come to realise that the doll has a complicated series of meanings, some deriving from early stages of development when they have a "transitional object" quality, while others serve a much more advanced state of symbolisation. We have noted regression in semi-symbolic play with dolls, just as in other areas of symbolisation, and consider this to be important evidence of disturbed development.

Ruth's dramatic first surrender of her stool ushered in a period of relative "submission" in other areas of behaviour, although Ruth refused to use the potty chair itself for many weeks thereafter. Subdued and even sad at times, she was no longer interested in the potty chair, the toilet and its flush, or in her father's showering to which she had rushed excitedly at every opportunity. All genital, anal, and urinary exploration and curiosity had ceased in relation to her own body, the changing of other children, and her parents.

The toys she now played with were small toy horses that she placed at either side of her as she sat rocking in a small chair. She clung to the baby doll and its carriage. Broken toys and crayons continued to distress her and she refused to use them.

At twenty-two months, Ruth was a quiet child whose constant eating companions were the two dolls at her sides, as Ruth insisted that they be fed while she fed herself. Her former anxious look of the narrowed eyes and tense face in the presence of strangers had returned, and her curiosity had become definitely limited in scope. The recognition of a definitive change in mood was her mother's first clear statement that Ruth would probably always be a "quiet" one who would be "afraid of strangers".

Comment

We are unable to assess the importance of the mother's new pregnancy and of the father's absence from home at such a crucial period of development in this child's life, although we were able to verify that the castration reaction itself had begun well before the mother's conscious knowledge of her pregnancy. The effect of pregnancies, as well as of brief and prolonged paternal absences has been studied in detail in several infants in our project. We plan to report this material at a later date.

Summary

In this paper we reported observations on the development of a child with a congenital defect that required repeated medical examinations and the constant wearing of a corrective device during her first year of life. The resulting early disturbance in body schematisation and in the developing mother–child relationship distorted and delayed the separation–individuation process and interfered with the establishment of an optimally stable maternal mental representation. Yet, with the development of free locomotion, there was a spurt in individuation and in symbolic development between Ruth's fourteenth and seventeenth months, as evident in the disappearance of stranger anxiety, the emergence of symbolic play, and in her enlarging verbal capacity. This ongoing individuation process brought her in due time to the awareness of anal, urinary, and genital anatomy and function, along with their appropriate sensations.

In this already vulnerable child, however, the discovery of the sexual anatomical difference and sexual sensations brought with it overwhelming disappointment and anger at the mother, with loss of self-esteem and the marked inhibited and depressive reaction that continues to characterise her. The incomplete and unstable fusion of the good and bad maternal images gave way under the impact of her anger; the maternal images were split and the bad image was projected on to other figures. A basic mistrust prevails, and it is likely that she will continue to have difficulties in separating from her mother. Another consequence of the distorted development of body schematisation and object relations was a concurrent split in the mental representation of her own body (the boy doll and eating companions) and a weakening of several aspects of ego functioning (such as general curiosity, play, and symbolisation).

Ruth's very early object relations, self-identity, and other ego functions appear to have been indelibly affected by bodily experiences in her first year. We observed the impact of the discovery of the sexual anatomical difference during her second year and attempted to delineate the fateful consequences for defensive organisation, object relations, mood, and style of play behaviour.

Follow-up at thirty-one months

A sister was born when Ruth was sixteen-and-a-half months old. Ruth seemed fond of the new baby and initially showed no hostility toward her. Just after the baby returned home, Ruth showed a spurt in doll play, but soon she abandoned it almost completely. Blocks became her favourite toy and the Empire State Building her favourite block-building project.

Toilet training had been accomplished before the baby sister was born. Although speech was advanced, the use of the personal pronoun "I" had not yet been achieved. Ruth continued to show marked anxiety in relation to even minor injuries. On one occasion she insisted on wearing long trousers to cover her scraped knee, long after the bandage had been removed. Following an injury to her lip, she refused to eat for three days and made persistent attempts to hide her face from the view of others. And her tolerance of separation continues to be well below the expected level.

In summary, Ruth's earlier difficulties in the areas of self-esteem, object relations, and other aspects of ego functioning, such as non-verbal and verbal symbolisation, were still in evidence as she entered the oedipal period; and the castration anxiety of her second year of life had never disappeared.

References

Galenson, E. (1971). A consideration of the nature of thought in childhood play. In: J. B. McDevitt and C. F. Settlage (Eds.), *Separation–Individuation: Essays in Honor of Margaret Mahler* (pp. 41–74). Madison, CT: International Universities Press.

Greenacre, P. (1953). Certain relationships between fetishism and the faulty development of the body image. *The Psychoanalytic Study of the Child, 8*: 79–98.

Greenacre, P. (1958). Early physical determinants in the development of the sense of identity. *Journal of the American Psychoanalytic Association, 6*: 612–627.

Mahler, M. (1963). Thoughts about development and individuation. *The Psychoanalytic Study of the Child, 18*: 307–324.

Mahler, M. (1966). Notes on the development of basic moods: the depressive affect. In: R. M. Loewenstein, L. M. Newman, M. Schur & A. J. Solnit (Eds.), *Psychoanalysis—A General Psychology: Essays in Honor of Heinz Hartmann* (pp. 152–168). New York: International Universities Press.

Pine, F., & Furer, M. (1963). Studies of the separation–individuation phase: a methodological overview. *The Psychoanalytic Study of the Child, 18*: 325–342.

Roiphe, H. (1968). On an early genital phase: with an addendum on genesis. *The Psychoanalytic Study of the Child, 23*: 348–365.

Werner, H., & Kaplan, B. (1963). *Symbol Formation*. New York: Wiley.

Discussion of Chapter Two

Phyllis Greenacre

I am always interested in studies of early development and welcome the opportunity to discuss this paper. It gives me the chance to compare direct observations of infants with my own findings that are predominantly from the analyses of adults. The two areas of symbol formation and the significance of early childhood play interest me especially. Since I discussed these in connection with Dr Galenson's earlier article on play and childhood thought, I shall not pay as much specific attention to them now, but my discussion inevitably overlaps somewhat the earlier one.

I would say at once that I do not know a great deal about vector structural analysis and in viewing my own data have proceeded along rather different lines. I would consider the second year of life as very rich in significant developmental potentialities. I have thought that the developmental sequence of the libidinal phases is not always as neat and orderly as our schema would present it; that there is always some overlapping of phases and that a premature activation of an aspect of a phase by a special stimulation may cause some unique individual patterning of the normally developing phase; but such premature and intense stimulation produces a reaction under strain. Furthermore, prolonged and excessive stimulation causes a kind of overflow into adjacent phases and may bring about a partial regression *or* a precocious invasion of a phase not yet maturing.

In addition, the reactions in any phase are accompanied by and interact with whatever is happening in the early ego development. For example, in the second year there is not only the heightened ambivalence to the parents as separation progresses, but also the trauma of toilet training with the awareness of the need to relinquish the stool, as well as the momentous discovery of the anatomical differences between the sexes. But equally important is the fact that this is the period of learning to walk, an achievement that is a landmark in the infant's separation problems and also brings him into a different perceptive relationship to his own body as well as to that of others and even to inanimate objects. He can now view them from different and changing angles in contrast to those slants to which he has been accustomed; and he must harmonise the new perceptions with the old. It also means a gradual consolidation in his own body image, and a greater independence from that of the mother. In as much as his reaction to outer objects is in part due to his own body perceptions, there is a new alignment of perceptual fragments, some of which may remain as symbols, in which the part serves as the symbol not only of the whole but of several different wholes. At any rate, there is a proliferation of symbol formation.

In the account of Ruth's development, I was impressed that the spurts of active development at fourteen months and again at sixteen months correspond with the times of achievement of standing alone and then of walking. The increasing richness of perceptual awareness goes on concurrently with and gets additional content from the toilet training and the discovery of the genital anatomical differences. These events are in a reciprocal way influenced by the erect posture and locomotion since this makes it much less comfortable for the infant to keep his stool in his diaper and carry it around with him, and at the same time it makes his own genitals and those of others more visually accessible to him. It is apparent I think that I tend to proceed in my understanding by building up a series of horizontal planes involving developmental patterns.

I was also impressed by the flare up of stranger anxiety that occurred on Ruth's entrance to the nursery school. I should like to offer some considered speculations and to ask some questions in regard to this situation. We learn that Ruth had had severe stranger anxiety during the latter part of her first year, and that there were other fears also, namely, the fear of the noise of the vacuum cleaner, a fear of the periodic physical examination, a fear of the paediatrician, and a fear of lying down in the tub to have her hair washed. All of these had disappeared or been ameliorated by the time that she came to the nursery during her twelfth month.

This was about the time that the wearing of the perinea pillow pad was discontinued. I should like to ask more about the actual timing of this removal—did it occur before or after her coming to the nursery, and what was the technique of stopping it. Was it summarily discontinued in a way similar to the weaning process or was it done gradually, with the child allowed to finger it and play with it at times. I would further be interested to know whether during the earlier period she seemed glad to have it replaced after changing and whether she ever developed any baby words or syllables to designate it. I am questioning, I think, whether she regarded it as a friend or an enemy. In connection with this it seems significance that while the use of the pillow might emphasise the genital area, yet in its softness it would have much more of a breast quality and might have been quite comforting. It would certainly then make greater an inner connection between the vaginal area and the mouth, a connection that is often true in girl children anyway. But in any case I would think its removal about the time of her coming to the nursery might have complicated her stranger anxiety.

The other symptoms of fear during the first year occurred about the same time and I would think of some possible connection with each other and conceivably with the renewed stranger anxiety. Here I would ask about the paediatrician: was Ruth taken to his office for examination and how often? How did she show her fear? Was there a removal of the pad? And were there periodic X-ray examinations to determine the state of the pelvis? Was there a nurse in attendance: I ask these details because it occurred to me that the first days at the nursery might in some way remind the child of going to the paediatrician's office if examinations were done there rather than at home. Even the seeing of some additional children might have brought some reminder of such visits. I have myself had patients who had suffered fears of vacuum cleaners, of telephones, of sewing machines, especially of whirring noises; and some where states of anxiety or even of panic in adult life were triggered off by fear of going under a hairdryer in a beauty parlour. Some years ago there were many women who were panicky of the medusa-like contraption of the electric permanent wave machines. Naturally, there are many different contributions to these states but the commonest sources of such anxiety in childhood seemed to be hospital or doctor's office experiences with X-rays or with anaesthetics. It seems possible that this child's fear of the vacuum cleaner and even of lying down in the tub to have her hair washed might have come from such sources. This together with the perineal pad problem would give the child an easy pathway of displacement from genital area to the head.

According to my experience there is some sensitivity to genital excitation in the second year of life, especially evident in patients who have suffered early traumatisation. I have thought that this was not a true early genital phase but was part of a greater excitation of the entire body to which the genital responded in its own way also. Such a situation of excitation might be a factor contributing to a body phallus identification later. I have several times had patients who had worn braces of one kind or another in early infancy and have found that these devices have a permanent registration both in dreams and in later somatic sensations even when the patient has no conscious memory of the early experience. It will be interesting to see what sort of illusory penis this child develops, if any, in view of the pillow breast-penis given her in her first year.

It would seem to me that even by the second year of life, this child's situation was so "loaded" that it would be difficult by vector analysis to dissect out in a way that would be to any degree predictively precise as to what zones might determine the direction of any possible creative ability as foretold in the child's play. Thus in this child the sequelae of the oral sensitisation certainly overlaps with the early toileting sensations, even when training was not yet specifically undertaken. The early interest in her labia was possibly not only looking for the phallus, which has been seen on the little boy, but it may also represent a lower mouth and derive some stimulation of interest from this source as well as from the genitals. This same problem of a mixture of simultaneous stimulations from different zones rises again in the interpretation of the biting of her own fingers. One must remember that the mouth is still a focus of interest and aggressive impulses in connection with the progressive eruption of teeth. And also that the fingers may even then have symbolic meaning. I have seen a girl child only a little over two years go into a real panic at the sight of a new maid who lacked one finger on one hand. I would also comment on the child's bending over to look between her legs. Certainly this would seem and doubtless was a looking for the phallus. But I have seen something similar in a group of children all less than three years old. The youngest who was about sixteen months old and was exhilarated in having learned to run and navigate freely, started a game of bending over and looking at the world upside down from between her legs. She was extremely merry about this and soon had the older nursery children doing the same thing. I thought this bit of play followed the mastering of walking and that she was experimentally looking at the world from every angle possible including those that she had abandoned.

As the authors have pointed out, the second year of life is one of extensive symbol formation mostly based on resemblances of body parts to each other or to external objects in whatever senses these may be registered. I believe that walking and talking represent a nodal period of consolidation in development that brings into more reliably constant constellations the perceptive fragments that have been experienced—laying around as it were—with loose associative connections, characteristic of primary process. Such associative connections are still retained in our dreams and in our lapses into magic thinking. But they are the stuff of similes, metaphors, and ambiguities of poets and in one form or another are part of the creative representations of artists in whatever media they may work. To a varying degree, they are part of the richness of sensual experience generally. When concretised they become part of the distressing symptoms in some psychoses. It is my impression that in not specially gifted persons, the making of things (in that sense creative work) is more related to practical needs and is more influenced excretory functions than is true in general in artists. It is then more a question of useful productivity than of artistic creativity.

I think in this paper the authors have indicated admirably the developmental background of symbol formation as it leads to and also becomes differentiated from the sturdy reliable and expectable reality appreciation and how the latter is based in the stabilisation of the mental representations of the infant's own body. I am not sure, however, in what sense the authors use the term *creativity*—whether to designate the special capacity of unusually gifted people to make original works of art in whatever medium, or whether it is with the connotation of a high degree of useful productivity, the potential for which is probably greater in most people than they can actually materialise.

If it is used in this latter sense, then I think I would agree with them. But I am inclined to think that in the very gifted individuals of greater or even less genius, there are inborn qualities that may influence the modality of expression, and also allow the gifted one peculiar ability to react to more different perceptual realities in life than is true for most of us, and perhaps to react more strongly. There are other qualities as well that may already be predetermined at birth. But I cannot be certain of this and believe my ideas have to wait verification or revision until more work is done both on longitudinal studies extending into adulthood and on individual infant differences at birth. Now when everyone is equal, and some more so, the thought of infants being differently endowed at birth is especially unpopular.

There is one more comment I would make concerning Ruth—that has to do with the occurrence of sexual excitement at this period. I thought it was rather clear that in her case there was a very great emphasis on urination involving a degree of envious excitement that was especially strong after the father's demonstration of his urinary prowess. This intimacy with the father may also have had some seductive quality to it. I have seen this excitement on urination in other little girls, generally a bit older than Ruth, when it seemed due to an angry uncertain competitive effort that combined with urinary pressure, to increase any sexual excitement that might be incipient anyway. (My observation occurred in a nursery school to which I had access about thirty years ago.) The present case of Ruth seems to be an almost classical example of the interest in fire and water works being part of situations of eroticised urinary functioning. What is especially noteworthy is that it occurred at so early a time.

CHAPTER THREE

The influence of hostile aggression on the development of expressive language

Eleanor Galenson

Among the most frequent developmental deviations in infants who are at "psychological risk" is delay in the acquisition of expressive language, commonly known as speech. Data from psychoanalytically informed infant observation and treatment offer intriguing insight as to the role of disturbances in the libidinal and aggressive impulse balance during a critical period in the second year of life. Factors that contribute to this imbalance in some children and their parents will be described, and a direction for preventative and therapeutic intervention will be suggested.

Reports in the psychiatric and psychoanalytic literature of cases of "elective mutism" in children usually do not distinguish between those children who have *never attained* the use of expressive language and those suffering from an *inhibition* of expressive language that had already developed. Expressive language usually begins to emerge during the middle of the second year, following the period of receptive language acquisition. The infant not only comprehends the meanings of familiar words, but can now utilise *socially accepted* words to communicate his or her personal subjective experiences and share them with others.

While many factors undoubtedly influence this process of language acquisition (constitutional endowment, language exposure, the presence of siblings, etc.), a major influence appears to be the nature of the mother–child relationship I will propose that it is the balance between libidinal and aggressive aspects of this relationship that affects the development of speech in a profound way.

A specific connection between speech and the sphincteric aspect of anality was first proposed by Greenacre (1969). She wrote:

> It may be significant that speech begins and is then elaborated during periods of special spurts of development of the body sphincters. The muscles of the mouth, pharynx and larynx which play such an important part in speech have rather complex sphincter-like activities. Clinically we know that the infant's speech may be much affected by the vicissitudes of sphincter control in other parts of the body. There may still be such a degree of plasticity in the body organization forming the basis of self-image that synchronous and similar body developments of early childhood affect each other through avenues of easy displacement. (p. 361)

Yet another connection between speech and anal phase development was suggested by Stone's (1979) evolutionary view of the development of the aggressive drive. Stone proposed that transformation of oral aggression facilitates the emergence of speech; oral cannibalistic fantasies that accompany the onset of teething are gradually deployed from mouth and teeth to hand activities under normal circumstances, leaving the mouth free for the development of the function of speech. At the same time, oral rage is gradually replaced by bodily sensations relating to sphincter activity, and the struggle between retention and expulsion becomes an *internal* one, unlike the feeding interaction of the first year.

Both Greenacre and Stone emphasised the importance of drive activity during the first two years in regard to both its bodily expression and the incipient ego function of social communication. Data from psychoanalytically informed infant research and clinical experience offer support for their hypotheses. Direct infant observational research findings indicate that there is a decisive turn in the management of oral aggression between the eighth and tenth months. As oral aggression intensifies with the eruption of teeth, infants normally develop a greater adaptive capacity to cope with delay as well as a greater repertoire of active affectionate behaviour toward their care-takers. But this developmental phase is also characterised by mother–infant interchanges that are mildly teasing in quality—an admixture of affection and controlled aggression in both members of the dyad.

However, if hostile aggression has been intensified during the infant's first year due to either physical or psychological trauma, or if the maternal response to the infant's budding aggression is unduly restrictive (Galenson, 1986), such infants become intensely negative in their behaviour toward their mother and other people as well. It is this libidinal–aggressive imbalance that appears to interfere with the developing symbolic function, specifically in regard to the emergence of expressive language. Under these circumstances, infants are unable to communicate fantasies and affects through the socially agreed upon vehicle of speech, and may indeed be impeded in the actual development of fantasies, as well as in their deliverance to the social world. Certain types of first-year experience appear to be particularly traumatic and apt to stimulate hostile aggression. These include prolonged separation from the mother, serious body illness, serious injuries, and surgical procedures.

Normally, the passage through the anal phase during the second year heightens separation anxiety because of the threat of anal loss. This gives rise to the sphincter struggle between retainment and discharge, opposing impulses that colour much of the psychological functioning of this period.

When excessive trauma of the type mentioned above occurs during the first year, the mouth becomes invested with excessive oral aggression, which cannot be adequately discharged subsequently through the normal anal channels, and the mouth is not available for the verbal expression of ideas and feelings under these circumstances. Another potential source of distortion of symbolic development is the similarity between the sphincteric structure of the mouth and larynx and that of the anus (Greenacre, 1969). Anxiety regarding anal loss, particularly when it has been preceded by an earlier experience of object loss, leads not only to an intense anal sphincteric struggle between retaining and discharging anal contents, but the use of oral and laryngeal sphincters that are needed for the development of speech may be inhibited until the anal struggle is resolved.

Analytically informed observation of the development of a little girl during her second year provides support for the hypotheses described above. Julie, a sturdy twelve-month-old girl who was the younger of two sisters, had been developing well during her first year.

She was securely attached to her mother as her primary care-taker and had also spent time during each week with a part-time care-taker. She gradually adapted to her new circumstances and became attached to a new part-time care-taker, but she refused to acknowledge Anne, her former babysitter, when Anne visited the family in their new home three months later.

In her attempts to master these separation experiences, Julie developed a large repertoire of hide-and-seek games, as well as other play that involved the theme of organising inanimate objects of various kinds according to their appearance and function. Shoes were lined up meticulously side by side, blocks were gathered in piles, and puzzles became a favourite pastime. This type of obsessional play helped Julie to organise her new outer world and her inner world as well.

This behaviour was readily accepted by Julie's family and by her new care-taker. Soon Julie, now fifteen months old, began to object to wearing diapers, insisting she could withhold her urine and soon her stool as well, until she got to a potty or toilet. This self-imposed toilet training was due in part to her desire to be able to do whatever her two-and-a-half year older sister did. Despite her parents' clear communication that they did not expect Julie to conform in this way, and indeed were often at their wits end when Julie insisted on finding a proper place to urinate during a family drive, Julie would not, and mostly did not, wet or soil her diaper during the day, although she could not exert this excessive control at night and agreed to wear diapers when she went to sleep.

Julie continued to control her family's activities in this way for the next four or five months, and she often had temper tantrums when her parents could not or did not conform to her toileting needs. In parallel with this struggle, Julie's symbolic development took a remarkable turn; not only did her formerly rich and free semi-symbolic play become repetitive and passionately obsessional, but she also remained stationary in her language development. Clearly able to satisfy her needs and wants by communicative gestures, she also understood what was said by others, but she continued to vocalise many idiosyncratic word like utterances and only a handful of identifiable single words. Expressive language was definitely delayed.

As Julie approached her twenty-fourth month, her behaviour began to alter in several areas. Her favourite transitional object, a blanket ("Blankie") was used for comforting as before, but Julie added an increasingly large family of "baby dolls", as she now began to call them. She fed, washed, undressed, and comforted them and began to actually *speak* to them in a kind of "baby talk", if one can use that term to describe the speech of a twenty-four-month-old child. This spurt in semi-symbolic play, and the equally impressive advance in her language that accompanied it, was truly astonishing. Julie soon began to use quite advanced sentence structure, language that appeared to have been readied silently, only waiting for a critical developmental push before it could appear. This new developmental step had been preceded by a real resolution of the anal and urethral sphincter battles. Now sphincterally competent, she could easily control her urination and defecation during the day, although not yet at night.

Julie continued to show the determined personality of her second year; she soon began to insist on learning how to "read" and do "arithmetic"—nascent activities that seemed to serve this striving and sturdy child very well. It remains to be seen whether her early separation experience will affect her later on, but this psychologically competent toddler had managed to use a variety of ego capacities as she dealt with the exaggerated aggression of her second year, without coming into serious conflict with her environment. She was certainly aided in great measure by her parents' capacity to abstain from responding to her hostile aggression with an aggressive response of their own. Not all children are reared under such fortunate circumstances. Nor are early traumas recognised for the influence they may exert during this highly vulnerable period of the first two years of life.

Conclusion

My research and clinical data from both normal and pathological infants suggest that conflicts over oral aggressive impulses that normally emerge during the last quarter of the first year may be intensified by anal phase conflicts over sphincter control and the accompanying anxiety during the second year. Important precipitating factors include a change in the infant's relationship with his or her primary care-taker, particularly if there is a break in the continuity of this relationship at the highly vulnerable age when object permanence is just beginning to evolve and separation anxiety is peaking.

In addition to its nutritive function, the mouth carries out the important sphincteric function of speech. This function may become involved in conflict when the anal sphincteric function of retention and loss begins to express both positive and negative affects, as well as anxiety. While receptive language may be proceeding normally in its development, an infant who is engaged in serious anal conflict as the result of earlier object loss may be unable to utilise the oral sphincter for the production of speech. Such infants usually acquire a complicated gestural repertoire that temporarily serves communicative purposes in lieu of speech. When the conflict over the issue of object and anal loss is resolved, either through the infant's own capacities or through intervention from the environment, both anal and oral sphincters become available for their appropriate function and the symbolic function proceeds to develop in the form of semi-symbolic play and speech.

If my hypothesis concerning the dynamic relationship between oral and anal aggression is correct, it would elucidate many of the puzzling features of distortions in language development, particularly the delay in the emergence of speech. I suspect that it is precisely in those instances where the mother–child relationship has been invaded by an undue degree of hostile aggression that the dynamic relationship between the libidinal aggressive drive balance and language development will be evident. I believe this is the situation in many single-parent families where the mother cannot help her toddler to modulate the normal, early hostile ambivalence of anal phase development in the absence of paternal support for both mother and child.

References

Galenson, E. (1986). Some thoughts about infant psychopathology and aggressive development. *International Review of Psychoanalysis*, 13: 349–354.

Greenacre, P. (1969). The fetish and the transitional object. *The Psychoanalytic Study of the Child*, 24: 144–164.

Stone, L. (1979). Remarks on certain unique conditions of human aggression (the hand, speech and the use of fire). *Journal of the American Psychoanalytic Association*, 27: 27–33.

PART II
INFANTILE ORIGINS OF SEXUAL IDENTITY

Introduction to Part II

Lucy LaFarge

For the contemporary reader, Galenson and Roiphe's work on infantile sexuality is best known for their groundbreaking and controversial formulations concerning female psychosexual development. On returning to the papers selected here, and the larger series collected in the 1981 volume *The Infantile Origins of Sexual Identity*, the reader becomes aware that the papers take groundbreaking positions in many other areas as well. In fact, in bringing these papers to publication in the 1970s Galenson and Roiphe placed themselves at the centre of many of the most heated psychoanalytic controversies of their time; and many of the controversies that they addressed remain unresolved to the present day. In addition to their reformulation of female development, their revised timetable for the early development of sexuality suggested the possibility of a new, biphasic sequence of castration reactions for the boy. The expressed thrust of the research—to trace the relationship between psychosexual development and the development of object relations and ego functions—touched upon emerging questions about the primacy of the psychosexual in light of a growing emphasis within the field upon external and internal object relationships. That the authors' data consisted of observations of preverbal children raised questions about the certainty with such data could be observed and understood. And finally, the relationship between the data of child observation and the adult clinical process remained uncertain. How could such observations inform the adult analyst? How directly could they be translated into the clinical material of the adult patient?

Beyond their controversial nature, these papers are remarkable for the quality of the data that they present. Each child is presented as a recognisable individual. In line with the object relations approach of the authors, the mothers accompanying the children are highly individualised as well, and the impact of their personalities upon their infants is considered in depth. Parents and infant are seen to interact in a resonating system, where influences flow in both directions, and the vicissitudes of the child's development stir powerful responses in the parents as well as the reverse. To an unusual degree, the authors highlight the importance of the parents' fantasies, conscious and unconscious, in the formation of the child's experience. And, perhaps more unusual, the authors consider the fantasies and experiences that the children's behaviour evokes in them as they hypothesise about the behaviour's meaning.

A revised timetable for psychosexual development

In their introduction to *The Infantile Origins of Sexual Identity*, Roiphe and Galenson lay out the task that they had set for themselves. "It is the interrelationship existing between instinctual-phase development, self-object differentiation, and other aspects of ego development that has been of particular interest to us" (Roiphe & Galenson, 1981, p. ix). Building upon Roiphe's earlier exploration of early castration reactions, their focus would be upon early psychosexual development and its matrix in object relations:

> Our work has centered upon the later months of the first year and the second year of life, a period of rapid growth and development. We have been particularly interested in elucidating the vicissitudes of libidinal-drive development not only as it was interwoven with other sectors of development in the child but also as it seemed to affect the very fiber of the child–parent relation. (Roiphe & Galenson, 1981, pp. ix–x)

In pursuit of these goals, Galenson and Roiphe established a research nursery, structured along lines similar to that of Margaret Mahler, and over a period of seven years observed sixty-six infants. Their results led them to construct a timetable for psychosexual development in which awareness of genital difference emerged much earlier than the timetable Freud had established and traditional analysts continued to maintain.

Freud (1923e) had argued that both the boy and the girl became aware of genital difference at age three to five, in the context of an early genital organisation where penis and clitoris became the leading zones of sexual excitement. The discovery of genital difference was a developmental organiser for both boy and girl; it marked the moment when the developmental trajectories of the two sexes were believed to diverge and the differential entry of each into the oedipal phase.

Galenson and Roiphe's observational data placed an early genital phase and the consequent awareness of genital difference much earlier, at age fifteen to nineteen months. Both boys and girls were seen to develop genital awareness in train with anal and urinary awareness. Galenson and Roiphe's data overwhelmingly supported this finding. As Elizabeth Lloyd Mayer wrote in her review of *The Infantile Origins of Sexual Identity* for *The International Journal of Psychoanalysis*:

> To my mind, the authors have offered ample and most convincing evidence for the existence of their hypothesized early genital phase. Indeed, I would guess that simple perusal of Roiphe & Galenson's case presentations by even the most psychoanalytically naïve reader would lead that reader to the independent hypothesis that there certainly must exist something very like an early genital phase which regularly emerges during the second year of life. (Mayer, 1983, p. 366)

Galenson and Roiphe's observations also provided strong support for the conclusion that the boy and the girl had widely different reactions to the discovery of genital difference. Only two of the boys studied showed serious disturbances in response to the discovery of genital difference, and these had had earlier disturbances in the maternal relationship. In the usual course of development, the boy's strongest castration reactions occurred later, under the dominance of phallic–oedipal dynamics. By contrast, all the girls studied showed definite reactions to the early discovery of genital difference and eight manifested severe castration reactions. The girl's discovery of genital difference was observed to instigate and shape the next phase of development as, in the sphere of ego development, the girl either moved toward a period of rapid ego expansion or toward a reliance upon regressive ego mechanisms, and, in the sphere of object relationships, either turned toward the father or became entrenched in a hostile dependent relation with the mother.

However, the meaning of these findings remained in question. Early critics asked whether the early castration reactions observed in some boys by Roiphe and Galenson bore the same meaning as, or even a linear relationship with, the castration reactions of the phallic–oedipal phase (Ritvo, 1972). And critics also questioned the meaning that Galenson and Roiphe ascribed to the girl's discovery of genital difference:

> Genital difference, then, is understood as disturbing to the girl *because and apparently only because* it reveals her penisless state. Was that truly the nature of the data? I find myself wondering whether it was the nature of the data selected for presentation because, in the minds of observers, only data which referred to the presence or absence of a phallus was considered relevant to identifying genital experience and concern. (Mayer, 1983, p. 368)

Female psychosexual development

It was in their formulation of female psychosexual development that Galenson and Roiphe encountered the greatest conflict, for here their conceptualisation was at odds with both the tenets of traditional psychoanalysis and the revisionist views of female development, that had begun to emerge within psychoanalysis and outside the field in response to a burgeoning feminist movement.

From the early years of the psychoanalytic movement, it had been noted that Freud had adopted a "phallocentric" model of psychosexual development for both sexes. A brief sketch of Freud's model of female development would go as follows: both the boy and the girl were thought to see themselves as masculine until the phallic phase. Following her discovery of genital difference, the girl developed a sense of herself as feminine, viewing femininity as defective masculinity. Her disappointment led to a loosening of the tie to the mother and a turn toward the father, who, she hoped, would give her the baby that would substitute for the lost penis. For the girl, anger and envy were primary and universal reactions, and her subsequent development reflected her attempts to master, undo, and compensate for her painful sense of injury. Already castrated, she had less motivation than the boy to give up forbidden oedipal desires and consequently the superego that she internalised was weaker than the boy's (Freud 1925j; 1931b).

During the period when Galenson and Roiphe published their findings, psychoanalysts had begun to question Freud's views on the weakness of the female superego (Jacobson, 1964) and the centrality of penis envy in female development (Grossman & Stewart, 1976; Schafer, 1974). Longstanding critiques of Freud's modelling of the girl's development as an inferior form of masculine development were beginning to gain momentum in mainstream psychoanalysis, and new ideas concerning a line of female development in which the experience of being female was primary were beginning to take hold.

While Roiphe and Galenson proposed a radical revision of the timing of the discovery of genital difference, they affirmed Freud's placement of this discovery as an organiser of female development. Acknowledging the girl's earlier sense of her femininity, they nevertheless saw this primary femininity as less critical in the shaping of her developmental trajectory than the discovery of genital difference, which was prompted by emerging genital excitement. As Galenson wrote in her 1990 review of their findings:

> We do not consider the discovery of the sexual difference and the new genital sensations of the early genital phase as merely several of many variables which influence the growing sense of identity. They are unique, exemplary, and of equal importance to the oral and anal aspects of psychosexual development which have preceded them ... We believe that Freud's original position regarding women was correct in so far as his premise that penis envy and feminine castration complex exert crucial influences upon feminine development. However, these occur earlier than he had postulated. They are closely intertwined with fears of object and anal loss, and they shape an already developing although vague sense of femininity stemming from early bodily and affective experiences with both parents.
> (Galenson, 1990, p. 177)

And significantly, as Mayer observed, Roiphe and Galenson also continued to understand the girl's reaction to genital difference exclusively as castration–the experience of lacking what the boy had. Their conceptualisation maintained the phallocentric definition of femininity that was currently under assault by feminist–revisionist analysts in the field.

In the decades immediately following the publication of *Infantile Origins of Sexual Identity*, the psychoanalytic conceptualisation of female development moved sharply toward a focus on primary femininity—the girl's fundamental experience of the self as female and her pride in her own body (Elise, 1997; Tyson, 1994), and her experience of a set of genital anxieties linked to her own female genitals (Mayer, 1985). Emphasis on the girl's experience as something in itself, rather than something defined in relation to the boy's experience led to opposition and at times neglect of Roiphe and Galenson's work.

More recently, psychoanalytic views of femininity, and of gender and sexuality in general, have begun to engage with the complex, ambiguous currents of both, and to discover, or re-discover the bisexual, or even multi-sexual nature of both the girl and the boy (Chodorow, 2004; Kulish, 2008; Moss, 2012). Infant observation supports the idea that castration anxiety arises during the girl's second year while female genital anxieties emerge slightly later, during the phallic–oedipal phase; it is difficult to establish separate developmental lines for the two kinds of anxieties, and in clinical work with adults, the two are often mingled neither concept can replace the other (Olesker, 1998). In this new context, we can see that Roiphe and Galenson's observations of the girl's castration reaction illuminate a moment in female development, that, while not exclusively defining of femininity, remains of key importance.

Male psychosexual development

Despite some doubts on the part of early critics, Roiphe and Galenson's formulations concerning male psychosexual development were much more easily integrated into contemporary trends in psychoanalytic thought than were their formulations concerning the girl. The authors observed that strong reactions to the discovery of genital difference were relatively rare in boys. Most boys responded to the discovery with a brief upsurge in masturbation followed by an increase in general motor activity. For these boys, they felt, castration became important only later, during the phallic–oedipal phase. However, four of the boys studied manifested intense reactions to the discovery of genital difference. There was an upsurge of poorly contained aggression toward the mother, intensification of early infantile masturbation, and a turning toward inanimate objects, which the authors saw as precursors to adult fetishes. The boys who had an intense reaction to the discovery of genital difference were those with a history of early difficulties that had impinged upon the stable representation of self and object. These findings pointed to a potentially biphasic experience of castration for the boy: the first kind of castration reaction emerged during the second year and reflected the narcissistic conflicts that could be activated by the discovery of genital difference; the second kind emerged later, during the phallic–oedipal phase and reflected oedipal dynamics.

The identification of an early phase of male castration anxiety, which became important for boys with a history of early disturbance in bodily experience or object relationships, resonated immediately with the experiences of those adult analysts who struggled with the problem of perversion. These observations confirmed Greenacre's (1953, 1968) earlier idea of the rootedness of perversion in an early disturbance of bodily experience and identity formation; and opened a new line of interpretation of more primitive meanings and functions that the boy's experience of a phallic or "castrated" body could hold. As Charles Socarides wrote in his review of Roiphe and Galenson's work for *The Psychoanalytic Quarterly*:

> The investigations of Roiphe and Galenson are extremely useful in their apparent confirmation and explication of clinical research findings derived from the analysis of adult patients with sexual perversions—as to the existence of early pre-oedipal castration anxieties, disturbances in gender-defined self-identity, and separation anxieties connected with threatened object loss and other conflicts during the pre-oedipal years. (Socarides, 1984, p. 458)

The idea that perversion serves different functions, and must be understood differently at different levels of object relationships, remains a useful way of conceptualising the treatment of the difficult and heterogeneous group of patients with perversions (Meyer, 2011). And our understanding of the larger group of men for whom perversions are not dominant symptoms is deepened by the recognition that later castration reactions, clearly linked to the phallic–oedipal phase, also bear the more or less subtle imprint of the boy's early response to the recognition of genital difference.

Psychosexual development and object relations

Among the explicit aims of Galenson and Roiphe's work, the tracing of the interweaving of psychosexual development and the development of object relations remains very much an unfinished project in contemporary psychoanalysis. At the time when these two authors wrote, instinct retained its traditional central role in psychoanalysis, while the development of object relations had only begun to come to centre stage, largely through Margaret Mahler's work on separation and individuation (Mahler, Pine, & Bergman, 1975). As successors to Greenacre and Mahler, Galenson and Roiphe might be seen as mapping a representation of the body and its instinctual zones onto a larger map of developing self and object representations and marking the points where the two lines of development intersected and shaped one another. From another perspective, it is also possible to see the two lines of development as two different aspects of internal representation "the psychical representation of the body as a body of drives that are felt . . . [and as] a body that is objective and located according to anatomical space . . . [particularly through] the role of vision" (Birksted-Breen, 1996).

In the decades since Galenson and Roiphe wrote, these two modes of representation have often been explored as separate lines of study, and North American psychoanalysis has generally emphasised the objective body that is seen, often to the exclusion of the body of drives—an outcome that these authors would have decried. Particularly in the area of female psychology, the task of weaving together the connections that Roiphe and Galenson traced—between the body of drives and the body that is seen, and between fantasy and external reality, remains in its infancy (Kulish, 2008).

The nature and value of child observational data

At the time when Roiphe and Galenson published their work, the status of child observational data remained very much in debate within the field. Thus on the one hand, one reviewer of their volume could express the wish that they had drawn bolder conclusions:

> If the adult analyst has an overall criticism of this volume, it is that it is too modest, too conservative, and too careful. Considering the experience with children and adults that these researchers represent, regrettably, they are too chary of making predictions from their observations for adult functioning and psychopathology. (Oremland, 1985, p. 684)

On the other hand, Solnit, in his discussion of one of the papers (Solnit, 1972), observed that the authors' reconstructions tended to be adultomorphic and argued that data from the psychoanalysis of adults and children was required in order to confirm or disconfirm formulations drawn from child observational data—particularly data from the inherently obscure preverbal era.

In the decades following the publication of *The Infantile Origins of Sexual Identity*, the observation of infants and children in research settings has burgeoned. In a sense a reversal of the status of the data that this research generates has occurred, with infant observational data, which is potentially replicable, seen as more "scientific" and more certain than the data of the individual psychoanalytic case.

However, the relation of child observational data to the analysis of adults remains controversial. Where the child observer or even the child analyst, who listens to material from adult analysis, often hears the direct expression of behaviours and experiences from early life, the adult analyst is more likely to hear the same material as an expression of the early that has been transformed by a long series of later experiences and now has come to serve a different function. The reconstruction of early experience has become less fashionable in analysis as analysts, particularly in the US, have come to emphasise the intersubjective nature of the analytic situation and the emergence of material within the relational field established by patient and analyst (LaFarge, 2012). The adult analyst often values child observational data for the rich store of hypotheses that it affords (Michels, 1999). Child data permits us to imagine our adult patients differently than we would otherwise. If the child analyst must be grateful for the rich store of observational data found in the papers collected here, the adult analyst must be grateful for the exciting breadth of hypotheses that they afford—hypotheses that break an old frame for seeing early psychosexual development and open a new and complex early world to our imagination.

References

Birksted-Breen, D. (1996). Unconscious representation of femininity. *Journal of the American Psychoanalytic Association, 44S*: 119–132.

Chodorow, N. (2004). Psychoanalysis and women: a personal thirty-five year retrospect. *Annual of Psychoanalysis, 32*: 101–129.

Elise, D. (1997). Primary femininity, bisexuality, and the female ego ideal: a re-examination of female developmental theory. *Psychoanalytic Quarterly, 46*: 489–517.

Freud, S. (1923e). The infantile genital organization: an interpolation into the theory of anxiety. *S.E., 19*: 141–153. London: Hogarth.

Freud, S. (1925j). Some psychical consequences of the anatomical distinction between the sexes. *S.E., 19*: 243–258. London: Hogarth.

Freud, S. (1931b). Female sexuality. *S.E., 21*: 223–243. London: Hogarth.

Galenson, E. (1990). Observation of early infantile and sexual erotic development. In: E. M. Perry (Ed.), *Handbook of Sexology, (Vol. 7, Childhood and Adolescent Sexuality)* (pp. 169–178). Elsevier Science Publishers, Biomedical Division.

Greenacre, P. (1953). Certain relationships between fetishism and the faulty development of the body image. *The Psychoanalytic Study of the Child, 8*: 79–98.

Greenacre, P. (1968). Perversions: general considerations regarding their genetic and dynamic background. *The Psychoanalytic Study of the Child, 23*: 47–52.

Grossman, W., & Stewart, W. (1976). Penis envy from childhood wish to developmental metaphor. *Journal of the American Psychoanalytic Association, 24S*: 193–212.

Jacobson, E. (1964). *The Self and the Object World*. New York: International Universities Press.

Kulish, N. (2008). Primary femininity: clinical advances and theoretical ambiguities. *Journal of the American Psychoanalytic Association, 48*: 1355–1379.

LaFarge, L. (2012). The screen memory and the act of remembering. *International Journal of Psychoanalysis, 93*: 1249–1265.

Mahler, M., Pine, F., & Bergman, A. (1975). *The Psychological Birth of the Human Infant*. New York: Basic Books.

Mayer, E. L. (1983). Review of *The Infantile Origins of Sexual Identity* by H. Roiphe and E. Galenson. Madison, CT: International Universities Press. *The International Journal of Psychoanalysis*, 63: 365–369.

Mayer, E. L. (1985). Everybody must be just like me: observations on female castration anxiety. *International Journal of Psychoanalysis*, 66: 331–347.

Meyer, J. (2011). The developmental and organizing function of perversion. The example of transvestism. *International Journal of Psychoanalysis*, 92: 311–332.

Michels, R. (1999). Psychoanalysts theories. In: P. Fonagy, A. M. Cooper, & R. Wallerstein (Eds.), *Psychoanalysis on the Move: The Work of Joseph Sandler* (pp. 187–200). New York: Routledge.

Moss, D. (2012). *Thirteen Ways of Looking at a Man: Psychoanalysis and Masculinity.* New York: Routledge.

Olesker, W. (1998). Female genital anxieties: views from the nursery and the couch. *Psychoanalytic Quarterly*, 67: 276–294.

Oremland, J. (1985). Review of *The Infantile Origins of Sexual Identity* by H. Roiphe and E. Galenson, Madison, CT: International Universities Press (1981). *The Journal of the American Psychoanalytic Association*, 33: 678–684.

Ritvo, S. (1972). Unpublished discussion of object loss and early sexual development by Herman Roiphe and Eleanor Galenson. Scientific Meeting of The New York Psychoanalytic Society, 11 January, 1972. Archives & Special Collections, A. A. Brill Library, New York Psychoanalytic Society and Institute.

Roiphe, H., & Galenson, E. (1981). *The Infantile Origins of Sexual Identity.* New York: International Universities Press.

Schafer, R. (1974). Problems in Freud's psychology of women. *Journal of the American Psychoanalytic Association*, 22: 459–487.

Socarides, C. (1984). *The Infantile Origins of Sexual Identity.* The *Psychoanalytic Quarterly*, 53: 454–459.

Solnit, A. (1972). Unpublished discussion of object loss and early sexual development by Herman Roiphe and Eleanor Galenson. Scientific Meeting of the New York Psychoanalytic Society, 11 January, 1972. Archives & Special Collections, A. A. Brill Library, New York Psychoanalytic Society and Institute.

Tyson, P. (1994). Bedrock and beyond: an examination of the clinical utility of contemporary theories of female psychology. *Journal of the American Psychoanalytic Association*, 42: 447–467.

CHAPTER FOUR

Early genital activity and the castration complex

Herman Roiphe and Eleanor Galenson

Roiphe's (1968) paper, "On an early genital phase", described a series of observations on normal toddlers and young psychotic children that suggested to him that children, both boys and girls, between the ages of fifteen and twenty-four months, normally and regularly demonstrate a marked increase in manipulation of their genitals, including frank masturbatory behaviour; they also show curiosity about and reactions to the anatomical differences between the sexes. A sharp upsurge in sexual interest and activity was thought to follow from the increase in endogenous genital sensation that children of this age experience. That endogenous genital sensation probably results from a change in bowel and bladder function, independent of any toilet training efforts, in the early months of the second year. This early sexual activity normally is concerned with the consolidation of the self and object representation and serves to establish a primary schematisation of the genital outline of the body. As far as can be determined, such early sexual development is free of any oedipal content (Roiphe & Galenson, 1973).

In 1970 Roiphe further reported that some children who had already shown evidence of such sexual arousal developed moderate to severe castration reactions after they had observed the anatomical difference between the sexes. He stated in that paper that these castration reactions appeared to develop only in children who had had earlier experiences that served to interfere with a stable body schematisation, such as severe illness, birth defect, and surgical intervention; or experiences that interfered with a stable object schematisation, such as loss of a parent and depression in, or gross emotional neglect by, the mothering figure.

In her paper on perversions Greenacre (1968) offered a formulation concerning early sexual activity and castration reactions in the second year of life. She stated: "It is now a common observation that fear of castration in boys and penis envy in girls occur earlier than used to be thought—i.e., well before the phallic phase, quite commonly about the age of two" (p. 51). From our reading of the psychoanalytic literature, we cannot agree with Greenacre that it is now "a common observation": that castration reactions occur about the age of two. Other than our own work (Galenson & Roiphe, 1972; Roiphe, 1968; Roiphe & Galenson, 1973) and a paper by Sachs (1962), we have been unable to uncover any detailed or comprehensive presentation of castration reactions occurring in the second year of life.

Greenacre (1968) continues:

In the earlier years, these problems [i.e., castration reactions in the second year] are much more involved with body narcissism in the investment of their own body parts as possession. I have thought that toward the end of the second year there was regularly some enhancement of genital sensitivity (phallic or clitoral) that occurred simultaneously with the increasing maturation of the body sphincters. (p. 51)

She refers to Anna Freud's (1951) comments in discussing observations at variance with established analytic findings concerning chronology:

Penis envy, which we expected to see in girls in the phallic phase, appeared with extreme violence according to some of our recordings in girls between eighteen and twenty-four months. In these cases the responsible factor may have been the bodily intimacy between boys and girls as it exists in a residential nursery where the opportunities for watching other children being bathed, dressed, potted, etc., are countless. (pp. 27–28)

Anna Freud tentatively suggests that the provocative force of the observation of the anatomical difference between the sexes produced extremely violent reactions of penis envy in these children. This thesis, however, does not explain the curious age clustering, nor does it establish the conditions for the narcissistic cathexis of the genitals implied in such a reaction (cf. Freud, 1923e; 1925j).

In order to investigate systematically sexual development in the second year of life, we have established a research nursery at the Albert Einstein College of Medicine, patterned on the model developed by Mahler at the Masters Children's Center (cf. Mahler & Furer, 1960; Pine & Furer, 1963). The children, who are about one year of age when enrolled, attend the nursery with their mothers four mornings a week for two hours each day throughout their second year. The nursery is set up as a large indoor playground where the children have ready access, visually and physically, to their mothers. Each mother–child pair is assigned its own observers, who follow them throughout the year. The following case illustrates "typical" observations made possible by our investigations.

Suzy was a dainty, small-boned child of thirteen months when she entered the programme. She had already worked as a model for many months and was capable not only of making the rounds of the modelling agencies with her mother in a quiet, poised manner but also of sitting through one- or two-hour sessions of photography, patiently doing as she was told. Her birth was normal; her early development was reported as "good". She had been walking for three months when she first came to the nursery and was sure-footed and agile.

She was an only child. Her mother, an attractive young woman who worked intermittently as a model, had gained forty-five pounds during her pregnancy. In the early months she had been so eager to show that she was pregnant, that she had worn maternity clothes long before they were necessary. She dressed herself and Suzy with style and flare. She was proud of her little girl's appearance and reacted grievously to each bruise, cut, or scar her daughter suffered. Suzy's father, energetic and ambitious, was considered a loving and devoted husband and father.

At thirteen and fourteen months Suzy showed very little interest in her genitals. Occasionally when exposed during the changing of her diapers, she would touch her genitals but this activity seemed of no more importance to her than her curiosity about the rest of her body.

At fifteen months she suddenly began to show definite and pervasive curiosity about the genitals of other children. As soon as any child was taken to the changing table at the nursery, Suzy would come over and watch intently as the diaper was being changed. No matter what she was doing, she never missed an opportunity to witness the whole procedure. Regardless of how involved she was in any activity, there always seemed to be some measure of attention focused on the changing table. In all other ways, in her interests and play, she seemed no different from any of the other children.

The first time this behaviour was observed, a little boy about her own age was being changed after a bowel movement. He touched his penis and pulled at it during the process. Suzy, with her eyes riveted on the boy's genitals, pointed to his penis and then touched herself, through her diaper, in the genital area. She then began to wipe the area with a paper towel. Her mother took it away from her but Suzy quickly got another. On subsequent occasions when she watched a little boy being changed, she either tried to touch his penis or pointed to it and then either touched her genital area if fully clothed or her genital directly if she were being changed and was exposed. Her mother always tried to stop her by taking away the towel with which she wiped herself, or by removing her hands from her genitals when she began to masturbate, or by placing her on the toilet when she clutched her genital area, apparently assuming that Suzy had to urinate.

During this same period, when a little girl was being changed, Suzy would watch intently but without pointing or making any effort to touch the genitals of the little girl. Then she would clutch her backside. This difference in behaviour in response to observing the anatomical difference between the sexes persisted without variation over a period of several months. Her consistent tendency to clutch her backside whenever she saw a little girl exposed was interpreted as an incipient denial of the anatomical difference between the sexes by way of displacement to the rear.

When Suzy was seventeen months old, she began to lift her skirt and giggle excitedly. During this same period she often made an effort to lift the skirts of the women in the nursery, never the little girls, and tried to peer under their dresses. She did the same at home to her mother, who became quite upset by this behaviour. It was only at this point that we learned that Suzy had been showering regularly either with her father or her mother since the age of twelve or thirteen months. We were unable to learn whether she had ever made any effort to touch her father's penis or to explore her mother's pubic area. However, her intense curiosity about the genital anatomy of adult women, betrayed by her persistent effort to look under their skirts, probably reflected perplexity from having seen pubic hair. The difference between her genital and her mother's may have raised the question of whether her mother had a penis hidden somewhere. Her mother, apparently with some appreciation of the relationship between Suzy's recent sexual curiosity and the experience of exposure, discontinued the joint showers.

When Suzy began showering with her parents, she also started to hold food in her mouth for a long time when she was fed. Her cheeks puffed, she would hold the food in her mouth in spite of her mother's mounting irritation. So long as her little daughter was passive, complaint, and showed off well, the mother was able to read her cues and provide for her needs. However, when Suzy developed a will of her own and seemed to react to the narcissistic insult from having observed the anatomical difference between the sexes, discord developed between mother and daughter. We speculate that some of this behaviour was related to a fantasy of acquiring a penis by eating one.

It would seem that the intensity of Suzy's sexual curiosity was stimulated by early and repetitive exposure to her nude parents. However, the timing of the appearance of Suzy's sexual curiosity and her behaviour are common to all of the children we have studied thus far, no matter what their experiences have been. Moreover, the behaviour of Suzy's parents, while perhaps different in degree, is by no means different in kind from that observed in most families we have studied, regardless of social, economic, or cultural differences. While the number of families (thirty-five) in our research is too limited to make any general inference, we are struck by how common it is for parents of children of this age to expose themselves before their children.

Before proceeding with the further vicissitudes of Suzy's sexual attitudes and behaviour, let us review the history of her toilet training. From the age of eight months, she had been placed on the toilet by her mother after breakfast and lunch without much success. The family word for urination was "tee-tee" and for bowel movements, "blinkie". (This unusual word was derived from the parents' observation that Suzy would blink her eyes when she had a bowel movement.) By the age of seventeen months, she was already using these words either in an anticipatory fashion or to indicate that she had wet or soiled herself. When she used the toilet, her parents would applaud, make a big fuss, and wave bye-bye to the bowel movement. Over a period of a month she attained reasonably reliable sphincter control, particularly over her bowel movements.

At eighteen to nineteen months of age, after some six weeks of established toilet control, Suzy developed an interesting confusion in language concerning toilet activities. She began to say "blinkies" when her diaper was wet or when she held her genital area, usually a signal that she had to urinate. At other times she would lift her skirt in front in an exhibitionistic manner and say "hiny", a word that she had consistently used earlier to refer to her backside.

This behavior of Suzy's should be viewed against the background of our observations of how children learn to name the parts of the body. In our experience with thirty-five children and their families, all the boys by the age of eighteen to nineteen months have been told the word for the penis and the backside, for urination and bowel movements. Up through the second year, none of the boys have been given a term for the scrotum or testes, although by this time most of them show some interest in these body parts (cf. Bell, 1961). The girls, while they have been given separate and distinct names for toilet functions and for the backside, have not been given any discrete word for their genitals. After their little girls have shown intense sexual curiosity, a few mothers have given them a word for their genitals.[1]

To return to Suzy's sexual curiosity and behaviour, let us consider the developing confusion over body parts and functions that arose when she was seventeen months. It will be recalled that Suzy had taken every opportunity to observe children being changed and had manifested consistently different behaviour when seeing little boys and little girls exposed. With boys she pointed to or attempted to grasp the penis and would then hold her own genitals. When she observed a girl, she did not point or touch, but would clutch her own backside. This behaviour reflected her observations of the anatomical difference between the sexes. She also displayed intense curiosity about the genital anatomy of adult women by attempting to peer under their dresses. During this period and up to the age of nineteen months, there was progressively more intense sexual activity and exploration on Suzy's part. In the bath or on the changing table she would engage in genital masturbation. Whenever she saw her mother's breasts, she would touch them and was often seen touching or pulling her own nipples.

In the nursery, Suzy would often undress the dolls, scrutinise the area between their legs, and then say "hiny". This doll play became increasingly elaborate: she would pretend to shower the doll, place her on the toilet to have a bowel movement, wipe her, and then wash her hands. Her play reflected the underlying bodily concerns that Suzy was struggling with at this time.

At nineteen months, there was an abrupt cessation of most of the sexual activity described above. She no longer went to the changing table to watch the other children while they were exposed. She no longer made any effort to peer under women's skirts. All of her genital masturbatory activity stopped. The only behavioural remnant, which was probably a derivative of the earlier sexual interest, was a persistent tendency to touch her mother's backside and breasts as well as her own.

As we have seen, some two months earlier there began some confusion about naming body parts and functions—she would say "blinkies", her word for bowel movement, when she was already wet or had to urinate; when she lifted her skirt and held her genital area, she would at times say "hiny", her word for her backside. At nineteen months, this was no longer an intermittent practice; it became her consistent behaviour. The word for urination entirely dropped out of her vocabulary. When she used the toilet to urinate, she wiped her backside. Earlier, when she wished to refer to her genitals, she would use the functional name, "tee-tee"; now she always referred to it as her "hiny". During this time she developed a mild anxiety when the toilet flushed. This anxiety varied in intensity over the ensuing months. She also developed transient and shifting fears of birds, dogs, horses, and other animals. From time to time she would be seen scrutinising her finger or leg with some apprehension, dolefully saying "boo-boo", her word for a cut or sore, when as a rule no sign of injury was apparent.

When Suzy was almost twenty months old, a little boy her own age spent the day with his mother at her house. She followed him into the bathroom when he went to urinate. She reached out to touch his penis and said "pee-pee", a word never used before by her or her mother to refer to either the penis or urination. For several days after this experience all the earlier sexual behaviour—for instance, going to the changing table, touching her own genitals and masturbating, lifting skirts, etc.—flared up again but in a short while disappeared. On three other occasions over the next several months when a boy visited and she had the opportunity to witness him urinating, this behaviour reappeared.

It is an unfortunate limitation of the observational method that children so young have limited verbal capacity. Accordingly, the meaning of such an intriguing detail of behaviour as Suzy's consistent tendency whenever she saw a little boy's penis exposed to either point or reach out to touch it must remain open to question. Perhaps this behaviour reflects some shock-like response to the perception of the anatomical difference between the sexes (cf., Greenacre, 1956) with some effort to establish through touch that the penis is real, or it may already betray a partially inhibited aggressive impulse to take the penis.

It is possible, we feel, that both interpretations may be true. Suzy's persistent need to repeat the observation of the penis over and over again in a relatively unvarying manner suggests that she reacted to the sight of the penis in a traumatic fashion. The repetitiveness seems to point to a need to establish the reality of the percept. The tendency to touch the penis suggests an effort to re-enforce the visual perception by using a more primitive perceptual modality. That this same behaviour may also serve the fantasy of aggressively grasping and acquiring the penis seems equally probable and entirely in keeping with the principle of multiple determination of behaviour. In a similar fashion, clutching the backside when she saw a little girl's genitals, referring to her genitals as a "hiny", dropping the word for urination and subsequently using the word for a bowel movement to signal urinary urgency, all seem to point to a profound denial of genital difference. At the same time, this behaviour seems to signify an incipient restitutive fantasy along the lines of the well-known stool = penis equation. In any event, it seems likely that this wide array of behavioural phenomena reflects a fairly severe castration reaction. This interpretation of Suzy's development is supported by the development of fear of the flush of the toilet, fear of animals, and her scrutinising her body for cuts and wounds.[2]

By the time Suzy was twenty months of age, there was a complete deterioration of her toilet control, which persisted over the next few months. Her mother's irritation over this lapse in control was considerable. It seems to us that this deterioration of toilet control was a direct outcome of castration anxiety. Confirmation of the castration concern was seen in Suzy's statement to her mother: "Michael has a pee-pee. I have no pee-pee. Why?"

This case, as well as several others we have studied, illustrates how bowel and bladder control in the second year may break down as a consequence of castration anxiety. Along these lines, it is our impression that the constipation that tends to develop at the end of the second year and many cases of intractable enuresis may be related to castration anxiety developing in the second half of the second year.

One of the unexpected findings of our research is that the whole process of toilet training is subject to the influence of the "minor" castration insults, such as a child of this age may quite readily come by in the ordinary course of events. For example, a little boy sees his mother exposed and is constipated for several days; a little girl whose bladder control has been reasonably reliable for some time sees a boy urinate and begins to wet for about a week. We have been accustomed to thinking about the training situation as something that the child does for the parents. Thus we interpret the training experience too rigidly in terms of the struggle for independence that is characteristic of this phase of development. We wish to add that the vicissitudes of the child's sexual interests, curiosity, and activity, also typical of this period, appear to have an influence upon the whole training process and may be at the centre of some of the psychopathology that perhaps begins at this time.

Following the deterioration of Suzy's control of her bowels and bladder there was a profound general behavioural regression and negativism. When she came to the nursery, she would refuse to get out of her stroller. She would sit there for a considerable time in a sullen and distressed state. She would not permit her mother or the nursery teacher to remove her jacket. She would scream if any of the children tried to touch her. When she was finally coaxed out of her stroller, she stayed close to her mother. If her mother were momentarily out of sight, Suzy would panic and could not be reassured until her mother picked her up and comforted her. This, indeed, was a contrast to the confident, competent, cheerful little girl of only a few months before, who would come into the nursery eager and smiling and seek out children or adults quite independently of her mother. Her earlier play with dolls rapidly became constricted and all but disappeared. Suzy's mother became perplexed, frustrated, and angry. She seemed quite unsympathetic and responded sharply and harshly to Suzy's negativism and clinging.

Thus we see that in this child the process of sexual arousal and the discovery of the anatomical difference between the sexes produced a castration reaction that affected her psychic development. Her overwhelming anger and disappointment with her mother are reflected in the almost paralysing hostile dependence that developed toward the mother. Suzy clung to her mother and demonstrated a sullen mistrust of other adults and children. Such a development does not augur well for the developing individuation thrust appropriate for this age. These developments are in accord with Mahler's (1966) ideas about the particular vulnerability of the child at this time. The characteristic ambivalence of the child toward the mother, which is aggravated by castration anxiety, seems to call forth an early defence mechanism of splitting the good and bad mother images and of turning of aggression against the self.

Concurrent with the undermining of the child's developing object relations is the indication of an interference with and weakening of several aspects of the maturing ego functioning. Most dramatic was the pervasive inhibition of Suzy's curiosity in general and of her sexual curiosity in particular; parallel with this was a marked inhibition and regressive deterioration of play. An outstanding effect of Suzy's castration anxiety was a loss in self-esteem and the emergence of a depressive mood.

Mahler (1966, 1967) has described the period from about fifteen to twenty-two months, the so-called rapprochement sub phase, as a period of particular vulnerability. This is a time when the child's self-esteem may suffer abrupt deflation. The collapse of the child's belief in his omnipotence, together with an uncertainty about the availability of the mother, tends to foster a hostile dependency. Mahler also states that in a number of presumably normal mother-toddler relationships, rapprochement occurs with conspicuous drama and may even constitute a crisis in the relationship. When both timing and behavioural indications are taken into consideration, Suzy seemed to show just such a crisis in her relationship to her mother. It is interesting that in this case, as well as several others we have studied, it is the mobilisation of castration anxiety that seems to precipitate the so-called rapprochement crisis. It would be worthwhile to investigate the question of whether there is any regular relationship between the castration reactions, such as we have described, occurring during the second year of life and Mahler's rapprochement crisis.

Summary

This paper, one of a series of reports on the findings of an investigation of sexual development in the second year of life, examines systematically a set of hypotheses that had been developed by Roiphe earlier:

1. All children between the ages of fifteen and twenty-four months normally show evidence of a sexual arousal as indicated by a sharp increase in the manipulation of the genitals, including frank masturbatory activity; they also show evidence of sexual curiosity, particularly about the anatomical difference between the sexes.
2. Children in the second year of life who have already experienced such sexual arousal and who have had the occasion to observe the difference between the sexes will develop distinct castration reactions provided there have been earlier experiences that tend to produce an unstable body image or experiences that tend to result in an unstable object representation.

In the present paper longitudinal data on one of the children studied are presented in detail in order to illustrate the typical behavioural phenomena of early sexual arousal and moderately severe castration reaction. It should be emphasised that this early sexual development is involved with the consolidation of the body-self schematisation and developing object representation and does not, as far as we can determine, have any relation to typical oedipal wishes.

The emergence of the castration complex in this little girl, as with several others in our research, had fateful implications for some of the major developmental currents during the second year of life. It resulted in a far-reaching inhibition of both sexual and general curiosity, marked constriction in play, and symbolic confusion regarding anatomical parts and functions. There was an intensification of ambivalence toward the mother. Anxiety about separation from the mother increased and self-esteem and mood were markedly depressed.

Notes

1. We believe that to omit naming such an important part of the body reflects a cultural manifestation of the castration complex. It suggests how early and how fundamentally cultural attitudes toward little boys and girls diverge. (cf., Abraham, 1911)
2. Apropos of the fear of the flush of the toilet, we note that in earlier papers (Roiphe, 1968; Roiphe & Galenson, 1973) we suggested that castration anxiety that is encountered during this period of development has some connection with earlier anxieties concerning body dissolution and object loss.

References

Abraham, K. (1911). On the determining power of names. In: *Clinical Papers and Essays on Psychoanalysis* (pp. 31–32). New York: Basic Books, 1955.

Bell, A. (1961). Some observations on the role of the scrotal sac and testicles. *Journal of the American Psychoanalytic Association, 9*: 261–286.

Freud, A. (1951). Observations on child development. *The Psychoanalytic Study of the Child, 6*: 18–30.

Freud, S. (1923e). The infantile genital organization: an interpolation into the theory of anxiety. *S.E., 19*: 141–153.

Freud, S. (1925j). Some psychical consequences of the anatomical distinction between the sexes. *S.E., 19*: 243–258.

Galenson, E., & Roiphe, H. (1972). The impact of early sexual discovery on mood, defensive organization, and symbolization. *The Psychoanalytic Study of the Child, 26*: 195–216.

Greenacre, P. (1956). Re-evaluation of the process of working through. *International Journal of Psychoanalysis, 37*: 439–444.

Greenacre, P. (1968). Perversions: general considerations regarding their genetic and dynamic background. *The Psychoanalytic Study of the Child, 23*: 47–52.

Mahler, M. (1966). Notes on the development of basic moods: the depressive affect. In: R. M. Loewenstein, L. M. Newman, M. Schur, & A. J. Solnit (Eds.), *Psychoanalysis—a General Psychology: Essays in Honor of Heinz Hartmann* (pp. 152–168). New York: International Universities Press.

Mahler, M. (1967). On human symbiosis and the vicissitudes of individuation. *Journal of the American Psychoanalytic Association, 15*: 876–886.

Mahler, M., & Furer, M. (1960). Observations on research regarding the "symbiotic syndrome" of infantile psychosis. *The Psychoanalytic Quarterly*, *29*: 317–327.

Pine, F., & Furer, M. (1963). Studies of the separation–individuation phase: a methodological overview. *The Psychoanalytic Study of the Child*, *18*: 325–342.

Roiphe, H. (1968). On an early genital phase: with an addendum on genesis. *The Psychoanalytic Study of the Child*, *23*: 348–365.

Roiphe, H. (1970). Unpublished paper.

Roiphe, H., & Galenson, E. (1973). Object loss and early sexual development. *The Psychoanalytic Quarterly*, *42*: 73–90.

Sachs, L. J. (1962). A case of castration anxiety beginning at eighteen months. *Journal of the American Psychoanalytic Association*, *10*: 329–333.

CHAPTER FIVE

Object loss and early sexual development

Eleanor Galenson and Herman Roiphe

In an earlier paper describing observational research on toddlers, Roiphe (1968) suggested that children of both sexes between the ages of fifteen and twenty-four months regularly show a marked increase in the manipulation of their genitals, including frank masturbatory behaviour, and curiosity about and reactions to the anatomical difference between the sexes. It was proposed that this sharp upsurge in genital interest results from the rather sudden increase in endogenous genital sensation experienced by children of this age. This sensation is probably caused by a change in bowel and bladder functions, unrelated to any efforts at toilet training, in the early months of the second year. Early sexual interest and activity in children normally serve to consolidate the representations of self and object and to establish a primary schematisation of the genital outline of the body. This early sexual development seems to be without oedipal resonance.

It was found that some children who had already given evidence of this sexual arousal developed moderate to severe castration reactions after observing the anatomical difference between the sexes. These castration reactions appeared to develop only in children with two kinds of past history. One group had undergone experiences that interfered with a stable schematisation of the body, such as severe illness, birth defect, or surgery. The other group had suffered experiences that interfered with a stable object schematisation, such as loss of a parent, neglect by the mother, or the occurrence of depression in the mother. Some of the children suffered both kinds of experience.

Over the past four years this sexual development in the second year of life has been studied in our research nursery at the Albert Einstein College of Medicine in thirty-five normal children.[1] These children attend the nursery with their mothers four mornings a week throughout the second year of life. The nursery is set up as a large indoor playground where the children can easily see and go to their mothers. Each mother–child pair has its own observers, who follow the child's development throughout the year. The developmental records include data from the mother obtained from direct questioning by the observers, direct observations in the nursery by the staff, and home visits and videotapes.

Billy was a sturdy, smiling little boy of eleven months when he came to the nursery. He crawled everywhere, babbling as he went, investigating his surroundings and toys, showing relatively little anxiety over the strange setting and the many strange children and adults.

He was the first-born and only child of parents in their late twenties. The pregnancy was uneventful and the birth normal. His development during the first year seemed to be excellent, except for a disturbance of sleep that continued throughout his second year of life. Except for occasional nights, he woke at least once and not infrequently three and four times each night. When Billy was only four weeks old and could hardly have been expected to sleep through the night, his mother had been disturbed and even anxious over his night waking. Unfortunately, though we learned much about this family, the boy's persistent sleep disturbance was never understood. Undoubtedly, what we needed was information about the fantasy life of the mother, which is often lacking in studies based on direct observation. Analysis of young mothers of infant children with early developing and persistent sleep disturbances has rather often revealed in the mother conflicts over separation. Billy's father's work required regular and frequent absences throughout Billy's infancy, and both parents expected the father to be inducted into the army sometime during Billy's first year. When Billy was nine months old, his father did enter the army and he remained away from the family until shortly before Billy's second birthday.

When Billy first attended the nursery, he had been without his father for two months and had not, to the best of our knowledge, shown any direct reaction to his father's absence. Shortly after his first birthday he began to walk and at thirteen months of age he began to evidence mild but quite definite signs of separation anxiety, which became increasingly prominent in the next few months. Although he had formerly been left briefly from time to time with a relative or neighbour without becoming anxious, he now began to show decided uneasiness and apprehension at such times. It was particularly notable that when so left by his mother, he reacted with distinct anxiety to certain noises, such as loud television set or the buzz of the doorbell.

At this point, Billy's mother reported that she had decided to leave the bathroom door open whenever she used the toilet in order to familiarise him with its use. Before this, she had regularly closed the door when she used the bathroom. Upon closer questioning, it was apparent that Billy became anxious and could not tolerate this separation from his mother. (We were surprised to learn how commonly parents of young children with no regular domestic help leave the door open when they use the toilet.)

A particularly instructive description of Billy's reactions to separation when he was around fourteen months old was afforded us when one of his observers, a young woman with whom he was quite familiar, was asked by his mother to sit with him in their own apartment while she ran some errands. Immediately after she left, Billy made for a plant in a corner of the living room and had to be restrained. He then wandered into his mother's bedroom, dreamily looked out the window, and called for his mother. After being comforted by the observer, he darted for an open bookshelf and began to tear one of his father's books. He was restrained from doing this with some difficulty. (Both activities were consistently forbidden Billy by his mother; usually a verbal restraint sufficed but occasionally she slapped his hand when he was particularly persistent, as he was on this occasion.) After a short while, he walked to his mother's night table, looking back at the observer, who did not stop him. He put his hand toward the drawer, looking back at her, and then pulled it out a little, again looking at her. Becoming aware that this must be forbidden activity, she stopped him.

What did this behaviour mean? Parents frequently must resort to sharp verbal prohibitions early in the child's second year, either to protect him or because they require an orderly house. Such admonitions can produce remarkably persistent inhibitory effects; children often evidence well organised memory and self-observation. One nineteen-month-old girl, angry because another child took a toy from her, was heard to voice her mother's admonition: "Now it's Suzy's turn, soon it will be yours. Don't pull Suzy's hair, make nice". Meanwhile, the child petted Suzy's head but with her rage mounting, the petting became rougher and rougher until her fist closed around a handful of hair. This tiny conscience demonstrates the self-observing function of the ego and it speaks to the ego in a restraining fashion. Its transitional nature is reflected by its concrete tie to the object; that is, the words are the mother's very own words and its structure closely parallels the character of the object representations as its integrity is still very much influenced by the vicissitudes of drive tension.

More playful examples of such defiance of the mother's prohibitions in her presence were displayed by Billy, and most of the other children, on a number of occasions. For instance, Billy once reached for an electric wire and then coyly and expectantly looked at his mother. When the expected "no" was spoken, he chuckled and then, in high spirits, approached the forbidden bookcase, again looking archly back at his mother—and so on.

This commonplace, playful, defiant behaviour reflects the toddler's maturing strivings for independence, modified by his still intense infantile dependence on his mother. Such behaviour seems to imply that the youngster has a will of his own and can act even in opposition to the mother's wishes. The child is maturing, for he is behaving in a way that looks forward to his becoming relatively autonomous. But he still expects and invites his mother's disapproving response, thus showing that he still needs closeness and mutuality with her.

Billy's defiant behaviour when he was left by his mother in the care of our research observer, however, was more complex. His mother's absence caused him to feel a profound sense of inner depletion and a longing for reunion with her. In his defiant behaviour, which both anticipated and required her response, we believe that Billy attempted to evoke the presence of his mother by magical–omnipotent means. He might have sought to evoke her presence in a number of other ways. But he was angry with her for leaving him and therefore chose to behave in a way that defied her prohibitions and elicited her disapproval. This behaviour served to express the child's independent strivings at a time of enhanced longing for his mother. By it, he denied his longing through the implicit assertion that he was independent of her and did not need her. This is an impressive display of the richly textured and multi-determined character of even a fourteen-month-old child's response to an experience of separation.

On this same occasion after the incident with the night table drawer, Billy became very cranky. The observer picked him up but he was not really comforted by this. At his insistence he was placed in his crib where he quickly found a hidden pacifier and put it into his mouth. He was then taken out of the crib, but after a few moments the observer remembered that his mother did not like him to have the pacifier outside the crib and removed it from him. He became enraged and inconsolable until it was returned to him; then his mood changed and he lay down on the couch next to the observer. He began to play with the pacifier, taking it out of his mouth, chuckling, and putting it back again, chewing on it and then spitting it out with his tongue; he continued thus for about five minutes until his mother returned. The earlier behaviour had shown Billy attempting to deal with the separation by calling forth his most advanced, independent repertory of behaviour.

When this effort failed, there was a sharp regression as evidenced by his resort to the pacifier. Unable to call up the image of his mother in a magical–omnipotent fashion by behaviour that implied reciprocal interaction with her, he turned to the pacifier to evoke a fantasy of his mother's presence in a more primitive and concrete way. In his removal of the pacifier and chuckling, it was he who abandoned the object rather than being abandoned in his chewing and spitting out of the pacifier, his angry rejection of the object was clearly demonstrated.

During the next two months, numerous incidents reflected Billy's conflict over separation. On several occasions at the end of a nursery session, he looked intensely apprehensive as he saw another mother and child leave the nursery, and ran crying to the open door. Under ordinary circumstances, Billy could, of course, discriminate between his mother and the other adults in the nursery. However, as he became anxious over separation he sometimes reacted to some other woman's departure as if she were his own mother.

When Billy was a little older than fourteen months, he developed, in the nursery and at home, a series of games that involved his ears, eyes, and mouth. At first, he very frequently cupped his hands over his ears, then removed them, as if he were exploring the role of the ear in hearing. This activity, which produces a rush of sound like the "roar of the ocean" one hears when holding a conch shell to the ear, has two startling effects. One is a marked withdrawal of attention from the outer world and a centring of it on one's own body. The other is a feeling of pressure and fullness in the ear with a distinct sense of the body–rind as a demarcation between the outside and the inside. It seems as if the rush of sound were coming from inside the ear rather than outside, as we ordinarily hear sounds. After three weeks Billy stopped doing this but began to withdraw it. This was followed by a third repetitive activity: a rapid up and down oscillation of his index finger very close to his eye, brushing against his eyelashes. The finger placed deep into the mouth elicits a gagging response and a feeling of nausea arising deep within the body; similarly, the rapid oscillation of the finger close to the eye produces a flickering effect and the sense that the visual locus is inside the body.

These effects produced on himself by Billy have several important characteristics in common. All dramatically shift attention from its usual locus outside the body to one inside and produce a particularly sharp sense of the body–rind as a distinct demarcation between inside and outside. All produce the illusion that sensation essentially evoked outside the self (though by the self, acting on the self) comes from within the self. A child in the midst of a struggle over separation (as were Billy and most children his age) is acutely aware of a deficiency, an emptiness within the self; he is aware of an inner longing that can be satisfied only by the mother, a figure located outside the self. Billy's experiments with his own body were probably an effort to master the sense of inner emptiness and depletion and the acute awareness that the nourishing centre of his being was located outside the self. This sense and this awareness are brought into sharp focus by the reactions to separation so common in children of this age. In this connection we recall Bishop Berkeley's famous paradox about perception and psychic reality (cf. Fraser, 1871). The rose we gaze at is outside in the garden, but our perception of it involves processes within our bodies. This paradox is a real problem in the child's development of a body schema, and is resolved only through varied and circuitous routes, some of which have been demonstrated to us by Billy. We must emphasise how difficult it was for us to empathise quickly with such behaviour as Billy displayed in his repetitive games. For some time we felt sure the behaviour was significant, but we were baffled by it. It was not until we tried out his actions on ourselves that their significance became apparent.

During Billy's struggle with separation and self-definition, his mother left him, at age sixteen months, in their own apartment in the care of his paternal grandmother while she joined her husband on his leave for two weeks. During this period, he continued to attend the nursery and there was very little observable change in his behaviour except that he seemed somewhat subdued and absolutely refused any milk. Before this, he had taken many bottles of milk, particularly when he awoke at night. At the same time his grandmother reported that he ate solid foods well, perhaps even voraciously. When his mother returned, he showed immediate recognition of her and expressed genuine pleasure at seeing her again. Except for the first twenty-four hours when he resumed drinking his milk, he continued his refusal of it in spite of extraordinary efforts by his mother. She tried mixing the milk with chocolate syrup and with a variety of vegetable colourings until she hit upon a mixture of orange juice and milk, which he accepted, curds and all. This continued for some three months before he once again drank plain milk. With his mother's return, he ate even less solid food than he had before she left, and this continued throughout the remaining time that we followed this child. The bottle of milk that Billy formerly took on falling asleep and during his night wakings, besides its nutritive function, seemed to be a transitional phenomenon—a representative of the object that he used to soothe himself to sleep (cf. Winnicott, 1953, 1965). Except for the first twenty-four hours after his joyous reunion with his mother, he refused milk for three months out of anger because he had been separated from his mother. It seems probable that this anger was split off and externalised and the partial image of the bad mother projected on to the bottle of milk, which was then rejected.

Within a very few days after his mother's return, Billy's separation reactions seemed to increase in intensity. He appeared chronically apprehensive and unhappy, and seemed little able to involve himself with things or people, children or adults. Earlier he had a pleasurable, babbling curiosity about everything in the nursery; now it was difficult for him to get involved in any sustained activity. The other children his age were by now developing more or less elaborate symbolic play (Galenson, 1971) and at times a surprisingly rich social involvement with adults and other children, while Billy's development seemed quite impoverished in these reports.

Billy now kept an anxious eye on his mother in the nursery. If he lost sight of her or she left for even a brief period, he broke into an anxious, miserable sobbing and was inconsolable until reunited with her. At the end of the nursery sessions, he often burst into tears and attempted to follow a mother and child who were leaving, although he had shown no particular involvement with that pair during the morning. During this period he developed a close relationship with the young woman who served as one of his observers. If she was already there when he came into the nursery in the morning, he insisted on being held in her arms for at least five minutes. He especially could not tolerate her departure from the nursery, even for brief periods. For some months, when hurt he often went to her in preference to his mother. After about three months when these acute separation reactions had largely diminished, Billy distinctly avoided this preferred closeness to his observer.

About one week after his mother's return, Billy was in the bathroom along with all the other children, playing with the toilet flush and seat cover and with the water. A group of observers had gathered outside the door to watch. One by one, all the other children wandered out, leaving only Billy. He crowded into a corner between the toilet and the wall and bent over slightly, touching his abdomen and pelvic area with his hands and gazing fixedly at the floor for about a minute or two. He then covered his eyes with his hands and squatted. This tense, almost manneristic withdrawal was highly disturbing to the adults, and the observer nearest him held her arms out to him. He cringed but then allowed himself to be picked up by his own observer. In this instance, Billy's acute and profound withdrawal seemed rather clearly to be a reaction to the large number of adults in close proximity observing him. However, during the next week or so he interrupted his activity from time to time and lay prone on the floor with a rather dreamy, abstracted expression. We could determine no consistent context for this behaviour.

We believe that after his increasing separation reaction, which was much enhanced by the two-week-long actual separation, Billy developed profound ambivalence, dealt with by him in part by splitting the good and bad objects. His reaction to the adults in the incident in the bathroom probably resulted from projection of the bad object-image on to the observing adults. His strong attachment to his own female observer, often in preference to his own mother—for example, when he hurt himself and went to her rather than to his mother—suggests how much the relationship to the maternal object was marred by ambivalence.

Billy's reaction to separation was also shown by his response to noise. When he was thirteen months old, he became moderately apprehensive when the doorbell buzzed or the television blared. This sensitivity to sound had not been noted earlier and first appeared only when his mother was away. After his mother's return from her trip, he was extraordinarily sensitive to sound whether or not his mother was present. Some sounds, even the doorbell in a neighbour's apartment, threw him into a paroxysm of apprehension, probably because such sounds were at least symbolically associated with coming and going. Most of the sounds that provoked an anxious reaction can only roughly be characterised as loud and sudden. We can state with confidence that Billy's reaction to sound was quite ordinary before and that his later profound sensitivity was a variant of separation anxiety. As might be expected, along with this anxious sensitivity to sound, Billy seemed to develop an unusual interest in and discrimination of distant and barely audible sounds. He would stop in the midst of the general din of the nursery, repeat a sound to himself, and be satisfied only when he could identify its source. These sounds—the hum of a neon bulb, the roar of a jet airplane, the whir of a cement mixer—not only were not heard by the adults in the room until Billy drew attention to them, but even then they could often be identified only with difficulty and after utmost concentration.

This displacement of anxiety to the auditory sphere has clearly been a manifestation of anxiety in the presence of strangers in many of the children—though not all—in whom we have observed it. For example, an infant boy of eight months would break into almost inconsolable paroxysms of screaming that, with considerable difficulty, we found to be provoked by the high-pitched, barely audible sounds of a garbage truck or jet airplane. Just before the appearance of this sound sensitivity, the little boy had shown a very transient stranger reaction that disappeared and seemed to be replaced by the anxious reaction to sound. The appearance of sound sensitivity occurs, according to our experience, much less commonly in acute separation reaction than it does in stranger reaction.

It is difficult to explain this phenomenon. If we consider the external perceptual indications by means of which the infant builds his image of the mothering figure, it is clear that the tactile and kinaesthetic are sensors in close proximity and consequently are most immediate. The olfactory clues are intermediate; they permit some distance and may even linger after the object disappears. The visual and auditory spheres clearly permit greater distance. Hearing cannot be much focused in one direction or another and does not delineate the object so clearly. And the auditory sphere stands alone: it offers the slightest and most ephemeral sensory indication of the object, for the object may be heard in another room, giving no other sensory indication. This is not regularly true in any other perceptual sphere. Perhaps this is why anxiety is shown by auditory behaviour in these two early normal crises—separation reaction and stranger reaction—as the infant tries to establish an internal representation of the object. Winnicott (1953) described the infant's babbling when alone—his hearing himself produce sound—as a transitional phenomenon. Moreover, in adult analysis memories of sounds in another room at night often evoke only a rather isolated, though vivid association of an anxious feeling of loneliness and being left out. This is usually, and we believe correctly, interpreted as an early residue from the reaction to the primal scene. We suggest that the anxious involvement of the auditory sphere in the separation reaction may serve as an additional important determinant in such auditory memory residues from early childhood.

Finally, it seems probable that these considerations may illuminate hallucinatory phenomena in adult schizophrenic patients. At times the psychotic ego is flooded with unneutralised aggression and there occurs concomitant regression and deterioration in object representation. Many ego functions, such as sharp delineation of inside–outside, deteriorate, and introjective–projective mechanisms become prominent. We propose that the ensuing object loss anxiety and fears of dissolution of the self may evoke the primitive mechanism we have described in these children: the anxiety becomes manifested in the auditory sphere, in hallucinations of sound. In the separation reactions and stranger reactions of normal children we may speculate that the implicit strain in the relation with the object evokes a disruptive quantum of aggression that is dealt with by this primitive forerunner of defence—the somatisation of aggression in the auditory sphere.

A contributing factor in Billy's relatively marked separation reaction may be that his mother, whose husband was away for an entire year, suffered greatly from loneliness and consequently became too close to her little boy; she may have resisted his maturing tendency to grow away from her. Mahler and Gosliner (1955) and later Greenacre (1966) pointed out the importance of the father in the whole process of separation–individuation. The major developmental thrust at this period is separation from the infantile symbiotic relationship to the mother, in the process of which the child leans increasingly heavily on his father. With the absence of support from his father in this process, Billy was much more threatened by his maturing independent strivings.

At fourteen months when his separation reactions had been clearly established for several weeks, Billy showed increasing interest in his genitals. Until this time both our own observations and his mother's reports showed that Billy handled his genitals only casually and infrequently during changes of diaper and in his bath. But from fourteen months through the remainder of the time we followed him, we have consistent reports that at virtually all changes of diaper and during baths he handled his penis, squeezing and pulling it, in a concentrated and persistent fashion. Erections were observed only irregularly. (We have found that erections occur regularly in little boys at this age—as contrasted with the first year of life—only when some degree of bladder control is attained.) Billy did not handle his scrotum and testicles until he was seventeen months old, at which time there were a number of reports of scrotal manipulation with testicular retraction (cf. Bell, 1961).

At about this time Billy began to show a remarkable fascination with the toilet, as did most of our children. In the nursery, as at home, he would spend long periods flushing the toilet, putting paper in and watching it disappear with evident glee. He did not seem to show this interest in the flushing of his own stool; it was not until he was eighteen months of age that he displayed manifest anxiety with the flushing of his stool. His mother showed no interest in training Billy when he first displayed interest in the toilet at fourteen months. In fact, she made only the most desultory and inconsistent efforts to train him when he reached eighteen months. When he failed to learn, she dropped it altogether. She permitted him to come into the bathroom to watch her use the toilet, offering the rationalisation that she wanted to familiarise him with its use: this seemed more a response to his intolerance of separation than the beginning of any consistent training effort.

When Billy was between fifteen and sixteen months old, his mother several times reported that he would, with a concentrated expression, clutch his penis for a minute or two, his whole face would flush, and he would strain as if with a bowel movement. This interesting behaviour, which was observed over a two- to three-week period only, tends to suggest how indistinctly differentiated the genital sensation is from the anal, at least early in development. During this same period on numerous occasions Billy was observed to clutch his penis when frustrated in an activity or angry with his mother. These observations led us to infer that his burgeoning separation reaction evoked a much greater than ordinary degree of hostile aggression, which may have liked to a precocious sadomasochistic phase.

At fifteen months, Billy developed an interesting ritual on going to sleep that persisted throughout the ensuing months. Holding his bottle pressed against his penis, he would lie down and fall asleep this way. The ritualised holding of the bottle suggested a transitional phenomenon, the bottle standing for the object. The appearance of a transitional phenomenon at this time in Billy's life does not come as a surprise since he was clearly struggling with a moderately severe separation reaction with the underlying threat of object loss (cf. Mahler, 1968). However, his clutching his penis suggests a concomitant castration reaction. On numerous occasions he had seen his mother exposed. Moreover, he had many times been observed to clutch his penis when frustrated or angry with his mother. In an earlier paper, Roiphe (1968) commented on the relation between fear of object loss and castration anxiety:

> The major thrust of development up to this point has been the differentiation of the self from the object and the internalisation and solidification of the object representation ... there is the developmental precipitate of the early genital phase, which opens the channel of genital arousal. At this juncture, the specific anxieties of the contiguous phases, object loss and castration, are indissoluble. The later castration anxiety of the phallic phase is genetically linked to that of the early genital phase, and by virtue of this, has a direct developmental connection to the anxiety of object loss ... Nevertheless, the castration anxiety in the phallic phase no longer has the direct and immediate resonance of object loss ... since in the intervening period the object representation has become further solidified so that the constancy of the representation is to a large extent insured. (p. 357)

From the age of sixteen and a half months when Billy was at the height of his separation reaction, he also began to masturbate frankly and openly. Several times he lay on a ball or some other toy, hands tucked underneath in the genital area, and rocked back and forth in a concentrated and withdrawn manner. This preferred masturbatory posture was similar to his ritual on going to sleep. That ritual served to comfort the child in the face of the anxieties over object loss and dissolution of self with which he was struggling. (His fears of dissolution already included anxiety over castration since he was experiencing genital arousal with concomitant increased narcissistic investment of the penis.) Perhaps, then, the underlying masturbatory fantasy during this early period of genital interest and activity is entirely pre-oedipal and is concerned with the consolidation of object representation and self-representation. As to self-representation, we believe that during this early phase of genital arousal, a primary genital schematisation takes place. We should make clear that when we speak of masturbatory fantasy at this stage in development, we mean a feeling state, a "feeling fantasy', so to speak, rather than a coherent thought or visual fantasy. It is probable that the several occasions on which Billy was observed in the nursery to interrupt his activity and lie prone on the floor with a dreamy and withdrawn expression represented a masturbatory variant.

On a number of occasions Billy straddled his mother's leg and rubbed himself back and forth. She seemed largely oblivious to the meaning of this activity, explaining that he liked to play rocking horse on her leg. However, she was alarmed when on one occasion, while she was changing a diaper and applying lotion to the whole perineal area, Billy took hold of her hand and placed it directly on his penis. On another occasion, while his mother was playing with him and tickling him under his arms and chin, he again took her hand and placed it on his penis, beginning to rock back and forth in a state of excitement. This latter incident suggests that the general erotisation of his body surface was already becoming centred in penile sensitivity, something we should have expected only in a much older child.

In Billy we observed the development of an unusually clear pattern of erotic masturbation. This intensification of the early infantile masturbation seems to have been related to the exploding separation reaction that followed on his mother's two-week absence. We have already pointed out that the severe separation reaction in this child evoked a much greater than ordinary degree of hostile aggression; this in turn may already have led to a precocious sadomasochistic phase and thus to an intensification of the pattern of sexual arousal usually characteristic of this age. It may be argued that Billy's mother, who was without her husband for the entire year, suffered sexual deprivation and in some way stimulated her son's open masturbatory activity, thus acting out her own sexual impulses. This is an acceptable variant of the more general hypothesis we suggest.

Some time ago Billy's family moved to another part of the country. Reports we have received suggest that at age three and a half Billy shows marked evidence of a persistent and pervasive separation conflict. He not only continues to be profoundly intolerant of being left by his parents, but also reacts with anxiety even when friends of his parents who are relatively strange to him leave the house or are seen off at the airport.

Summary

Our experience leads us to believe that there is an endogenously rooted phallic sexual current that, by the middle of the second year, becomes increasingly influential in a child's development. We believe that the developing object relationship and body schematisation give shape to this emerging sexual current and the primary genital schematisation that takes place at this time in the child's life. We have in this paper offered some evidence to suggest that the underlying "feeling fantasy" of this sexual arousal involves the consolidation of the object representation and the self-representation. Early experiences that tend to challenge the child unduly with the threat of object loss and body dissolution result in a faulty and fluctuating genital outline of the body at a time when the genital schematisation normally undergoes a primary consolidation.

Note

1. Our research methods are based on those developed by Mahler (1963, 1968) at the Masters Children's Center (cf. also, Pine & Furer, 1963).

References

Bell, A. (1961). Some observations on the role of the scrotal sac and testicles. *Journal of the American Psychoanalytic Association, 9*: 261–286.

Fraser, A. C. (Ed.) (1871). *The Works of George Berkeley.* Oxford: Clarendon.

Galenson, E. (1971). A consideration of the nature of thought in childhood play. In: J. B. McDevitt & C. F. Settlage (Eds.), *Separation–Individuation: Essays in Honor of Margaret Mahler* (pp. 41–74). Madison, CT: International Universities Press.

Greenacre, P. (1966). Problems of over-idealization of the analyst and of analysis. Their manifestations in the transference and countertransference relationship. *The Psychoanalytic Study of the Child, 21*: 193–212.

Mahler, M. (1963). Thoughts about development and individuation. *The Psychoanalytic Study of the Child, 18*: 307–324.

Mahler, M. (1968). *On Human Symbiosis and the Vicissitudes of Individuation, Vol. 1: Infantile Psychosis.* New York: International Universities Press.

Mahler, M., & Gosliner, B. J. (1955). On symbiotic child psychosis. Genetic, dynamic and restitutive aspects. *Psychoanalytic Study of the Child, 18*: 325–342.

Pine, F., & Furer, M. (1963). Studies of the separation–individuation phase: a methodological overview. *The Psychoanalytic Study of the Child, 18*: 325–342.

Roiphe, H. (1968). On an early genital phase: with an addendum on genesis. *The Psychoanalytic Study of the Child, 23*: 348–365.

Winnicott, D. W. (1953). Transitional objects and transitional phenomena. A study of the first not–me possession. *International Journal of Psychoanalysis, 34*: 89–97.

Winnicott, D. W. (1965). *The Maturational Process and the Facilitating Environment. Studies in the theory of emotional development.* New York: International Universities Press.

Discussion of Chapter Five

Albert Solnit

In this paper Doctors Roiphe and Galenson continue their systematic reports of direct observations of toddlers in the second year of life. These systematic and intensive observations made by multiple observers in a research nursery, patterned on the model developed by Margaret Mahler at the Masters Children's Center, have been used to illuminate questions about normative and deviant development in the second year of life. An earlier paper had suggested that children between the ages of fifteen and twenty-four months undergo an earlier genital phase characterised by manipulation of their genitals and other masturbatory behaviour. It was presumed that there was a sharp upsurge in endogenous genital sensations. It was further assumed that these endogenous genital sensations resulted from a change in bowel and bladder functions, independent of any toilet training efforts, in the beginning of the second year of life. This change in bowel and bladder functions referred to the child's increasing maturational capacity to withhold urine and stool as neuromuscular development progressed.

In Roiphe's 1968 report the emphasis is placed on genital arousal evoked by this dawning capacity for bowel and bladder control that in turn sets in motion the recognition, at least potentially, of sexual differences. Roiphe also attempted to relate or associate the functional control of bowel and bladder with the mental and perceptual process of self and object awareness and therefore with the psychic capacity for self and object representation.

Although Roiphe allowed for precocious evocations of these capacities, he pointed out that there was mounting evidence from his group's systematic observations that there were normative patterns that required us to consider an earlier genital phase as a regular feature of development in the second year of life. There is also the suggestion that anxiety and loss can evoke a precocious response initially.

In the observations of Billy and in the case report of Billy and his family we hear persuasive evidence that suggests the association of object loss and early sexual development in the second year of life. However, in many areas of this report alternate inferences may be competitive, in terms of their heuristic value, with those formulated by the authors.

For example, the advent of aggressive energies in the beginning of the second year of life is often in advance of the ego's dawning capacities to curb or transform these drive elements. Thus, the child, in this period, begins to walk, to voluntarily control the sphincters and to use words, at the same time as he has temper tantrums, shows a reluctance to go to sleep and vigorously protests the loss of the love object in periods of separation. Much of Billy's behaviour can be understood as derivative of the conflict evoked by the demands of the aggressive drives in connection with the object ties.

Another example would relate to the series of "... curious and highly interesting autogenous games which involved his ears, eyes and mouth". The authors risk abstract and somewhat adultomorphic inferences such as "Billy's autogenous [self-generating or produced independently of external influence or aid] behaviour seems to represent an effort to master the sense of inner emptiness and depletion and the acute awareness that the nourishing centre of his being is located outside the self . . ."; or that each of these autogenous effects serves to shift the focus of attention from its ordinary locus outside the body to one inside or produces a particularly sharp sense of locally of the body–rind and a remarkably distinct and clear demarcation of the inside from the outside. It also has the tendency to produce the delusional effect that a sensation that is essentially evoked outside the self, although in these instances by the self on the self, is experienced as coming from within the self.

We are sharply reminded of this adultomorphic tendency when the authors state, "It was not until we finally reproduced these effects on ourselves that their significance indeed became apparent."

I would suggest that Billy's behaviour had autoerotic as well as auto-aggressive components and that such behaviour in his case could also represent regressive efforts to deal with separation or threatened loss. In two places the use of the concept or interpretation of ". . . a profound sense of inner depletion and a longing for closeness . . ." seems to be extravagant since in the first place it is related to defiant behaviour and in the second place, to autogenous behaviour. Neither defiance nor autoerotic or auto-aggressive behaviour is likely to reflect a profound sense of inner depletion.

What is missing throughout are descriptions of Billy's language development that might assist us, through these evidences of mental activity, in selecting the inferences or the interpretations of Billy's behaviour that we would find most clarifying in terms of understanding and explaining present and future behaviour.

Methodologically, in such important research we should keep in mind that experiences in the early part of the second year of life can be reconstructed to some extent in adult analysis, but it is also true as Freud pointed out in "Remembering, repeating and working-through":

> There is one special class of experiences of the utmost importance for which no memory can as a rule be recovered. These are experiences which occurred in very early childhood and were not understood at the time but which were subsequently understood and interpreted. One gains a knowledge of them through dreams and one is obliged to believe in them on them most compelling evidence provided by the fabric of the neurosis. (Freud, 1914g, pp. 147–156)

There is good reason to believe that Freud, from his own experiences including the interpretation of one of his own dreams, was referring to reconstructions in the second and third year of life.

I mention this because, whenever possible, the use of direct observations to corroborate psychoanalytic propositions or to modify psychoanalytic theory may require psychoanalytic observations in children and adults, since psychoanalytic hypotheses themselves are generally derived from the psychoanalytic interview situation. Ernst Kris pointed this out in his brilliant 1947 paper on "The nature of psychoanalytic propositions and their validation", in which he stated that the psychoanalytic interview situation is the most important testing ground for the validity of psychoanalytic hypotheses (Kris, 1947).

In referring to experiences in the early part of the second year of life and the reconstructions of these experiences that are so early in life that they cannot be recovered as memories, I refer to reconstructions of psychic reality more often than to real or actual events in the life of the child. At the same time, I follow Ernst Kris' idea that psychoanalytic observations can in many instances help us decide between alternative hypotheses, though they may not provide criteria for verification.

The emphasis in this paper on the assumption of an earlier chronology in sexual development raises general and specific questions. In general, there may be a speed-up of psychosexual development as is so frequently reported in the psychoanalytic literature of the 1950s and 1960s (Kleeman, 1965, 1966).

However, there is also a persistent tendency in the literature to overlook the question of what are the preponderance of psychosexual phenomena at a given phase and to forget that the very young child characteristically expresses a wide range of polymorph infantile sexual behaviours. In fact, the richness of this study of Billy also emphasises his orally influenced regressive behaviour as much as it does his genital arousal. It raises the question, what constitutes a "phase"? What criteria shall we use to distinguish the generally polymorph infantile erotic activities in the first three years of life from the patterning or preponderance that we characterise as a phase? When we speak of a phase are we referring to a level and pattern or organisation of behaviour as well as to the erotic behaviour; or are we concentrating on the erotic behaviour as the most important indication of a particular phase of psychosexual development? I would presume that the concept of phase refers to patterns and levels of behaviour that have psychic representational equivalents that are crucial for our understanding, as well as to patterns of erotic behaviour. Stimulation that is excessive, as when Billy's mother applied lotion to his perineal area or tickled him may evoke precocious genital reactions, characterising seductive activities of the mother to which Billy responded in kind.

The description of Billy's altered reactions to sounds were fascinating and significant. Anxiety in anticipation of loss can heighten the awareness of the outside world and can be manifest reactions to the "dangers" of the outside world, focused particularly on outside sound in Billy's case. I would like to suggest that this is a useful illustration of the displacement not only of anxiety but of threatening hostile feelings on to the outside world where they can be recognised, differentiated, and mastered. This is very likely is a forerunner of later defences, such as externalisation, intellectualisation, and projection as a way of warding off the discomfort of the inside noises and warding off the anxiety caused by angry feelings and thoughts about the cherished love object.

Finally, I believe the authors have posed a challenging and important task, that of correlating the psychic activity of object and self-representational capacities with psychosexual development. Their on-going studies will continue to raise productive questions, to require a consideration of theory refinement and to compel us to be aware of the strengths and weaknesses of our methodological resources.

In my discussion of this important presentation I have not had the time to applaud the richness and value of this phenomenological study by Doctors Roiphe and Galenson and their colleagues. I should like to indicate my pleasure in having the privilege of discussing this paper by quoting John Donne:

> That then this Beginning was, is a matter
> of faith, and so infallible.
> When it was, is matter of Reason,
> and therefore various and perplex'd.

(Donne, 1651, p. 22)

References

Donne, J. (1651). In: A. Raspa (Ed.), *Essayes in Divinity* (pp. 1–221). Québec: McGill-Queens's University Press.

Freud, S. (1914g). Remembering, repeating and working–through. *S.E., 12*: 145–156.

Kleeman, J. A. (1965). A boy discovers his penis. *The Psychoanalytic Study of the Child*, 20: 239–266.

Kleeman, J. A. (1966). Genital discovery during a boy's second year: a follow-up. *The Psychoanalytic Study of the Child, 21*: 358–392.

Kris, E. (1947). The nature of psychoanalytic propositions and their validation. In: L. Newman (Ed.), *The Selected Papers of Ernst Kris* (pp. 3–23). New Haven: Yale University Press, 1975.

Roiphe, H. (1968). On an early genital phase: with an addendum on genesis. *The Psychoanalytic Study of the Child, 23*: 348–365.

CHAPTER SIX

Observation of early infantile sexual and erotic development

Eleanor Galenson

Gender identity

As a general term, identity is usually understood as the view of oneself as an individual with a sense of wholeness and continuity over time. From the psychoanalytic object relations point of view, a sense of the self is the reciprocal of the sense of the other, usually the primary care-giver to begin with, both evolving interdependently and having important mutual effects. The sense of identity, in contrast to that of a gender role is, according to Stoller, a private experience of self in relation to others; it may be conscious or unconscious. "Core gender identity", a term first used by Stoller (1968), refers to an individual's cognitive and emotional conviction of being male or female in relation to members of the same and opposite sex, while sexual identity is at once a broader and more delineated concept—one that begins to evolve towards the latter part of the second year of life but that continues to evolve throughout life. It pertains to the kind of man or woman the individual is, particularly in the sexual area.

While gender identity becomes more and more complex and is affected by a variety of experiences and factors (Money & Erhardt, 1972), there are periods that have proven to be particularly critical in this respect. It has long been recognised that the oedipal drama makes for a crisis in the boy's sexual identity, when a more definitive identification with the father normally takes place. The oedipal crisis is not as crucial a turning point for girls with regard to their sense of gender and sexual identity, although oedipal conflicts and their resolution exert lasting effects with respect to the girl's relationships with both parents. With pre-puberty, there is a revival of the ambisexual struggles of the pre-oedipal period, but the new sexual capacities in both sexes, along with the maturation of the body and the appearance of secondary sex characteristics, give new aspects to gender and sexual identity. But what about pre-oedipal influences upon the issue of gender identity?

Literature review

A brief summary of the literature regarding infantile sexuality begins with Freud's (1905d) remark that the masturbation of early infancy seems to disappear after a short time but may persist without interruption until puberty. Spitz and Wolf (1949) reported that infants of mothers confined to institutions developed autoerotic behaviour during their first year only if they had been able to establish a tie to the mother of good enough quality, a finding corroborated by Provence and Lipton (1962). Progressive steps in the acquisition of gender identity have been the subject of infant observational research during the past fifteen years. Kleeman (1965, 1966, 1971) described the genital development of five infant girls and one infant boy as beginning with random fingering of the genitals during the first year and proceeding to genital self-stimulation of a different quality towards the end of the second year, coinciding with the emergence of genital pride and exhibitionism as well as castration anxiety.

In a series of publications Galenson and Miller (1976), Galenson and Roiphe (1971, 1976, 1979), Galenson et al. (1975), Roiphe (1968, 1973), and Roiphe and Galenson (1973, 1981) verified Kleeman's initial findings and expanded the knowledge of the development of gender identity, with data derived from their study of seventy normal boys and girls.

The boy usually discovers his penis during bathing or changing—a situation of intimacy and being cared for by the mother, between six and eight months of age, some two or three months before the girl's discovery of her genitals. This initial genital discovery is followed in both sexes by casual touching and intermittent self-handling of the genitals during the next few months. Boys and girls show a difference in the quality of their genital play as well, girls' genital play being less persistent, less focused, less frequent, and seemingly less intentional than the boys, a difference probably due to the more direct mechanical stimulation of diapers and cleaning experienced by the more exposed male genitals, as well as differences in parental handling.

Toward the end of the first year, when intentionality and upright locomotion begin to emerge, intentional reaching for the penis in the boys was noted for the first time and was now accompanied by evidence of pleasure as well. This early genital play appears to be an aspect of bodily discovery. While a mild to moderate degree of erotic pleasure was often noted during the genital self-stimulation, the infant was not self-absorbed nor was there evidence of mounting arousal.

Although most of our mothers had not yet begun to toilet train their infants, both boys and girls began to show increased negativism and ambivalence, along with direct anal-zone awareness and anal-derivative play between their twelfth and fourteenth months. The richness and complexity of anal-phase behaviour indicated that a new level of psychological organisation had indeed been attained. Fears of anal loss emerged subsequent to anal-derivative behaviour and usually reached their peak intensity near the middle of the second year.

Emergence of anal-phase behaviour

At the anal zone itself, anal-phase emergence is marked by variations in bowel patterning, diarrhoea or constipation, and such behaviours as squatting, flushing, straining, and grunting, accompanying or directly preceding defecation. The infant might either signal for or begin to resist diaper change. There was definite interest now in the stool itself and in exploring the anal area, and gestures and words supplied by the parent for the act of defecation and its product also appeared.

Further phase-related changes were bouts of directed aggression as well as ambivalence, those drive-connected affects identified by Freud (1905d) as characteristic of the anal phase. Ego reflections of this new level of organisation included anal curiosity, as the infants investigated the anal areas in other people, in toy animals and dolls, and invented many play sequences in which the form, structure or other attribute (such as an olfactory interest) resembles that of the anal area itself or the stool. The toilet apparatus itself—the flushing mechanism, the lid, bowl, and water—were a never-ending source of interest, delight, and also of some anxiety to the youngsters at this time.

Emergence of urinary awareness

The richness of this aspect of our research data was particularly rewarding in view of the paucity of this type of material in the infant observational literature. In our infants, urinary-zone awareness emerged between the twelfth and fourteenth months in most instances; usually, although not always, after anal awareness had developed and independent of attempts at toilet training. Urinary-derivative behaviour followed soon afterwards. Direct zonal manifestations included changes in urinary diurnal patterning and changes in behaviour that either directly preceded, accompanied or followed urination. The infants now paid selective attention to wet diapers; the girls would squat to look at and touch the urinary stream and the boys would handle the penis itself as well as the urinary stream as they experimented with interrupting and then resuming urination. Both boys and girls now liked to play in the puddles of urine they had produced. They became intensely curious about the urinary function in others (adults, peers, and animals) and their play was now rich in many sequences involving pouring and squirting liquids, whether with faucets, hoses, watering cans, or the mouth. In all these forms of urinary-derivative behaviour, the structural similarity to the urinary act itself was unmistakable.

Most of our subjects succeeded in being permitted to observe the parents' toileting at this period of their development, in spite of parental modesty in several families. Particularly in the boys, the new excitement and exhibitionistic pride in urination was coupled with clearly discernible scoptophilic development. Their intense urinary curiosity then became enmeshed in the early genital curiosity that soon appeared. Both boys and girls tried to grasp and sometimes mouth the father's urinary stream. As far as we could determine, this behaviour was not connected with an undue degree of parental exposure, but was simply an expression of the intense curiosity and interest evoked by a newly discovered zonal experience in themselves and then in others.

A decided difference between the boys and girls was noted in their response to the mother's urination. The girls consistently clamoured to be with the mother during her toileting, but the boys' interest was far more difficult to delineate. Some boys developed curiosity about the mother's urination even before the father's, but many of the boys seemed to avoid it at any time. It appears likely that the boy's interest in the mother's urination rapidly becomes intertwined with his emerging awareness of genital sensations and genital anatomy, an awareness that apparently promotes the development of a defensive denial in relation to the mother's perineum.

It was in connection with the development of exhibitionistic pride in the boys as well as their urinary technique or posture that the degree of the father's availability and his emotional involvement with his son appeared to play an important role. Where the father was more available in general to his son, the father's interest in the boy's urinary progress and technique became an important aspect of their mutual involvement; these boys tended to adopt the upright urinary posture some months before those whose fathers were less emotionally available to them or absent altogether. Paternal availability and support for the boy's growing sense of his male sexual identity during the second part of the second year of life is crucial in providing the boy with confirmation of his own phallic body image and allowing him to eventually acknowledge the absence of a penis in his mother—a process that apparently extends over many months to the middle or even the end of the third year of life.

We were especially impressed by parental reactions to the infant's urinary curiosity and exploration. The young child's natural impulse to explore the male urinary stream by both oral and tactile measures aroused considerable uneasiness in even our most psychologically sophisticated fathers. Some continued to allow occasional touching, while others rapidly banished the little girl from the bathroom during their urination, although she was permitted to re-enter during bathing, showering, and shaving.

The parents' need to repress erotic feelings aroused by the primitive childish curiosity is striking. In several instances, within a week or two many parents had forgotten all about the very information they themselves had offered. This tendency seems to be greater on the part of the father vis-à-vis his little daughter than between mother and son.

With increasing self-object differentiation at the beginning of the second year, the anal and urinary zones become heightened sources of anxiety as well as pleasure; stool and urine are not only gradually invested with psychological significance as body parts that can be lost, but also seem to represent some aspect of the mother. This appears to apply especially to the stool, for anal loss is now almost invariably associated with some degree of anxiety. It is in the midst of the anal-urinary elaboration that genital self-stimulation of a qualitatively different variety emerged for the first time in our infants.

Emergence of the early genital phase

Between the fifteenth and nineteenth months in the group of non-traumatised girls and boys we studied, heightened genital sensitivity began to serve as a source of focused pleasure that was far more intense than that which the earlier forms of genital self-stimulation had provided. During the early weeks of this increased genital activity repetitive intense genital self-stimulation, either manually or by such indirect means as straddling objects, rocking, and thigh pressure, occurred in both boys and girls, and they explored their genitals by visual and tactile means. Accompanying evidence of erotic arousal included facial expressions of excitement and pleasure, flushing, rapid respiration, and perspiration. In the boys, masturbation was largely manual, penile erections were often part of the genital excitation (although these often occurred at other times as well) and the testicles were often included in the self-stimulation. The infant frequently made affectionate gestures and touched the mother's body during or after the genital self-stimulation.

In the girls, the new quality of genital self-stimulation observed consisted of manual, repetitive rubbing, squeezing, and pinching of the labia at the areas of the mons and clitoris. Because the genital area is so small at this age, it is usually impossible to decide whether the vaginal opening is stimulated at the same time. However, several of the mothers reported that the little girl's finger had actually been introduced into the opening of the vagina itself, although this was not the main site of stimulation.

In both sexes, open affectionate behaviour to the mother as an accompaniment of the new genital self-stimulation began to disappear after the first few weeks, and was soon replaced by the familiar inward gaze and a self-absorbed look. This development seems to indicate that a fantasy feeling-state had now become a regular concomitant of the genital self-stimulation, and that this new type of genital activity is true masturbation. Furthermore, various forms of non-verbal yet clearly symbolic behaviour accompanied the new genital activity, indicating the presence of some concurrent, albeit rudimentary, fantasy state. For example, many of the little girls in our study used nursing bottles, transitional-object blankets, stuffed animals, and dolls for direct masturbatory contact. We think it likely that this early fantasy formation includes a partial memory of the earlier maternal contact of changing and bathing, since the genital manipulation so often involves these typical "mother–me" objects. Concrete objects are then gradually discarded, and masturbation approaches the adult model, although some people never relinquish concrete objects entirely (Greenacre, 1968).

The emergence of genital-derivative behaviour in all our infants who were developing normally followed the emergence of true masturbation. This genital-derivative behaviour could be traced in almost every sector of the infant's functioning. In the girls, doll play increased remarkably and the quality of the play itself changed in that dolls were continually undressed, the crotch area examined, phallic-shaped objects were placed first at this area, and the dolls themselves were often used for masturbation or were placed beneath the genital area at bedtime. Many girls then adopted one of the dolls as an obligatory companion during both waking and sleeping hours.

The boys' use of "phallic" toys such as cars, trucks, airplanes, and other objects that could be put into motion increased markedly during the early weeks of the genital phase. Furthermore, the strutting body posture and phallic pride of the boys was in sharp contrast to the flirtatiousness of the girls who lifted their skirts and exposed their genitals.

As the signs of specific endogenous genital responsiveness mounted, curiosity about the sexual difference emerged in both boys and girls, curiosity that soon led to visual comparisons; the boys stared at the father's penis and then at their own during those increasingly frequent times when both were naked together either in the shower or during the father's toileting. Both boys and girls tried to see and touch their mother's breasts and to peer beneath the skirts of women and dolls.

Discovery of the sexual anatomical difference

After the emergence of curiosity about sexual difference, the reactions of the normally developing boys and girls diverged. After an initial period in which both boys and girls appeared to suffer a shocked reaction consisting of an ubiquitous denial of the genital difference, with displacement of interest to the mother's breasts, the umbilicus, and the buttocks, virtually all the girls went on to develop pre-oedipal castration reactions. These reactions included a recrudescence of their recently allayed fears of object-loss and self-disintegration and a variety of other regressive symptoms, depending upon the severity of their reaction. However, there were also developmental advances in most of the girls in that they showed far more elaborate fantasy play and early attempts at graphic representation. While this may have represented to some degree the use of denial through fantasy, the new developments, we believe, reflected the girls' defensive efforts to cope through ego advancement with the anxiety provoked by their recognition of the genital difference.

With regard to object relations, the recognition of the genital difference led in all the girls to a definite heightening of the already present ambivalence of anal-phase development, but also to the emergence of a new erotic and flirtatious interest in the father in all but a very small number of girls. This erotic turn to the father is an important preparation for the positive oedipal attachment soon to appear.

Eight girls in our sample developed very severe pre-oedipal castration reactions. All of these girls had experienced an important threat to either the developing body image or to their maternal relationship during their first year, as had been predicted by Roiphe. In all the girls, however, the pre-oedipal castration reaction affected almost every area of behaviour. At the genital zone itself, manual masturbation was frequently replaced by indirect stimulation and some girls abandoned masturbation entirely, while several continued to masturbate but without pleasure. In several girls we observed distinct signs of shame and embarrassment during their fifteenth to eighteenth months, particularly with regard to loss of urinary control. When urine trickled down their thighs, leaving puddles on the floor, they appeared ashamed and uncomfortable—reactions confined to the girls only and apparently related to the dawning awareness of the urinary-genital anatomical differences.

With regard to ego development, it was impressive that those girls who had previously differentiated boy from girl verbally now frequently confused the two and their use of the word "boy" often dropped out altogether.

It was in the area of genital behaviour that the difference between the sexes was most impressive. The girls showed a far greater tendency to use regressive oral and anal comforting measures, such as mouthing and sucking, anal masturbation, and anal and urinary retention. Displacement of masturbation to other body parts was most common. Oral and anal-phase anxieties of object and anal loss were intensified and were now reflected in renewed fears of separation, while the castration anxiety was evident in their intense concern over minor bruises and scratches and in their avoidance of broken toys.

The changes in the form of masturbation and its total inhibition in some little girls represented their efforts to deny the sexual difference by avoiding the whole genital area, an avoidance that soon disintegrated in most of the girls as sexual pressure rose and as denial of the anatomy of their genitals began to interfere with their developing sense of reality.

These pre-oedipal castration responses to the sexual differences appear to act as organising influences from this time onwards. Perhaps it is in its effect upon developing object ties that the effect of the castration reaction in girls is most striking. While both boys and girls had developed a special relationship with the father toward the end of the first year as part of their growing sense of separateness from the mother, it was in the midst of their castration reactions, as described above, that most of the girls made the erotic turn to the father, seeking out the mother only at times of distress. These were the girls who had had a relatively successful experience during their first year. However, where the earlier relationship with the mother had been of poor quality, or if the girl had suffered important bodily traumata during her first year or had experienced the birth of a sibling during the second part of the second year, hostile dependence upon the mother was enormously aggravated in the wake of the discovery of the sexual anatomical difference.

These early events in the psychosexual sphere also exert a marked influence upon the girl's developing libidinal attachment to the father, determining whether a definitive erotic shift toward the father takes place toward the end of the second year, or whether the tie to the mother persists and becomes intensified and even more ambivalent. The milder castration reaction appears to facilitate the girl's turn to the father as her new love object with a continuing, albeit less intense attachment to her mother, while the more profound castration reaction seems to lead to a predominantly negative oedipal constellation, with the mother as the primary and ambivalently loved object.

Finally, we noted the occurrence of mood changes in many girls that occurred concurrently with their pre-oedipal castration reactions. Mahler (1963) described the sadness and the loss of zest and enthusiasm in many of the little girls during the same chronological period, a change in mood that she attributed to the rapprochement crisis. We believe that these mood changes, which may range from very mild reactions to the establishment of a basic depressive mood seen in one of the girls in our study, can probably best be identified as reflecting developments in both the psychosexual and object-relations spheres.

As stated above, the symbolic function in girls advanced in complexity.

Under the impact of the pre-oedipal castration; many girls developed a special type of attachment to dolls or other inanimate objects, different from the earlier type of doll play in that the dolls and other objects may serve as "infantile fetishes" in support of the sense of femaleness.

We have also described the expansion of play in most of the girls. However, those girls who suffered the most intense castration reactions showed, in contrast, a considerable constriction in their fantasy life in that imaginative play of all types became sparse and stereotyped. This went hand in hand with a restriction in their general intellectual curiosity, and their exploration of the world about them became definitely narrower in scope at this period of critical transition between preverbal and verbal methods of communication.

In contrast to the girls, the boys seemed less overtly disturbed by their discovery of the anatomical differences, all but four of the boys showing only a minimal degree of overt reaction to this discovery, and experiencing a brief upsurge of masturbation, lasting only a month or so. This was followed by a decline of direct manual masturbation, together with a definite increase in the intensity of their general motor activity. Both of these latter developments appear to reflect the boy's anxiety in relation to his recognition of the genital difference, with its implied threat of castration and regression to the more symbiotic type of passive attachment to the mother. Their apparent lack of overt disturbance can be ascribed to the boy's continued attempts to deny the sexual difference, a denial that can be supported by avoidance of confrontation with the mother's genitals and those of his female peers, and by the boy's turn toward the father in non-erotic identification with him.

From time to time, the boys' denial of the genital difference broke down, and evidence of anal–genital confusion emerged. Attempts at toilet training met with strong objection for a period, until the anal–genital confusion once again subsided. There were also renewed regressive requests for the bottle, increased attachment to transitional objects and heightened anxiety over separation. Furthermore, the boys tended to avoid witnessing the mother's genitals and her urination.

Our original postulate stated that all infants would show evidence of passage through an early genital phase sometime between eighteen and twenty-four months of age. This condition was satisfied in all seventy subjects, except that the time of onset was several months earlier in most. We also assumed that circumstances that interfered with the developing sense of body intactness or with the mother–child relationship would affect the way in which the infant experienced the early genital phase. This condition was also satisfied in all the predisposed girls, but not in all the predisposed boys.

However, we did not expect to find the striking difference in *overt* reaction between the randomly selected male and randomly selected female infants, with regard to their reactions to perceiving the anatomical difference between the sexes, although we now recognise that their greater motor activity may well have served as a discharge route for the underlying pre-oedipal castration anxiety.

Another group of boys among the randomly selected twenty-three boys differed in that the onset of the early genital phase was delayed, occurring well beyond the beginning of their third year. The parents of one of these infants were extremely inhibited emotionally, especially with regard to sexuality; two other boys in this group were emotionally remote from their parents, who were having serious marital problems. The remaining three boys with delayed genitality were locked in an overly close and erotic relationship with their mothers, and developed moderately severe castration reactions and transient confusions in sexual identity during their third and fourth years.

Conclusion

In our view then, Freud's original position that sexual-drive organisation exerts a special and exemplary role in development remains a valid one, although drive organisation is in turn considerably and extensively influenced by events in the sphere of object relations. Very early genital-zone experiences during the first sixteen months of life contribute to a vague sense of genital awareness and undoubtedly exert an influence over many ego functions.

With the process of separation and individuation, the genital zone emerges as a distinct and differentiated source of endogenous pleasure, somewhere between fifteen and nineteen months of age, exerting a new and crucial influence upon the sense of sexual identity, object relations, basic mood and other aspects of ego functioning. This era constitutes an early genital phase, preceding that of the oedipal period, and the later oedipal constellation will inevitably be shaped by the pre-oedipal developments we have described.

We do not consider the discovery of the sexual difference and the new genital sensations of the early genital phase as merely several of many variables that influence the growing sense of identity. They are unique, exemplary and of equal importance to the oral and anal aspects of psychosexual development that have preceded them. The emergence of the early genital phase, including the pre-oedipal castration reaction, reactivates and becomes fused with earlier fears of both object and anal loss, and is therefore particularly threatening to the child's still unstable sense of self and object.

The subtle differences in parental handling of the infant during the first year or so probably contribute to an incipient sense of sexual identity. But it is only with the emergence of genital awareness—and endogenous precipitate of anal and urinary awareness—that differences between boys and girls can be clearly discerned. These differences seem to mark the beginning of the divergent pathway each sex follows, a finding that strongly suggests that the second half of the second year of life is a critical period for the development of the sense of sexual identity. In girls, this period is characterised by a remarkable increase in semi-disintegration. The erotic turn to the father and a definite change in masturbatory patterns are further features that distinguish the sexual development in the girls. Although the girls appear to be more vulnerable than the boys, they also show advances in ego functioning.

The boys, in contrast, show far less *overt* disturbance as they defend against the pre-oedipal castration anxiety by a more profound denial and displacement. The father's availability plays a crucial role in support of the boy's distancing from his mother and increasing confirmation of his own phallic body image.

We believe that Freud's original position regarding women was correct in so far as his premise that penis envy and the feminine castration complex exert crucial influences upon feminine development. However, these occur earlier than he had postulated. They are closely intertwined with fears of object and anal loss, and they shape an already developing although vague sense of femininity stemming from early bodily and affective experiences with both parents. Furthermore, the pre-oedipal castration reactions vary in intensity from child to child to a marked degree, and they profoundly influence drive and ego development.

References

Freud, S. (1905d). *Three Essays on the Theory of Sexuality. S.E.*, 7: 125–143.

Galenson, E. & Miller, R. (1976). The choice of symbols. *Journal of the Academy of Child Psychiatry*, 15: 83–96.

Galenson, E., & Roiphe, H. (1971). The impact of early sexual discovery on mood, defensive organization, and symbolization. *The Psychoanalytic Study of the Child*, 26: 195–216.

Galenson, E., & Roiphe, H. (1976). Some suggested revisions concerning early female development. *Journal of the American Psychoanalytic Association*, 24S: 29–57.

Galenson, E., & Roiphe, H. (1979). Development of sexual identity: discoveries and implications. In: T. B. Karasu & C. W. Socarides (Eds.), *On Sexuality: Psychoanalytic Implications* (pp. 1–17). New York: International Universities Press.

Galenson, E., Vogel, S., Blau, S., & Roiphe, H. (1975). Disturbance in sexual identity beginning at 18 months of age. *International Review of Psychoanalysis, 2*: 369–397.

Greenacre, P. (1968). Perversions: general considerations regarding their genetic and dynamic background. *The Psychoanalytic Study of the Child, 23*: 47–52.

Kleeman, J. A. (1965). A boy discovers his penis. *The Psychoanalytic Study of the Child, 20*: 239–266.

Kleeman, J. A. (1966). Genital discovery during a boy's second year: a follow-up. *The Psychoanalytic Study of the Child, 21*: 358–392.

Kleeman, J. A. (1971). The establishment of core gender identity in normal girls. *Archives of Sexual Behavior, I*: 117.

Mahler, M. (1963). Thoughts about development and individuation. *The Psychoanalytic Study of the Child, 18*: 307–324.

Money, J., & Erhardt, A. (1972). *Man and Woman, Boy and Girl: The Differentiation and Dimorphism of Gender Identity from Conception to Maturity*. Baltimore, MD: Johns Hopkins University Press.

Provence, S., & Lipton, R. (1962). Point of view. *Infants in Institutions* (pp. 9–22). New York: International Universities Press.

Roiphe, H. (1968). On an early genital phase: with an addendum on genesis. *The Psychoanalytic Study of the Child, 23*: 348–365.

Roiphe, H. (1973). Some thoughts on childhood psychosis. *The Psychoanalytic Study of the Child, 28*: 131–145.

Roiphe, H., & Galenson, E. (1973). Object loss and early sexual development. *The Psychoanalytic Quarterly, 42*: 73–90.

Roiphe, H., & Galenson, E. (1981). *The Infantile Origins of Sexual Identity*. New York: International Universities Press.

Spitz, R. A., & Wolf, M. (1949). Autoeroticism: some empirical findings and hypotheses on three of its manifestations in the first year of life. *The Psychoanalytic Study of the Child, 3/4*: 85–120.

Stoller, R. (1968). *Sex and Gender, Vol. 1*. New York: Science House.

CHAPTER SEVEN

Review of
The Infantile Origins of Sexual Identity

Elizabeth Lloyd Mayer

Freud's early observations of his own children at play have been succeeded by increasingly systematic observations of children in naturalistic settings by psychoanalysts. Herman Roiphe and Eleanor Galenson are well established as pioneers in carrying out such observations; their observational studies and resulting theoretical innovations have received wide psychoanalytic publication and acclaim for some years. The current work, *The Infantile Origins of Sexual Identity* (1981), constitutes a compendium of their earlier published studies, edited and admirably integrated into a single volume.

Roiphe and Galenson describe the subject of their work as follows:

> It is the interrelationship existing between instinctual-phase development, self-object differentiation, and other aspects of interest to us . . . As our research proceeded, we became increasingly convinced that we had been engaged in raising the development of the sense of sexual identity from its vague beginnings during the earliest weeks and months to a definite conscious awareness of specific gender and genital erotic feelings and fantasies by the end of the second year. This definitive awareness has turned out to be a critical factor in ongoing psychological development and has therefore been designated as the beginning of a new psychosexual phase. (Preface; pp. ix–x)

With detailed case histories, Roiphe and Galenson substantiate their claims for the existence of an early genital phase, in which genital schematisation is the outcome of a normal and regularly occurring increase in spontaneous, endogenous genital sensation and arousal, typically commencing between fifteen and nineteen months of age.

They begin the book with two chapters based on Roiphe's previously published papers (1968, 1973) in which he set forth his conceptualisation of an early genital phase and his related ideas concerning pre-oedipal castration reactions. In these chapters, as in most of the succeeding ones, theoretical exposition is integrated with detailed single-case presentations. The case presentations are based on observational data obtained in the authors' research nursery. In Chapter Three we are offered a lucid description of the nursery setting and the author's observational method. This chapter offers the general reader a real feeling for the context in which Roiphe and Galenson have generated their hypotheses. In addition, this chapter will be particularly useful for investigators interested in the establishment or assessment of similar observational research. Roiphe and Galenson have included a physical plan of their research nursery, replicas of the flow charts used to record daily observations, and we are offered a vivid picture of daily life in their nursery, even down to the astronomical plumbing bills that apparently result from permitting a group of children in the second year of life free access to a common toilet.

Succeeding chapters go on to highlight aspects of Roiphe and Galenson's hypothesised early genital phase with much the same organisation followed in the first two chapters: single cases are used to illustrate particular phenomena in conjunction with the concept of an early genital phase. The infantile fetish, transitional object, development of symbolic function, development of play, effects of body traumata, and effects of object loss are among the many topics taken up. The authors see their work as extending and complementing the observational research of Margaret Mahler, by whom they have been much influenced. While Mahler's investigations have focused particularly on the development of object relations, Roiphe and Galenson have emphasised the integration of object relations with drive theory. Overall, Roiphe and Galenson have richly elaborated psychoanalytic understanding of the second year of life, offering the reader a plethora of charming and down-to-earth observational vignettes while expanding and speculating upon many aspects of psychoanalytic theory.

They have attempted to discover, in direct observation of one-year olds, the early roots of numerous phenomena with which clinical psychoanalysis has long been familiar. In this effort, Roiphe and Galenson have offered confirmation of much that psychoanalytic theories of development have postulated. They have also challenged certain ideas, first and foremost the age at which genital experience becomes a major organiser of psychological development.

As a compilation of previous work, *The Infantile Origins of Sexual Identity* is beautifully organised. The authors have managed to compose each chapter in such a way that each one stands on its own, yet leads naturally into its successor and has an important place in the book as a whole. They have avoided undue repetition, although they make their point—the existence of an early genital phase—often, each time with slightly different focus. In terms of organisation, I would quibble with the placement of Chapter Three (their description of the nursery setting and investigative method), since it seems to me that this section really should introduce the work, placing their entire research effort in a comprehensible context for the reader.

To my mind, the authors have offered ample and most convincing evidence for the existence of their hypothesised early genital phase. Indeed, I would guess that simple perusal of Roiphe and Galenson's case presentations by even the most psychoanalytically naïve reader would lead that reader to the independent hypothesis that there certainly must exist something very like an early genital phase that regularly emerges during the second year of life. The manifestations are, as Roiphe and Galenson put it, astonishingly protean, and the vignettes cited to document the existence of such a phase are appealingly close to the data of observation.

But, while their evidence for the *existence* of an early genital phase is compelling, I find certain aspects of the ways in which Roiphe and Galenson have elucidated the *nature* of that phase less convincing. To my mind, while effectively demonstrating the significance of early genital awareness and concern, they have over-extended themselves in the attribution of content to the fantasies associated with the genital experience of the child in the second year of life.

For example, we are presented with myriad instances of children compulsively clinging to certain objects that appear to have both reassuring and sexually arousing functions. On the basis of the observations presented, the conclusion that the children appear comforted and aroused by these objects seems close to the data and amply justified. However, when Roiphe and Galenson inform us concerning the content of the fantasies associated with the objects, I am sometimes hard-pressed to find the evidence. For instance, young Malcolm (Chapter Twelve) is observed to engage in a number of distressing behaviours in conjunction with a less-than-harmonious relationship with his mother. Based on the evidence reported, there seems little question but that Roiphe and Galenson are correct in suggesting his excessive anxiety over separation from his mother, significant disturbance in his sexual identity, and in pointing to the extent of his genital arousal and castration anxiety during his second year. But I find the attribution of meaning to Malcolm's actions at times to be overdone. In the midst of Malcolm's massive difficulty over separation from his mother he insists on carrying his mother's purse over his arm. Undoubtedly the act had meaning, but what? According to Roiphe and Galenson the act represented "his assertion of the presence of the female phallus—the pocketbook [which] he draped over himself in identification with his phallic mother" (pp. 234–245). I cannot find evidence for this interpretation and can only explain it as an inferential leap based on previously established psychoanalytic theory concerning boys with severe castration anxiety, theory that Roiphe and Galenson have very thoughtfully expanded in its application to the second year of life. But theory is theory, not observation. As *speculation*, their interpretation is certainly of interest since they are particularly interested in possible precursors to the development of perversions and fetishes and have contributed significantly to our knowledge in this area. But the line between speculation and observation is at times less explicit than the overall import of Roiphe and Galenson's work should demand.

Roiphe and Galenson are sensitive to the need for maintaining this distinction between speculation and observation as well as to the tremendous difficulty of doing so. In fact, to the extent that they have failed to do so, they have plenty of company, since the business of distinguishing observation from inference has plagued psychoanalytic research since its inception—inevitably, given the complexity of the phenomena under study, and the attribution of unconscious meaning to that which is directly observed. The phenomena that Roiphe and Galenson have set out to study are, after all, staggeringly complex: their subject includes the entirety of sixty-six children's conscious and unconscious psychological experience as it was observed two hours per day, four times per week, over ten months of each child's second year of life, supplemented by daily chats with parents, occasional visits to each child's home, etc. Precisely because of the awesome mass and complexity of such data, I find myself, in studying their work, wishing that I could be somewhat more informed regarding that which constitutes a direct observation and that which constitutes an inference on the part of the child observers. The problem of interpretation is particularly acute since the kinds of confirmation expected in reports of observations made in the clinical situation do not apply in the kinds of "naturalistic" observation undertaken by Roiphe and Galenson.

The other aspect of this book that I found somewhat problematic involves the way in which Roiphe and Galenson conceptualise the early genital phase of little girls. (In raising this issue, I am aware that I am succumbing to making the invariable psychoanalytic criticism: "Look at what *wasn't* understood in this rich mass of material, never mind what *was*!" I will nonetheless take the liberty of making the criticism, hoping that I have sufficiently emphasised the enormous amount that Roiphe and Galenson *have* contributed to our understanding of psychosexual development, meanwhile pointing to what did, indeed, strike me as a real stumbling block in their conceptualisations.) Roiphe and Galenson offer many and most convincing examples of the dramatically disturbing effect that the perception of sexual differences has on both boys and girls. This observation is, of course, nothing new to psychoanalysis; what *is* new, is the observation that this reaction occurs with great consistency during the second year of life, significantly prior to the oedipal phase. The reaction to genital difference acquires such force, according to Roiphe and Galenson, because of the distinct genital awareness and arousal that typically develops when the child is between fifteen and nineteen months of age. This point seems clear and strongly supported by Roiphe and Galenson's case reports of both boys and girls. And in fact, I find that their explication of the early genital phase in boys continues to be lucid and persuasive. But their view of the same phase in girls presents, to my view, certain paradoxical elements. (This is especially striking because eight of the eleven cases presented in the book are girls, while only three are boys.)

On the one hand, Roiphe and Galenson cite and apparently agree with those authors who have viewed the young girl as having an early awareness of her specifically female genitalia that precedes the discovery of anatomical difference, and makes an early contribution to her sense of femininity (Horney, Jones, Melanie Klein, Greenacre, Zilboorg, Stoller) They particularly mention previously published reports of early vaginal sensation. They also make the general observation that, with the emergence of genital awareness between fifteen and nineteen months, the play of girls differs from the play of boys, along the lines suggested by Erikson: their girls were building largely enclosed structures, while their boys built tall towers (p. 96). So far Roiphe and Galenson seem to be offering us a view of the early genital phase in girls in which genital experience and therefore genital mental representation are not defined solely by the presence or absence of a phallus. The implication is strong that there is something specifically female (i.e., not simply penisless) about the way in which the girl mentally represents her own genitalia at an early age. They seem to be headed in the direction of postulating some kind of primary femininity that precedes meaningful perception of the anatomic difference between the sexes.

Yet I find that actual observations related to such a mental representation are curiously lacking in Roiphe and Galenson's case reports. They describe, in their girls, very little verbalisation, play, or behaviour that refers to the female genitals except as genitals that are distressingly lacking a penis. Genital difference, then, is understood as disturbing to the girl because, *and apparently only because* it reveals her penisless state. Was that truly the nature of the data? I find myself wondering whether it was the nature of the data selected for presentation because, in the minds of the observers, only data that referred to the presence or absence of a phallus was considered relevant to identifying genital experience and concern. For example, at one point "genital-derivative" play is defined, for both boys and girls, as the placing of phallic-shaped objects in the genital area (p. 100). To be sure, this is *one* kind of "genital-derivative" play; but is it, as Roiphe and Galenson seem to suggest, the *only* kind? Indeed, in their formal "Guidelines for identifying genital awareness", Roiphe and Galenson list the following three categories as the possible categories of observation that should be noted as expressing genital-derivative play: dolls (inspection, exploration); toy animals (inspection, exploration); use of phallic-shaped objects for thrusting into holes, etc. (p. 65). While inspection and exploration of toys or dolls is non-specific with regard to content, it appears that the only more general category of play that deserves specific citation as "genital-derivative" is play that includes a thrusting phallic-shaped object. But what, then, of the enclosed spaces play cited by Roiphe and Galenson as strikingly typical of girls in their early genital phase? Apparently, such play would not be recorded as relevant observation because, as I examine the guidelines for data-gathering, there is simply no place for it. Such play does not fit into what has been defined as relevant to the child's gradual schematisation of his or (particularly) her genitals. Not surprisingly then, despite the general observation that this enclosed-spaces play predominated among the girls to such an extent that Erikson's ideas were "amply confirmed" (p. 96), we hear almost nothing of it in the case presentations. Instead we hear quite exclusively about concerns that one might lose the phallus if one has it and one is deficient without it if one does not have it.

This emphasis seems one-sided to me, although, as psychoanalysis has certainly maintained, it does reflect one side of female psychosexual development. While Roiphe and Galenson have greatly expanded our understanding of early psychosexual development, certain long-standing problems in the theory of female development remain, to my mind, unresolved in their work. It remains ambiguous to me how Roiphe and Galenson conceptualise the girl's mental representation of her own genitals that must proceed from the early genital arousal that they postulate equally for girls and boys. They have raised the issue themselves, and pointed in general terms to the different early body image developed by each sex, but is my impression that they have not searched their data for examples of how girls accomplish the mental representation of what their genitals actually *are*, except in terms of their penislessness. (As something of an exception to this trend, they make the general suggestion that the girl's development of symbolic function is given particular push by her attempt to conceptualise the less visible aspects of her genitals.)

A related issue is that Roiphe and Galenson view the girl's castration concerns entirely in terms of her conviction that she had been castrated (i.e., lost a penis), not in terms of anxiety concerning potential loss or damage to her female organs. Again, this is a familiar point of view in psychoanalytic theory, but I wonder whether its very familiarity led the observers to select observations conforming to this definition of castration reaction in girls rather than focusing as well on evidence of castration anxiety that is not exclusively phallocentric. For example, Roiphe and Galenson speak of little Kate's "passive confrontation *with her castration*" (p. 12, my italics), not with her *fantasy* of castration. I wonder if this speaks to a bias in the way their observations were made, that is, a penisless genital *is* a castrated one. Interestingly (and again, I find, somewhat paradoxically), they point to this bias in the parents of their female subjects, suggesting that the striking tendency of parents not to teach the girl a name for her genitals reflects a cultural manifestation of the castration complex. For similar reasons, perhaps, genital-derivative play, behaviour, or concern that does not refer to the phallus goes unnamed in Roiphe and Galenson's research.

Turning back, however, to what Roiphe and Galenson have accomplished, it seems to me that their research is very much of a piece with the recent trend in infant research: their book goes far in awakening (or re-awakening) respect for the enormously developed, differentiated, and complex capacities of the extremely young child. Increasingly, we seem to be recognising how very much is going on in the small human's life—earlier, and in more organised fashion, than developmental psychology has generally led us to believe. Roiphe and Galenson have done much to further that recognition and the implications of their work are far-reaching, both for our understanding of the second year of life and for our understanding of subsequent development.

Reference

Roiphe, H., & Galenson, E. (1981). *The Infantile Origins of Sexual Identity*. New York: International Universities Press.

CHAPTER EIGHT

Review of
The Infantile Origins of Sexual Identity

Jerome D. Oremland

This concise, clearly written book represents the distillate of the research findings from systematic analytically informed, cross-sectional, and longitudinal observations of the sexual and gender development of the infant and young child. From these, the authors develop integrated hypotheses, some of which have been published elsewhere as individual papers, regarding early gender development.

Starting with Freud's acknowledgment of the incompleteness in our information about the prefigurements of genital sexuality, Roiphe and Galenson have since 1966 methodically gathered evidence enriching our understanding, particularly of the second half of the second year of life and its relation to the development of sexual concepts, sexual activity, and sense of gender as part of the development of the sense of self.

They take that human dialectic that when studied as physical predominances we call male and female, when studied as behavioural proclivities we call masculine and feminine, but that from early on is subjectively experienced as an absoluteness of he-ness or she-ness and tease out its relation to the basic patterning in separation of self from object.

Using Margaret Mahler's extensions of Freud's basic phase-specific sequential developmental model, Roiphe and Galenson's laboratory, like Mahler's, is the natural nursery, their subjects infants and young children and their care-takers, and their instrument analytic eyes and interviewing with analytic knowledge. In this setting, Roiphe and Galenson made definitive observations that lead them to hypothesise that much earlier than even the boldest of Freud's assertions about the sexual nature of childhood, there is intense, specific, and *gender-bimodally differentiated behaviour* that is an important achievement of the separation–individuation progression.

They assert that this behaviour, which they label *the early genital phase*, arises with increasing specificity in body awareness and concomitant increasing self-definition and is not specifically linked to oedipal ideation. As contributors to this *early genital phase*, they emphasise:

1. the importance of spread of excitation, particularly associated with anal and urethral sphincter activities
2. the importance of unpurposeful but frequent maternal stimulation of the genitals in the course of caretaking
3. the direct observation of the genital differences between the sexes of the child.

They hypothesise that severe early disturbances in body image formation such as resulting from illness and injury and/or early disturbances in object relatedness, particularly loss, will cause intense and observable gender-differentiated disturbances with important and lasting consequences. These emphases are in keeping with Freud's most important formulations regarding the significance of the interaction of experience and developmentally determined fantasy.

Their observations indeed provide us with a rich store of surprisingly highly differentiated sexual and gender-related responses of boys and girls during the crucial second half of the second year of life. These include a range of responses that may reach a specificity, severity, and persistence marking them as precursors and contributors to the important gender-differentiated character traits and psychopathologies of the oedipal period. Closely related to these observations are hypotheses regarding the fetish about which these authors are contributing much to our knowledge.

What are some of the implications of this work for psychoanalytic theory and practice? Roiphe and Galenson's work corresponds to the increasing knowledge in all fields with regard to the human being that its capacity for differentiating and utilisation of differentiations is more primary, historically is more ancient, and evolutionarily more primordial than we ever thought. In some ways, this work is part of that ever necessary corrective that direct research-oriented observation provides to our tendency to regard development too simply rather than the actual complexities of the processes.

Implied in Roiphe and Galenson's schemata are both continuous and discontinuous lines (themes) of human development giving fuller meaning to Freud's zonal theory. In keeping with Erikson, Spitz, and especially Greenacre, zonal phasing becomes maturationally determined potentials, continuations, and predominances. There are both linear progressions and topographic accretions that comprise what we rather loosely call "early experience".

Of special importance was the amount of difference in the response of the very young boys and girls to observing the genital difference. The boys dealt with it largely by avoiding situations in which they would be exposed to the sight of the female genitalia, turning to their own genitalia (looking at, fondling, and more specific masturbation) for reassurance, and seeking the father when he was physically and emotionally available for identificatory support. It is tempting to suggest, as the authors do, that the boys' avoidance reflects the intensity of the defensive requirement, although this may be their pressing their data to meet theoretical expectations.

In contrast, the girls frequently manifested initial marked depression often becoming highly involved in various repair attempts that utilised a high level of symbolic fantasy and thought. More research is needed on these different developmental challenges and responses of boys and girls.

As a criticism of their work, in the crucially important area of response to observation of genital difference, I do not think they acknowledge enough that the child is dealing with two orders of difference. In their observations there is not enough differentiation between responses to the absolute difference between the sexes and the relative difference between the child and the adult, observations that might have provided valuable additional insight into the early precursors of competition, hierarchy, and envy, particularly in the male. In this regard, their report on Little Jeff's response to seeing his young adult uncle naked is particularly telling, though subject to several interpretations.

Strikingly absent in their observations is imitation of or unusual interest in the breasts or in the physical manifestations of pregnancy. Although breasts and the umbilicus were sometimes used in displacement upward, the absence of direct imitation of breasts or pregnancy perhaps indicates that such behaviour is more associated with later oedipal or early latency phases or that "breast envy" or "pregnancy envy" in boys or girls is really a lesser order of, or even an individual specific phenomenon, rather than an important regular contributor to personality matrix.

As would be expected by observing this age, there are confirmations and new considerations regarding anal and urinary zonal concomitances. This provides a corrective for the recent relative ignoring of these important contributors to personality matrix and psychopathology. Of particular interest is the differential response to stool and urine. It seems that while urination and defecation both become highly and differentially endowed with meaning, the urine stream rarely achieves quite the specific significance as "thing" as the stool does. Roiphe and Galenson's detailing of the importance of the stool as substance and object as part of the individuation of self from non-self is particularly enlightening.

The amount of verifying evidence that the stool can become "thing" for the replacement of loss in general, and often specifically for the "lost" phallus, is testimony to the aliveness of symbol formation during this period. The observations further enlarge our understanding of the role of things in various kinds of repairs during development. In general, Roiphe and Galenson's observations regarding bowel and urinary considerations are remarkably confirming of adult reconstructions regarding specific symptom formation.

Returning to their main hypotheses of an *early genital phase*, regrettably, to my mind, they use unverifiable theory when they suggest that their genital phase partakes of spreading excitation from the urethral and anal sphincters. Here I think misleading energic concepts insinuate themselves into their work.

In a similar vein, although I fully endorse their view that caretaking of the genital area is an important contributor to these behaviours, I would emphasise that this caretaking, especially the responsive interplay of the care-takers, gives content to rather than "awakens" the genitality. However, with little question, I would assert with them that these contents will have great and enduring importance as to how the genital area will be integrated into the body concept as a whole, and fateful significances regarding sexuality, genitality, and sense of gender.

This is related to another area of their work, from my view, that is open to question—namely their using as their extrinsic disturbing factors severe disturbance in body image, such as illness or injury, and severe disturbance in object relations, such as loss. Paradoxically, emphasis on such large events deemphasises experience as the important determinant in personality development, in general, and gender development, specifically. Close scrutiny often reveals that the use of cataclysmic external events often betrays a minimalisation of the singular importance of the *ongoing reciprocity* between external and internal.

It is the conscious and unconscious *responding attitudes* as they become internalised that are the great contributors, modulators, controllers, and disturbers of the human being's elaborate and multiple continuous and discontinuous developmental lines. It is the conscious and unconscious attitudes, interacting with phase-specific sequential developmental unfoldings, that give the fullest meaning to Freud's propitious term, *the complementary series*. It is of considerable significance that Roiphe and Galenson abandoned their control *vs.* experimental groups as they came to know each child more fully and intimately. With increasing knowledge of each child, it was increasingly difficult for them to differentiate out a group considered "trauma-free", even for the first year of life.

From the standpoint of intrafamilial interaction, another significant contribution is their detailing of the ever-changing importance of the father as maternal other and man in the infant and young child's life. This seems quite confirming of Mahler's and E. L. Abelin's suggestion of the importance of an early triangulation for self and suggestion of the importance of an early triangulation for self and gender definition as separation–individuation progresses. This early triangulation is separate from and, in fact, a necessary precursor to oedipal triangulation. What is most surprising in the Roiphe and Galenson material is how early the children's behaviour was *bimodally gender-differentiated* regarding father as man, again showing how early patterns of he-ness and she-ness are established.

Of special interest regarding parental interaction are the remarkable examples of sexually related inconsistencies in these generally well-meaning and well-informed parents. Regarding a number of specific incidents, the authors note "the needs to repress the erotic feelings aroused in the parent by the primitive childish curiosity is most striking" (p. 250). This, unfortunately, does not do justice to this complicated societal repressive process.

I would like now to move to another sector of their work, their studies of the fetish, because of its wide clinical and theoretical significance. Bak, Freud, Galenson, Greenacre, and Roiphe have given us some of our most important distinctions regarding fetish phenomena both developmentally and clinically. All agree at base that although there are a number of ways these are regarded, fetishes reflect a composite of developmental levels.

In a larger sense, the study of the fetish is the psychopathologic counterpart of the study of the part things play in development. The essence of the fetish, which makes it so intriguingly close to the transitional object, is the endowment of a non-responding connotative thing with meaning. This crucial capacity marks the shift from imitation to imagination and must not be confused with the specific motivation or purpose being served by this capacity. Roiphe and Galenson clearly denote that the transitional object as part of separation and differentiation of self and non-self both represents internal loss and an internal gain externally fashioned.

The essential question seems to pivot around evaluating the role of the primal object, the mother, in these special things: the transitional object, the infantile fetish, the amulet, and the adult fetish. The infantile fetish is illustrated by Roiphe and Galenson's little girl whose doll became her missing penis. She was repairing a loss through fashioning a symbolic substitution. Of special interest is her helping us to see the condensation involved. The previously experienced and partially mastered loss of the primary object (doll as transitional object) is used in the present mastery of loss of another, developmentally more defined, part-self concept. Closely related is the amulet, that is, a person (child or adult) clutching a cross. However, the amulet, as opposed to the fetish, carries a greater component of transmutations of the primary object into external object.

More complex still is the adult male fetishist who frantically attempts, in a like manner, to hang on to a multileveled condensed symbol of loss of the primary object and threatened loss of a further developmentally defined part-self concept compounded and intensified by oedipal vengeful retaliations and feared body mutilations.

What is clear from Roiphe and Galenson's observations is that it is too limited to specify the fetish as the illusional material penis as Freud attempted. Such specificity does not enough take into account the early precursor ideational accretions that Roiphe and Galenson's material demonstrate.

Closely related to the emerging capacity to endow things with meaning is the major achievement of the second year of life, an area maturationally tied to gender development, that unfortunately is under-represented in the Roiphe and Galenson study, language formation.

The developmental fact is that the male is much less proficient in language acquisition than his female counterpart. One cannot help but think that, for atavistic reasons, the little boy's acquisition of speech is delayed to insure his active-into-environment mode, motoric movement. He is deprived until later of the more efficient but less motoric-assertive-into-the-environment mode, speech.

The role of the differential rate and ease of the acquisition of speech enters into the various complex responses Roiphe and Galenson describe as a curious specific. While the little boy is struggling with words, at the same time his signal sign of gender, his penis, is easy to name. Whereas, the little boy has an easily nameable thing, the more word-proficient little girl's situation is more complex. Roiphe and Galenson observed the mothers' unwittingly reinforcing this difference. They frequently name, often with pet names, their little boy's penises. Rarely, if ever, was there anything comparable for the little girl's genital. The unclear and complex female genital continues un-nameable by most for life. Here again we see complex pushes toward the concrete and external in the male and a requirement to tolerate the ambiguous, the unclear, and the internal in the female, auguring bimodal proclivities.

In summary, Roiphe and Galenson's work is important for our increasing knowledge of early development. They contribute greatly by adding direct observations of that extraordinary period of life in which so many of the elemental marks of being human are indelibly put in place. As part of that mosaic, they have given us new and definitive ideas about the development of the body self, the sense of gender, and sexual functioning as they emerge in the course of self-definition.

Specifically, through observation, they have identified a bimodally sexually differentiated *early genital phase* that is a resultant of progressive self-definition. They suggest that the *early genital phase* is aided by the presence of the father as other and as male, and is a necessary precursor for later organised oedipal constructs. As part of this phase, augmenting and distorting it, is the direct observation of the genital difference between male and female. The response to this is surprisingly highly gender-bimodally differentiated and more related to threats to body intactness than to oedipal retaliatory fears. Likewise, they confirm the role of symbolic endowment of the faeces as "thing" as part of separation of the "me" and the "not-me," adding new dimensions to our understanding of the capacity to endow connotative objects with meaning in various loss repairs on multipsychosexual levels.

While methodological criticism will come from the broad cadre of psychoanalytic and non-psychoanalytic researchers in infant psychiatry, one cannot come away from this material with anything less than a fuller realisation of how early gender differentiations present themselves. From a larger perspective, these observations remind the adult analyst how complex and difficult are the early years of the human being. If the adult analyst has an overall criticism of this volume, it is that it is too modest, too conservative, and too careful. Considering the experience with children and adults that these researchers represent, regrettably, they are too chary of making predictions from their observations for adult functioning and psychopathology.

PART III

THE TRIPARTITE THERAPEUTIC MODEL

CHAPTER NINE

Treatment of psychological disorders of early childhood: a tripartite therapeutic model

Eleanor Galenson

While many therapeutic approaches to the psychological problems encountered in very young children have been utilised during the past two decades, there is a striking paucity of information in the literature or the rationale for the specific therapeutic modality, the details of the therapeutic work itself, and the clinical results. The consequence has been a burgeoning of methods of treatment of young children and their parents that cannot be evaluated systematically. We hope to encourage others to present their methods of evaluation and comparison by outlining the rationale as well as the clinical application of the tripartite therapeutic model that we began to employ in the late 1970s.

Our therapeutic model grew out of our experience in two contiguous fields:

1. infant observational research on early sexual development (Galenson & Roiphe, 1971, 1976, 1980; Roiphe & Galenson, 1981)
2. the treatment of psychological disorders of very young children and their parents in several therapeutic nurseries in hospital clinic settings (Galenson, 1984, 1986).

Our own model was based on Mahler's (Mahler, Pine, & Bergman, 1975) tripartite method of treating autistic children, modified to suit the requirements of other types of psychopathology. Mahler's inclusion of the mother as an integral member of the treatment unit, a unique and original approach, has remained an element central to our type of therapy.

Mahler's subsequent research concerning the complexities of the mother–infant relationship laid the ground work for others in the field who began to treat young infants and their parents. Fraiberg (1980) and others (Fraiberg, Adelson, & Shapiro, 1975) found that the birth of a new baby revives important pre-oedipal memories and regressive tendencies in all parents, along with new parental capacities. In this chapter we emphasise the pathological rather than the normal aspects of the parent–infant relationships that we have encountered in the infants and parents who have been our patients. It should be emphasised, however, that our familiarity with normal developmental unfolding was an essential prerequisite for the therapeutic work we carried out.

Beginning in 1978 all children under four years of age who were referred to us for treatment in our private practice were seen in conjoint treatment with their parents. Forty-five infants from the middle and upper socioeconomic sector constitute the group from which our clinical experience with this particular therapeutic model has been drawn. Most of the infants were not yet two years old when they were brought for consultation. Their presenting symptoms included disturbances in sleeping and eating, problems involving impulse control, excessive fearfulness, failure to develop speech, and difficulty in establishing social relationships with their peers. Six were adopted children; ten were the children of divorced parents or of parents who were contemplating divorce. Most of the mothers of the infants we have treated were in their early or mid-thirties, and almost all had a professional commitment outside the home. All but three of the pregnancies had been planned; several mothers were referred to us by therapists with whom they were then in treatment, because of their intense anxiety about their impending delivery and fears that the infant would be malformed, despite negative findings in the prenatal investigative procedures that had been carried out.

This failure to engage the mothers with issues relating to their unborn or young infants in the course of individual parental treatment appears to support Bibring's (1959) hypothesis that pregnancy brings shifts in the maternal psychic structure. It also supports Fraiberg's (1980) view that the baby is a special kind of "transference object" for all parents beginning at the time of conception, an object with whom some of the parents' early experiences and conflicts may be acted out for the first time. Our clinical experience with parents of very young children, accumulated in the course of fifteen years of infant observational research (Galenson & Roiphe, 1971, 1976, 1980), had already convinced us that conjoint treatment of the infant in the company of at least mother, and preferably both parents, was far more effective as a therapeutic model than individual therapy with one member of the family in addressing the various psychological disturbances of young infants. Fraiberg and her group were simultaneously developing an intervention technique in the Child Development Project at the University of Michigan. She found that data obtained when both mother and infant toddler were present differed from those obtained from the mother alone, a finding amply corroborated by our data.

Blos (1985) described the dynamics underlying the maternal psychic changes that appear to accompany the biological changes of pregnancy and the postpartum period. As the baby becomes the object upon which the mother unconsciously displaces her own early strong and conflicted feelings, remnants of forgotten but affectively charged memories become evident in her actions with her baby.

The primitive nature of the need states and the helplessness of the very young infant are probably responsible for reactivating the archaic remnants of the parents' unresolved early needs. This ego-syntonic maternal and paternal regression accounts for the enormous suggestibility and the intense quest for support that are encountered in so many new parents. We believe it is therapeutically unwise to accentuate this parental regression by authoritative counselling, a procedure that undermines the parents' already faltering sense of parental competence. Unfortunately, young parents who have consulted us had already relinquished their parental prerogatives to a nurse, housekeeper, or a parental guidance professional with whom they had established a strongly dependent relationship. This division in primary maternal care-taking leads to confusion in the infant's relationship to both care-takers. The confusion is increased when the mother continues to retreat from her role as primary care-taker. Although some mothers continue to share the care-taking role with the surrogate mother on more or less equal terms, in most cases the stability of this double maternal representation appears to be adversely affected by the split in care-taking between two people. Separation problems of many types and degrees of severity appear to be related to this splitting of the maternal role.

In contrast to mothers who surrender their babies to a care-taker are those whose early experiences with their own mothers lead to an over intense and exclusionary relationship with the infant. The latter group of mothers nurse the baby well beyond the first year and tend to exclude the father from involvement with the infant as well as with themselves. Marital disruption often ensues as the mother's earlier tie to her mother is now re-enacted with her baby.

In view of the fact that so many psychological disturbances of infancy are due to a disturbance of the mother–child relationship, whatever the nature of the maternal psychopathology may be, therapeutic intervention must be aimed at a firmer establishment of a more harmonious balance in this dyadic system. If this is to be accomplished, the emotional investment in the therapist on the part of both parent and infant must be a temporary one. The therapist should never displace the mother, except under those unusual circumstances where the mother is likely to remain emotionally unavailable to her infant. Maintaining an optimum balance in joint therapy is difficult; offering initial support to the mother without usurping her role goes contrary to the tendency of mothers of young infants who identify with the therapist. The mothers' identification with their own mothers is revived within the transferences that develop between therapist and mother on the one hand and between mother and baby on the other. However, it is the development of precisely these transference relationships that allows old, unresolved parental conflicts to be approached and more successfully resolved as mother, child, and therapist interact in the joint sessions. While in some mothers early maternal identifications serve to strengthen aspects of the sense of oneself as a mother, in other mothers this revival of archaic maternal and self-representations during pregnancy and following the birth of the child often contributes to confusion and conflict, with the new mothering role allowing old unresolved conflicts to surface once again.

One young woman whose mother had remained at home as the sole and intensely involved care-taker could not decide whether or when to leave her child to go back to work. She was overcome by guilty feelings at "abandoning" her infant if she left but was irritable and angry whenever she remained at home. This conflict spread to involve other areas, all of which involved the issue of separation. She could not decide when to stop nursing, when to decrease the number of bottles, when to allow her baby to negotiate the separation involved in falling asleep alone in his crib rather than in her arms, when to encourage her baby to play alone, walk alone, be alone, and so forth. Every variety of interchange between mother and child that involved some degree of separation had become a crisis.

For another mother whose mother had worked outside the home during her infancy, another type of conflict characterised the relationship with her infant. She had decided to rear her child herself, since her own childhood had been spent so unhappily, constantly yearning for her working mother. However, she soon came to realise during joint psychotherapy that she was jealous of her baby, who was now receiving the very maternal attention of which she had felt so deprived.

As to the effect of the birth of a child upon the father, it is probably true that no marriage is unchanged thereafter in its basic psychological structure. In several of our patients, marriages that were described as stable and harmonious before the pregnancy began to deteriorate even before the actual delivery occurred. In other instances the deterioration followed the birth of the child. Many fathers have described their feelings of being excluded from their former intimacy with their wives, feelings that could then be traced to the revival of ancient sibling rivalries that had never been resolved. These fathers found themselves competing with the baby for their wife's attention, especially if the mother left the home to work and divided her emotional investment between her baby and her work. Such fathers felt particularly guilty about expecting attention for themselves from their already stressed wife, while the wives rationalised their intense commitment to their infant as necessary for the establishment of a sound relationship with the child. In many instances these rationalisations concealed the mother's revival of her attachment to her own mother and the fulfilment of an unsatisfied yearning for her, a regression from the heterosexual oedipal attachment that had prevailed before pregnancy.

Our psychotherapeutic model consists of two or three joint sessions per week with the young child, the mother or father, and one of the two therapists, and a weekly session between the parent(s) and the second therapist. An unexpected finding in our treatment model has been the correlation of dynamic themes that emerged in the twice- or thrice-weekly therapeutic tripartite joint sessions and those that emerged in the weekly individual sessions with the parent(s). (The parents are informed at the outset that the therapist conducting the tripartite joint sessions is in constant communication with the second therapist.) As similar themes unfolded in both therapeutic settings, clarification of the infant's psychopathology in the light of the parents' unresolved pre-oedipal conflicts has been astonishing in its mutative effect on both infant and parental psychopathology.

While this therapeutic model is both costly and time-consuming, it has produced therapeutic results that one would not have believed possible in some of the severely disturbed young children we have treated. Furthermore, despite the complexities of this psychotherapeutic structure, there have been surprisingly few transferential problems—which one might expect when two therapists are involved in the treatment of both infant and parents. Close collaboration between the two therapists not only has provided rich material that was then utilised in interpretive work but also undoubtedly prevented serious transferential problems from developing.

The major variants in our approach to each of the cases involving the forty-five infants and young children from which our clinical data are drawn have been the intensity and type of parental treatment, adjusted according to the nature of parental psychopathology we found. In almost all instances the presenting complaint concerned the young child and the child–parent interaction remained the primary focus of the dynamic material we pursued with the parents until the treatment had taken hold sufficiently for the parent(s) to be invested in the work with the therapist who was treating the child and parent(s) jointly. For some parents this focus on the parent–infant interaction had to continue for the duration of therapy. Most of the parents, however, became accessible after some months to greater exploration of their own inner conflictual childhood residues, which were, of course, central to thief child's psychopathology. About one-third of our parents gradually developed an interest in more intensive individual treatment for themselves and continued psychotherapy with the individual therapist (E. G.), the person whom they had consulted originally about the child. It is this therapist (E. G.) who remains responsible for the many decisions that arise; it is self-evident that the transferential problems would be severe without an arrangement in which the ultimate responsibility rests with one therapist who considers the suggestions and tentative decisions of the therapist conducting the joint child and parent(s) sessions before arriving at an ultimate decision.

Regarding the age group for which this joint model of therapy has been appropriate, we have found the following to be true: separating parents from children who are less than three and a half or four interferes with, rather than aids, the treatment process. Much is gained when the mother and father alternate in joint sessions with their child, and this continues to be the case well into the middle of the third year of age of the child in treatment, or even beyond. It is only when oedipal material constitutes the major aspect of the child's dynamic themes that the child himself begins to request exclusivity with the therapist. And since most of our child patients reach oedipal phase development relatively late because of their pre-oedipal psychopathology, we have begun individual treatment of the child at a later age than is ordinarily the practice in either psychotherapeutic or psychoanalytic treatment of children.

Clinical illustration

The clinical material that follows illustrates the application of our treatment model to a rather severely disturbed young child and her equally disturbed parents.

Janet was brought for consultation at twenty-one months because she had never been heard to utter a word. Her gestures and other behaviour indicated that she understood even complex spoken language, and prior testing had ruled out an organic hearing impairment. The only child of a professionally successful mother and father past his professional prime and fifteen years the mother's senior, Janet had been left to the care of a nursemaid from the time of her birth. In addition to the delay in her language, Janet had been a very poor eater from her earliest months and was particularly recalcitrant on the rare occasions when her mother tried to feed her. At twenty-one months she sucked on her bottle often during the day, refused solids, and used several pacifiers at night.

The mother, Martha, had decided to have a child since "I was getting old and couldn't wait much longer"—a decision with which the father complied without much objection but with little enthusiasm. Once the child was delivered, Martha had little wish to see her newborn infant in the hospital, and she returned to full-time work within six weeks of Janet's birth. Janet had not developed a special attachment to her mother nor had she shown stranger anxiety during her first year, but she did cry at times during her second year when her mother sneaked out of the house each morning to go to work. She was now very easily frustrated and had begun to have severe temper tantrums.

On her first visit to our playroom with her mother, this tiny, frail, very pretty little girl left her mother immediately without a backward glance, handled a number of toys on the shelves, and appeared to ignore the therapist (E. G.). She made not a sound but communicated by gestures to her mother and then to the therapist exactly what she wished them to do. Furthermore, she complied with a number of quite complex requests from the therapist, indicating that she already possessed a well-developed capacity for receptive language. Our initial clinical impression of this clearly intelligent, auditorily intact child was that her marked delay in expressive language was secondary to a severe disturbance in the mother–child relationship. We hypothesised that there had been a split in her maternal mental representations between the strict nanny and the emotionally and physically distant mother. Because of these circumstances our treatment model was modified to include the nanny, who participated with therapist (B. F.) in one of Janet's sessions each week; the mother joined Janet in the two other sessions. In addition, the mother was seen individually twice-weekly by therapist (E. G.), who also met with the father whenever he was available.

The mother's history

Martha, the firstborn of two children, had been her mother's "perfect child" in every respect. Always obedient and helpful, Martha had been extremely close to her mother during the first ten years of her life, despite the birth of a younger sibling. Her father was rarely at home before her bedtime; he was friendly if distant. Martha's poor appetite was the only area of conflict between mother and daughter; Martha often threw food away surreptitiously and remained a poor eater throughout childhood, adolescence, and adult life. She was a totally different child in school, however, than she was at home; from her first year in nursery school at three years of age she was a fiercely disobedient troublemaker who was labelled as such until the end of high school. Yet despite this almost intolerable school conduct, she did well in her studies and her parents never discussed her deviant school behaviour with her or her teachers.

Martha did well academically in college. She had a series of love affairs during her adolescence and a brief marriage in her early twenties. After the divorce she entered a profession that was closely connected with her father's career and was highly successful in this work. Several years later she married her current husband, a man considerably older than she. She knew she did not love him at the time but had decided she was ready to have a child.

Martha had suffered from many bouts of depression since her adolescence; these were not relieved by several attempts at psychotherapeutic and psychoanalytic treatment over a period of fifteen years. Yet despite these recurrent periods of depression, she was able to continue to work and to enjoy much of her social life—as long as she took medication for her "headaches" and could relieve her evening moods by a rather heavy consumption of alcohol.

Martha's relationship with her mother changed at about ten years of age after a summer spent away from home. She then became quite ambivalent to her mother and continued to fight and then make up with her from then on throughout adolescence. She was extremely homesick during that first summer away from home, and her relationship with her father slowly changed after this first parting from her mother. She became closer to him and saw him daily in the course of her work, which had become the major source of satisfaction in her life. Her current marriage was unsatisfactory; she considered her husband too passive and was clearly contemptuous of him. It appeared that Martha had won out in the battle for her father, since her husband (and mother) were now the outsiders while Martha and her father were extremely close. Janet, Martha's child, seemed to represent Martha's younger sibling, who had been relegated to a nursemaid's care (just as Janet had been) while Martha and her mother maintained their intense attachment to one another during the first ten years of Martha's life.

Course of treatment of mother and child over the first ten months

Within two weeks of the beginning of treatment Janet's first word, "No", appeared as she played out many games involving regressive oral and anal themes during the joint sessions where either her nursemaid or her mother watched passively. The issue of separation pervaded Janet's play sessions during the next month or so, and she became increasingly angry and rebellious both at home and during her sessions. Instead of throwing her former tantrums, she now directed her anger at her mother, who was both annoyed and frightened, particularly since her daughter's behaviour reminded her of her own early misbehaviour at school. Martha began to wonder about the contrast between her own compliance with her mother's every demand at home and her rebelliousness at school. Then, as Janet became embroiled in issues of separation during the treatment sessions and wanted to have her mother sit close to her at all times, Martha began to think seriously for the first time about leaving her husband. But now for the first time she was acutely aware of her own fears of separation, as she saw Janet struggling with *her* separation fears during the conjoint sessions.

During the third month of treatment, Janet began to act out many forms of anal derivative play in her sessions, smearing paints and using Play-Doh and hammering toys. At the same time here was much outward-directed aggression, including resistance to having her soiled diapers removed, constipation, and overtly negative behaviour, as well as efforts to control her anger. Correlated with this emerging anality was the beginning of expressive language development. (Concurrence of anal-phase unfolding and the development of expressive language have long been recognised as a clinical constellation, probably signalling the relative degree of release of the expression of aggression from its prior inhibition.) However, the advance in one aspect of Janet's psychosexual development was accompanied by intense regression in other spheres. She initiated a "tiny baby" game, that she played endlessly and in which she took both the active and passive roles, discarding the baby and being discarded herself—a game in which her mother was able to participate to some degree.

However, as Janet's freedom to express her aggression increased, her mother became more depressed. Memories of Martha's first prolonged and intensely painful separation from her mother, when she attended overnight camp at ten years of age, now crowded in; during her individual sessions she described her suicidal ideation when she had not been allowed to return home. She also elaborated on the rebelliousness against her father, which slowly flowered into a solid and often secret alliance with him against her mother.

During the fourth month of treatment, twenty-four-month-old Janet began to protest remaining with her nurse when her mother left for work. This behaviour was now welcomed by Martha, in contrast to her previous feelings, and she herself decided to gradually replace the unempathic and authoritative nurse, after considerable preparation during the joint sessions. With this slight improvement in the mother–daughter relationship, new information emerged about the nature of Martha's "obsession" with her daughter since the time of her birth. Martha now described her fear of the delivery and of having a deformed child. She had been so frightened of handling the baby during her first two months lest she drop or hurt her that she had gone back to work to escape these frightening impulses; she had been only partially aware of her motivation at that time. She remembered that she had never liked young infants, since they were "unable to verbalise their needs", and she had attributed her difficulty with Janet to this lifelong intolerance of all infants. However, she now recalled that a major preoccupation as a little girl had been to remain her mother's "little girl", the price she now realised she had paid for retaining her mother's love. She said she had known that her mother would discard her if she behaved independently, and thought she had found a partial solution by splitting herself into the helpless, obedient "mama's girl" at home and the intelligent, angry, and rebellious child at school. This split became a permanent aspect of her self-representation. As an adult, the pleasant "phony" façade with which she faced the world hid her private depressed and angry feelings. She had thought everyone was like that and had never questioned this contradiction in herself.

By the fifth month of treatment, as mother and child became engaged in mutual play during the joint sessions, Martha decided to leave her work for several months while Janet became acquainted with the new nurse. This decision signalled an important shift in Martha's feelings; there was now a period of consolidation in the mother–daughter relationship, with tenderness both within and outside the sessions. It was significant that Janet developed signal anxiety for the first time now, as the libidinal ties to her mother strengthened. Also, modulation of all affects had increased; Janet was sad at times and angry at others, with many in-between stages that had not been present before. Janet spoke wistfully and sadly about her father when he was away from home on business trips, a sadness that Martha could parrot but did not really understand.

Just before the summer vacation, at twenty-seven months of age, Janet began to masturbate and explore her genitals for the first time, at least eight to ten months later than the usual time of emergence of the early genital phase. We thought that the impending summer separation had hastened the pace of the separation–individuation process, which had been so distorted by her difficulty in establishing a stable, unified maternal mental representation.

In a fashion parallel to what was emerging during the joint mother and child sessions, an important breakthrough occurred in the mother's individual treatment sessions with therapist (E. G.) as the summer separation approached. She now recounted for the first time her severe reaction to the death of a dearly beloved male friend several years previously, memories that brought much sadness and weeping for the first time. Janet's conception had been consciously planned by her mother as a replacement for this man whose loss the mother had never really mourned. Even now she could barely tolerate the painful feelings these memories evoked. As she wept, she began to understand how these forbidden sad feelings over the loss of someone she loved were connected with her earlier fear of separation from her mother and her need to repress hostility toward her mother lest this lead to a rupture between them. She also remembered sadness and yearning for her father—feelings that had to be hidden from her mother for fear of being abandoned by her.

At the end of the summer, twenty-nine-month-old Janet was a pleasant, sociable child who was now capable of advanced semi-symbolic play, interested in books, and able to use short sentences to express her wishes and needs. She often clung to her mother, however, and she had developed a rather severe sleep disturbance, which we ascribed to her advancing separation–individuation process. Janet now clearly experienced her anger and directed it towards the person whom she held responsible for her frustration—often, but now always, her mother. Her sense of herself as a feminine person was much more definite; she admired and wanted to wear shoes with high heels, and she loved earrings (both in identification with her mother and as possible phallic replacements). She explored her genitals and the genitals of dolls and animals during her joint sessions, and she was curious about her mother's genitals as well. Her human figure drawings now clearly demonstrated a knowledge of the sexual differences for the first time.

Martha reacted to Janet's increasing sense of separateness, as well as her femininity, with a paradoxical discouragement about her "lack of progress" and said she was afraid to return to full-time work because of its effect on Janet. It was only when Martha could begin to acknowledge her anger and anxiety about the summer separation that she began to wonder about her attitude toward her husband. It became clearer to her that he represented in part the father of her childhood, remote and unappreciative of her femininity as a child, a striking parallel to the long-delayed emergence of Janet's early genital phase.

Martha's professional life represented an identification with the father of her adolescence. But it was a situation fraught with potential danger because of the threat to the already highly ambivalent relationship with her mother. Martha began to understand why she had felt so threatened by the helplessness and dependency of her newborn infant: these traits had mobilised her fears of being drawn back into the early bondage to her mother, a bondage that had satisfied some needs but had so severely jeopardised her overall development. Small wonder that the birth of her baby had precipitated a major upheaval in Martha, interfering with the lifelong defences by means of which she had maintained the split self-representation of a compliant, obedient little girl attached to her mother and a competent, self-reliant person identified with her father.

Martha's marriage remained unstable and eventually disintegrated. Janet's early genital phase and genital derivative behaviour continued to emerge to a surprisingly full development, and her new exhibitionism and flirtatiousness was now enjoyed by her mother—and by her grandfather, in particular—but only half-heartedly appreciated by her father. Her language had become fluent and articulate, but her peer relationships were still unsatisfactory, since her need to remain in control so often interfered.

Janet's conjoint treatment continued for another year as she negotiated the separation and divorce of her parents. Her mother remarried when Janet was almost six years old, an event that caused an expected increase in Janet's oppositionalism, that continued until she slowly began to accept her stepfather as a more or less friendly addition to her family. Janet decided she wanted to stop treatment shortly after the marriage; her mother has continued in her individual psychotherapy and has come to realise the enormously crippling effect of her early symbiotic attachment to her infantile and angry mother. Yet she has not been able to free herself from this ambivalent relationship, and she continues to use pills in small amounts when under stress. Janet still needs to exercise control over her environment, obviously the remnants of her extremely traumatic and unsatisfactory early relationship with her care-takers.

Conclusion

We believe that this mother would not have been able to develop a relationship with her child if conjoint treatment had not been the vehicle for the unfolding of the mother's past maternal relationship through her direct exposure to her child's conflicts. There is a here-and-now quality, an aliveness that is provided by experiencing the child's reactions during the course of joint therapy and that cannot be conveyed through verbal channels. Young children utilise so many non-verbal channels for communicating, particularly in regard to affect, and can be adequately understood only if the adults, therapist and parent alike, join the child in the non-verbal areas of her life.

The task of basically revising the consequences of such a split maternal representation is extremely difficult and often not entirely successful. However, we hope this child will return for treatment at a later age for further individual therapy, therapy that we believe will be far more successful because of the early period of conjoint therapy in which she was joined by her mother.

References

Bibring, G. L. (1959). Some consideration of the psychological processes in pregnancy. *The Psychoanalytic Study of the Child*, 14: 113–121.

Blos, P., Jr. (1985). Intergenerational separation–individuation—treating the mother–infant pair. *The Psychoanalytic Study of the Child*, 40: 41–56.

Fraiberg, S. (1980). (Ed.) *Clinical Studies in Infant Mental Health*. New York: International Universities Press.

Fraiberg, S., Adelson, E., & Shapiro, V. (1975). Ghosts in the nursery. *Journal of the American Academy of Child Psychiatry*, 14: 387–421.

Galenson, E. (1984). Psychoanalytic approach to psychotic disturbances in very young children: a clinical report. *Hillside Journal of Clinical Psychiatry*, 6: 221–244.

Galenson, E. (1986). Some thoughts about infant psychopathology and aggressive development. *International Review of Psychoanalysis, 13*: 349–354.

Galenson, E., & Roiphe, H. (1971). The impact of early sexual discovery on mood, defensive organization, and symbolization. *The Psychoanalytic Study of the Child, 26*: 195–216.

Galenson, E., & Roiphe, H. (1976). Some suggested revisions concerning early female development. *Journal of the American Psychoanalytic Association, 24S*: 29–57.

Galenson, E., & Roiphe, H. (1980). The preoedipal development of the boy. *Journal of the American Psychoanalytic Association, 28*: 805–827.

Mahler, M., Pine, F., & Bergman, A. (1975). *The Psychological Birth of the Human Infant*. New York: Basic Books.

Roiphe, H., & Galenson, E. (1981). *The Infantile Origins of Sexual Identity*. New York: International Universities Press.

CHAPTER TEN

Gender disturbance in a three-and-a-half-year-old boy

Eleanor Galenson and Barbara Fields

In a review of their clinical experience with more than 500 gender-disturbed patients, Meyer and Dupkin (1985) examined their clinical observations with regard to the three major aetiological hypotheses concerning gender disturbance: (1) biological influences; (2) nonconflictual identification; and (3) conflict leading to defence formation. The non-conflictual identity hypothesis proposed by Stoller (1968) predicated on an extended blissful symbiosis with a covertly bisexual mother who has intense penis envy, and an absent or uninvolved father. The conflict–defence hypothesis proposes the occurrence of trauma in early childhood, with distortion in object relationships and separation–individuation, and subsequent oedipal conflict.

These hypotheses agree in one respect, namely, they propose that the origins of gender disturbance lie early in life. With this in mind, Meyer and Dupkin examined their data on twelve children from their ongoing study of gender disturbances—ten boys and two girls ranging in age from five to thirteen years at the time of initial contact. All patients satisfied the criteria for childhood gender disturbance (Meyer & Dupkin, 1985): the childhood onset of consistent cross dressing, the stated wish to be of the opposite sex, and the reversal of sex-typical roles in their imaginative play, games, and playmate preferences, criteria that were also satisfied by Green's (1974) sample.

None of the children had a history of blissful symbiosis and many had experienced multiple separations from parents, paternal absence or abandonment, and maternal bisexuality. Furthermore, precipitating factors included traumatic sexual overstimulation, repeated separation traumata, and maternal psychosis connected with childbirth. Subtle influences of parental psychopathology were also in evidence in the group, and none had any physical or psychological abnormalities. The presence of early traumata in the history of this group supports the conflict–defence hypothesis.

As Meyer and Dupkin emphasised, gender identity is now believed to normally emerge during the later preverbal and early verbal periods, and is clearly demarcated by two years of age (Galenson & Roiphe, 1974; Hampson & Hampson, 1961; Mahler, Pine, & Bergman, 1975; Money & Erhardt, 1972). Furthermore, the onset of fetishistic, transvestite, and gender-disturbed behaviour in children less than two years old has been described by a number of authors (Galenson et al., 1975; Green, Newman, & Stoller, 1972; Greenson, 1966; Sperling, 1963; Stoller, 1975, 1978). Meyer and Dupkin concluded that the ten children they reported appeared to have been relatively fixated in their development near or at the phallic–narcissistic states; that is, at about two to three-and-a-half years of age, and a number of their cases suggested an even earlier onset of developmental deviations. Their pathology can be understood as a pathological elaboration of the developmental issues of the phallic–narcissistic phase, which emerges in the early part of the third year of life.

Galenson and Roiphe (1971, 1974, 1980) postulated that there is an early genital phase of body-genital schematisation that emerges between eighteen and twenty months of age, a postulate that is critical for understanding both the early dynamics of normal gender formation and the early and subsequent psychopathology of gender disorders. In their view, children are vulnerable to profound disturbance and equally profound defensive measures at the time of gender formation. This takes place precisely because of the heightened sexual drives of the early genital phase, the incomplete discrimination of self and object, and the anal phase with its heightened aggression and ambivalence.

Galenson and Roiphe (1980) described three boys from their series who apparently resemble the children studied by Meyer and Dupkin

(1985) in demonstrating severe disturbances in body–genital schematisation during their second year. Difficulties in the early relationship with their mothers included heightened aggressive ambivalence toward the mother, and unusually intense identification with her. These three boys played with dolls extensively in a rigid, repetitious, and compulsive manner, and preferred to wear their mothers' clothing and jewellery.

The early genital phase, as proposed by Galenson and Roiphe, is a developmental sequence, which may be viewed as a "psychic organiser", in that the psychic system is restructured on a higher level of complexity. Through self-induced genital stimulation, the infant can now *actively* achieve the pleasure previously associated with passive maternal contact, and also the pleasure previously derived from a fantasy of the mother's presence. This shift in the passive–active balance would undoubtedly aid in consolidating differentiation of self from object, so that the act of masturbation and its accompanying fantasy state not only provide a feeling of closeness to the mother, but simultaneously enhance differentiation from her, specifically around the supremacy of genitality. In addition, masturbation and its fantasies provide something equivalent to trial action, offering specific satisfaction at the genital level and possibly facilitating repression of regressive pre-phallic fantasies of merging with the nonsexual mother of early infancy.

In the case of gender disturbance we will present, the diagnostic assessment and form of treatment were designed on the basis of gender identity formulations derived from the research data described above. While the details of the child's early development and his parents' response during treatment provide an unusual opportunity to understand the dynamics of the gender disturbance of this particular child, we do not postulate that all gender disturbances share these dynamic features, nor do we maintain that the trauma he sustained would eventuate in gender disturbances in all boys. However, the combination of circumstances this boy experienced were very similar to those postulated from our research data. In this case, they did indeed lead to a gender disturbance of profound severity.

Ben, a pleasant, obedient, intelligent boy of three-and-one-half years when we first saw him, had begun to attach his girl playmates' hair barrettes to his own hair at two years eight months, during a vacation with his parents and in the absence of the housekeeper who usually cared for him. Soon thereafter he began to wear his mother's jewellery, her scarves, and her t-shirts and insisted on wearing only pink or purple clothing. Simultaneously, he stated for the first time that he wanted to be a girl. A stutter that had appeared briefly at eighteen months now returned, and Ben began to be very fearful of his mother's even mild disapproval, constantly inquiring whether she still loved him.

By three years and three months, Ben was even more insistent on wearing pink or purple socks and shirts, and wore paper bracelets and necklaces that he made himself. He draped t-shirts or other clothing about his waist as a make-believe skirt and draped clothing over his head as "pretend" long hair. The "little purple pony", a feminine-looking horse with a long silky mane, and a doll with long hair became his favourite toys. At the same time, he said he wanted to kill people with guns and he had cut a swatch of his hair in order to look "like the Indians who attack their enemies". He would stroke and fuss with his mother's hair for as long as she tolerated it, and had become fascinated by the stories of Cinderella, Snow White, and Sleeping Beauty. Always playing the parts of Cinderella and Sleeping Beauty in these fairy tales, he would elaborate on his fear of the witches and the stepmother in these stories, yet insisted on hearing and playing them out, fearful yet obviously excited as well.

Ben had been an unplanned first and only child whose delivery was long and painful: he was separated from his mother in the hospital for the first three postpartum days because of her physical debility. His mother thought him an ugly baby when she saw him, and had stated again that she had wanted a girl. But she did nurse him for two months and then returned to her previous full-time professional work that required long hours away from home. Ben's first full-time nurse left abruptly during Ben's fourteenth month; the two weeks that followed were marked by his incessant crying whenever either parent left him, the first time he showed distress on separation from them. However, he quickly became attached to the second housekeeper as soon as she arrived, stopped crying when his parents left to go to work, and in fact often appeared to ignore them altogether. He gave up his bottles at two years ten months without difficulty (about two months after his cross dressing began) and he toilet trained himself by the end of his third year.

Linguistically advanced for his age, Ben was an obedient little boy who socialised well at the pre-nursery school he began to attend shortly before his third birthday. There, although he preferred to play in the girls' corner, his behaviour was not considered aberrant, and neither his fears of witches, his stutter, nor a sleep problem that had slowly worsened after his cross dressing began, caused concern on his parents' part. However, the mother's friend, a psychotherapist, urged the parents to seek consultation because of his concern over Ben's wish to be a girl.

Significant in the parents' background was the mother's life-long ambivalent relationship with her mother, a woman who berated her daughter constantly, and the maternal grandfather's rages that had terrorised the family. Also, Ben's mother described her own life-long fear of overt aggression, her severe anorexia from early childhood on, and bouts of anxiety that had led her to seek treatment for herself. Yet, despite these psychological problems, she had maintained a successful business career before Ben's birth and continued to do so afterwards.

The paternal grandparents were chronically ill and depressed people. Despite this background, Ben's father had been successful in building up his own business and had no serious psychological complaints. However, he described himself as over-conscientious and a worrier. It was he who tended to Ben's needs and wants on many occasions, as well as during the housekeeper's brief absences. The father described no homosexual fantasies or homosexual activities of any kind. The parents had been close to one another during the ten years of their marriage preceding Ben's birth, and still continued to enjoy their life together, despite Ben's difficulties.

When we saw Ben for the first time, he was a boyish, handsome, highly articulate child who made excellent social contact. However, Ben fluttered from one toy to another, simultaneously relating a story about "my little pony" that he had seen on television. A very bad witch had come from "the gloom", he said; she ate spiders and also melted "my little ponies" and ate them. (This theme of being the victim of attacking witches or bad queens was to be played out in endless varieties over the next few months of Ben's treatment.) Ben said he wanted to be a girl in answer to my query about his gender preference, and then immediately placed a toy pipe between his legs. Going to our playroom "little pony", he brushed the long silky mane with obvious and intense pleasure. Noting the anatomical dolls, he made no comment but quickly wrapped them up in blankets and pretended to feed them and put them to sleep. He asked for

"Sheera"—a female figure not in the playroom—saying he planned to dress as Sheera for Halloween. He then pulled apart the legs of a doll, he called a stuffed dragon a "fairy", and drew "two monster spiders".

His second session was equally revealing. He brought his own doll, "Sheera", to the session and called our attention to her blonde hair which, he said, he loved to wash. He told us she was powerful and had a sword that he had not brought with him. In contrast to the first visit, Ben now appeared anxious and much more stimulated. He pretended to cook, handled and played with play dough briefly, and then anxiously washed his hands. This was followed by regressive play in which he pretended to be a baby girl while his mother took care of him. Other toys were touched very briefly in passing. These initial sessions proved prognostic of what was to come.

The treatment plan was as follows: Ben and his mother were to attend two sessions each week together and his father would accompany him for the third session. Both parents would gradually become actively engaged in the treatment process with therapist (B. F.). Both parents would also attend separate weekly sessions with the second therapist (E. G.). (This type of intensive conjoint treatment of children and their parents has been evolved gradually and has proved extremely effective in dealing with psychopathological disorders of many young children (Galenson & Fields, unpublished). Based on the premise that the child–parent relationship is already deeply disturbed, treatment is aimed at therapeutic dyadic and triadic restructuring of the entire family.

As treatment proceeded, it became evident that Ben's play was unusually literal and concrete in that he appeared unable to accept semi-symbolic substitutes. Thus, he would enact the part of the heroine of his stories and insisted that his therapist or one of his parents enact the other parts, rather than pretending to play. These enactments had a limited and repetitive quality, unusual in a child with such an excellent verbal capacity. Metaphor was unacceptable; he literally "became" the whole pony, for example, rather than identifying with partial aspects or qualities of the pony. This difficulty in substituting "the part for the whole" interfered with Ben's development in going from concrete to abstract thought, particularly in regard to matters pertaining to identity. His defensive, feminine identification had, in essence, invaded and distorted a specific aspect of his symbolic development (i.e., wherever body imagery was involved). This type of behaviour (i.e., the enactment of a character or event) frequently characterises patients with gender disturbances. They perform puppet play, as well as dramatic presentations, in which they "act out" their conflict over gender identity—using a female voice, body movements, and body decorations in a massive denial of their maleness.

It soon became evident that Ben's severe separation anxiety had been defended against by his feminine identification. As this defence was challenged by his therapist, Ben began to cling to his parents in our playroom and also feared the end of each session when he had to part with his therapist.

Our impression concerning the dynamics of Ben's psychopathology was as follows: the absence of an active autonomy push during his second year indicated a serious distortion in his separation–individuation process, a consequence of the trauma he incurred with the sudden loss of his first housekeeper at fourteen months and the concomitant emotional unavailability of his mother. Although he seemed able to substitute the second housekeeper almost immediately, we postulate that an unusual degree of hostile aggression had been provoked by this sudden loss, particularly in view of his tenuous attachment to his mother. The witches and other "bad" fantasy female characters in the fairy tales probably represented his split-off and projected anger at his nurse and mother, as he attempted to hold on to the "good" mother. When Ben's behaviour indicated a beginning awareness of his genital sensations and the male–female genital differences—somewhere between sixteen and nineteen months—he tried to become as much like his mother as possible in bodily appearance and particularly genitality. He therefore surrendered his phallic sexuality when it first began to emerge, he did this as a defence against the threat of separation from her that disidentification would entail. Every boy is faced with the need to acknowledge the genital difference between himself and his mother during the latter part of the second year, an acknowledgment that normally intensifies separation anxiety. Ben's props—the barrettes, skirts, and other adornments—served as phallic supports as well as substitutes in the unusually severe dilemma of reconciling his self-representation with that of his mother. He appeared to have adopted the defensive strategy of becoming the "phallic woman", partially preserving his masculinity, albeit in a fetishistic form.

We were also concerned with Ben's mother's psychopathology. Her exposure to her father's rages had made her intolerant from her earliest years of the expression of aggression in any form, either in herself or in those about her. This inhibition of aggression laid the groundwork for her highly ambivalent relationship with her mother, setting the stage for her serious chronic depression. The depression intensified with the birth of her son—a male like her father and therefore a potential aggressive threat.

We have postulated that Ben, an unplanned and unwanted male, aroused unbearable hostility in the mother, with infanticidal wishes against which she struggled by distancing herself emotionally from him. Ben's father, whose family constellation had required considerable repression of his own hostile aggression, had not actually surrendered his masculinity, but his basically passive attitude became evident as we got to know him. Yet, despite all these parental conflicts, Ben steadfastly maintained that he did not think he *was* a girl, but only that he *wanted to be* and *pretended* to be a girl. Furthermore, his good ego development as shown by his firm reality testing in general and his excellent language development support our view that despite the serious traumata he had sustained and despite his partial renunciation of his masculinity, a solid early relationship with his primary object, the first housekeeper, had been established. Furthermore, his father appeared capable of participating actively in Ben's treatment, although he, too, had hitherto maintained an emotional distance from his son.

Treatment included all three family members precisely because of both parents' severe intolerance of hostile aggression in themselves and others. As we began treatment, the mother had asked my "advice", as she put it, regarding her move from a full-time job to a part-time one. The mother's increased availability was enormously helpful, as it turned out. We agreed that the housekeeper would remain for the time being, but would slowly retreat as Ben's primary care-taker as the mother took over this role. We agreed that no new feminine "props"—pink and purple clothing, dolls, or other feminine equipment—would be purchased for Ben, but the current ones were to remain in place lest Ben be forced to use his "props" in secret.

During the first three months of treatment, Ben was encouraged to regress both at home and in his sessions. This was accomplished by responding to the many subtle signals he gave us: he wanted to be fed and cuddled by his mother, he spoke more babyishly, he fed and cuddled dolls, and began to want sweets incessantly. Only very gradually was his mother able to participate in this level of relationship with her son, one that she now realised had been denied to both of them during his infancy; her guilt over her earlier absences would often seriously depress her. Along with his regression, Ben began to challenge his parents with open anger and oppositionalism in every form. Temper tantrums, slapping and hitting, biting, deliberately urinating on the carpets, and so on turned Ben from the quiet passive boy of the first few months of treatment into a hellion whenever he was with his parents. His housekeeper, however, remained free from his attacks for the time being, and his school behaviour was unchanged.

But even as Ben attacked his parents, he also clung to them; he now began to imitate his father both by wearing his clothing and in many of his actions. Rough-and-tumble play became a regular and mutually enjoyable activity between them. At the onset of treatment Ben said he disliked his penile erections and questioned his mother apprehensively about whether his penis was in danger of getting longer. Now Ben anxiously noted small cuts and bruises on his body, and his handling of his penis became almost incessant. Some phallic-derivative play with guns and Superman emerged now and then during his sessions, but at home he still continued to "style" his mother's hair. It was interesting that his feminine play did not upset her nearly as much as his overt anger and oppositionalism and his newly emergent demands for sweets. The dynamics that had impeded Ben's phallic development were becoming more evident.

During the fourth month of treatment, Ben began to play out and verbalise fantasies of magically transforming himself into a girl ballerina by adding a scarf to his head or a t-shirt about his waist. The dynamic connection between Ben's anger at his mother, his fear lest this anger lead to separation from her, and his defensive use of female identification with a phallic mother in the face of this conflict now became even more evident. While interpretations of these connections seemed to be rejected as Ben seemed to ignore them, some effect was evident in that Ben began to cautiously explore female bodies. He tried to touch his mother's and his housekeeper's breast, commenting on the "big nipples", and he said to his mother, "You don't have a penis, do you?"

Both parents often expressed their discouragement with Ben's treatment. His mother was increasingly anxious and intolerant of Ben's insatiable demands for sweets, fearing he would "damage his teeth and body" and that he would choke on the candies he demanded. This fear of choking, the husband now remembered, had plagued her from Ben's earliest months. Ben's father was much more upset by the cross dressing and refused to participate in the fairy tale enactments during the therapeutic sessions.

By the fifth month of treatment, Ben began to articulate his fear of going to sleep because of the witches and robbers in his dreams that corresponded to the witches in his fairy tale enactments. His behaviour during the day began to show both masculine and feminine trends; while he continued to imitate and rough-house with his father and for the first time touched his father's pubic hair and penis in the shower as if to explore them, he also made believe that he had lost a leg, all this while saying he would always have "a boy's head and a girl's other parts". His fury still emerged periodically as he hit and provoked his mother in particular, but he would still dissolve in tears at her slightest reaction.

Gradually a new theme emerged at home and in his sessions: Ben began to question his mother about having a brother or sister, saying, "What if you have a baby and she's a girl?" He wanted to know how babies were born and where they came from, and he spoke of marrying his five-year-old girlfriend. Yet, as his fourth birthday passed, his tantrums, oppositionalism, and food demands once more became more intense and his feminine behaviour increased as if he had expected a magic birthday present that had not materialised. At the same time, however, he played he was a baby, looking for his old baby clothes and carrying a newfound transitional object, his "blankie". Although he was disconsolate *after* his birthday and obviously disappointed in all his gifts, he shortly thereafter asked his mother what a vagina was like and told her she would feel better if she had a penis.

After this birthday upheaval Ben's play slowly began to change in a fundamental way: he began to *pretend*, and for the first time was satisfied to use a variety of symbolic substitutes in his fairy tale plays. His imitations of both parents in their various activities increased, and he began to draw and make puppets with which he would then play out some of his fairy tales. Clearly the shift to defensive femininity appeared to be less urgent as a protection against the anxiety of separation.

Ben began to note that his father's arms were very big and asked if his own would someday match them in size. His enuresis and clinging behaviour slowly decreased, and he was now jealous of sharing his mother's attention with others. For the first time, he refused to go out with his maternal grandmother, saying that his mother could protect him better—a statement to which the mother responded with tears of relief as well as guilt over his "lost infancy".

His current status is best described in his mother's own words:

> These last three years have been the worst in my life; at first I felt I had no son at all; then I felt so guilty at what I had done to him, and now I am half a mother, but not very good at it yet, as I'm not good at my work either. As for Ben—while passing a stool recently, he said, "I don't really want to be a girl—I know I'm a boy, but sometimes my mind tells me something else".

And on a subsequent visit to a friend's house where there were many dolls and purple ponies, Ben played with these toys but he left without a backward glance at them—an almost unbelievable change from his behaviour six months previously.

Discussion

Ben was certainly not yet free of his defensive femininity, nor of the severe castration and separation anxieties that we believe led to this defensive elaboration However, his relationship with his mother has a distinctly different quality—a mutual tenderness and a playfulness that had previously been entirely absent, and a tolerance of a moderate degree of hostile aggression on both sides. Although Ben's shelves had been lined with toys, as had our own playroom, Ben did not play with them for many months (although he immediately noted anything that had been changed). He had not been able to experiment with the world of toys since they were not "the real thing", and he required the concrete object, rather than even a partially representative one. The defensive genital reconstruction whereby he had endowed his mother with a penis, while he partially castrated himself psychologically to conform with her, had severely inhibited the development of abstract thinking in this quite intelligent child.

We were particularly impressed by the emergence of intense hostile aggression as his fetishism was gradually challenged—rage that we assume had reached unusually severe proportions after the first traumatic separation from his housekeeper at fourteen months, leaving him with a barely viable, fragile maternal relationship. This maternal relationship had to be protected by projecting his hostility in the form of the witches and other females supplied by the fairy tales his parents told him. His oral rage was unusually intense and was an important aspect of his symptomatology. It appeared to be dynamically connected with his mother's severe intolerance of hostile aggression. We do not yet know whether it was Ben's *maleness* that was a particularly powerful stimulant for the re-emergence of the mother's pre-oedipal psychopathology, or whether the reawakening of her own oral experiences played an important role in her pathological reaction to Ben. But we are convinced that the joint treatment sessions during which Ben's anger and regression were acted out in a hundred different forms not only stimulated painful memories and affects in the mother, but were indeed essential for the formation of a positive tie of sufficient depth and strength to balance Ben's primitive rage at this same mother. This took place without the major splitting of the object that we assume had occurred during Ben's second and third years (Galenson, 1986).

It is likely that Ben would have maintained his perverse femininity had intensive treatment not been instituted at this age. While we are not certain of the outcome, we do not think Ben will become an acting-out homosexual, although some feminine wishes may well remain. We believe we have uncovered in this child the major aspects in the genesis of *one* type of homosexuality, and the dynamics of a perversion in formation. The conflict–defence hypothesis of gender disturbance is supported by the dynamic constellations uncovered during the treatment of this child.

References

Galenson, E. (1986). Some thoughts about infant psychopathology and aggressive development. *International Review of Psychoanalysis, 13*: 349–354.

Galenson, E., & Fields, B. (n.d.). Unpublished. "Separation disorder with gender identity instability."

Galenson, E., & Roiphe, H. (1971). The impact of early sexual discovery on mood, defensive organization, and symbolization. *The Psychoanalytic Study of the Child, 26*: 195–216.

Galenson, E., & Roiphe, H. (1974). The emergence of genital awareness during the second year of life. In: R. C. Friedman, R. M. Richart, & R. L. Van de Wiele (Eds.), *Sex Differences in Behavior* (pp. 223–231). New York: Wiley.

Galenson, E., & Roiphe, H. (1980). The preoedipal development of the boy. *Journal of the American Psychoanalytic Association, 28*: 805–827.

Galenson, E., Vogel, S., Blau, S., & Roiphe, H. (1975). Disturbance in sexual identity beginning at 18 months of age. *International Review of Psychoanalysis, 2*: 369–397.

Green, R. (1974). *Sexual Identity Conflict in Children and Adults*. New York: Basic Books.

Green, R., Newman, L., & Stoller, R. (1972). Treatment of boyhood "transexualism": an interim report of four years' experience. *Archives of General Psychiatry, 26*: 213–217.

Greenson, R. (1966). A transvestite boy and a hypothesis. *International Journal of Psychoanalysis, 47*: 396–403.

Hampson, J. L., & Hampson, J. G. (1961). The ontogenesis of sexual behavior in man. In: W. Young (Ed.), *Sex and Internal Secretions*, Vol. 2 (pp. 1401–1432). Baltimore, MD: Williams and Williams.

Mahler, M., Pine, F., & Bergman, A. (1975). *The Psychological Birth of the Human Infant*. New York: Basic Books.

Meyer, J. K., & Dupkin, C. (1985). Gender disturbance in children. An interim clinical report. *Bulletin of the Menninger Clinic, 59*: 236–269.

Money, J., & Erhardt, A. (1972). *Man and Woman, Boy and Girl: The Differentiation and Dimorphism of Gender Identity from Conception to Maturity*. Baltimore, MD: Johns Hopkins University Press.

Sperling, M. (1963). Fetishism in children. *The Psychoanalytic Study of the Child, 19*: 470–493.

Stoller, R. (1968). *Sex and Gender*, Vol. 1. New York: Science House.

Stoller, R. (1975). *Sex and Gender*, Vol. 2. New York: Jason Aronson.

Stoller, R. (1978). Beyond gender aberrations. Treatment issues. *Journal American Psychoanalytic Association, 26*: 541–558.

CHAPTER ELEVEN

Psychoanalytic approach to psychotic disturbances in very young children: a clinical report

Eleanor Galenson

The literature dealing with the subject of childhood psychosis is voluminous, but two major themes dominate this literature: the first concerns the issue of continuity *vs.* discontinuity; that is, psychosis that occurs in children below three or four years of age, or "early onset psychosis", as we shall call it, the same psychological entity as psychosis with onset in later childhood and adolescence. The second theme concerns the question of aetiology—the old nature–nurture issue. Related to the latter is the evaluation of therapeutic intervention.

Concerning the identity of early with later forms of psychosis, much current opinion favours the view that early onset psychosis is a pathological process that is different from the later form (DeMeyer et al., 1973; Rutter, 1972; Szurek & Berlin, 1973), although many disagree with this.

One finding upon which there is general agreement in this otherwise most contradictory body of literature is that the ratio of boys to girls in early onset psychosis is between two to four boys to one girl. Also, there is a generally accepted impression that there is a gradual increase in incidence of psychosis in girls as they get older.

Genetic data and studies implicating brain dysfunction, as well as disorder of perceptual and sensorimotor integration are inconclusive and equally contradictory. Furthermore, there remains the problem of whether the aberrant parameters are primary or secondary to the disease process itself (Call, 1983; DeMeyer et al., 1972; Mykelbust, Killen, & Bannochie 1972; Ornitz & Ritvo, 1976; Wing & Wing, 1971).

Among the many studies regarding a genetic aetiology of childhood psychosis, Rimland (1964) reported an unusual number of monozygotic twins who were autistic, and Rutter (1967) added eight cases of his own. However, Rutter concluded that the data on twins still remained questionable because of inadequate reporting on zygosity and diagnostic criteria. Furthermore, Pollin and colleagues (1966) suggested that the concordance of schizophrenia in twins might derive from concordance in prenatal central nervous system (CNS) damage rather than agreement in genetic origins. One must conclude that the influence of genetic factors in infantile autism is still unclear.

Evidence for primary central nervous system abnormality in childhood schizophrenia has consisted of the report of excessive prenatal at-risk factors (Bender & Faretta, 1973, for example), but the presence of neurological "soft" or "hard" signs (DeMeyer et al., 1972, and others) has not been confirmed by others (e.g., Bomberg, Szurek, & Etemad, 1973). Some workers found abnormal electroencephalogram (EEG) patterns in psychotic children (DeMeyer et al., 1972), while others did not (Treffert, 1970).

In regard to the literature describing environmental rather than constitutional aetiological factors, there seems to be general agreement that in those children who become schizophrenic later in childhood, parent–child relationships do show typical disturbances. But since these same constellations have been found in families with nonpsychotic children, their aetiological significance is not clear (Frank, 1965).

In regard to early onset psychosis, there is no general agreement even as to the presence of parental psychopathology. However, psychoanalytically oriented studies that utilise intensive and reconstructive evaluations report that there is a profoundly conflictual parent–child relationship in their cases. Mahler and others (Bettelheim, 1967; Mahler, 1965, 1968; Mahler, Pine, & Bergman, 1975; Ruttenberg and colleagues, 1983) espouse the view that the mother's prime function is to ensure that the infant receives those experiences that will lead to integration and structuralisation of the early ego, experiences that they feel are absent in cases of childhood psychosis. However, none of these workers excludes the possibility that certain predisposing factors may render the child more vulnerable.

Several normal developmental studies point to a reciprocal interdependence between genetic and environmental factors. Within the framework of this general reciprocal relationship among variables, it now appears that there are certain critical factors, as well as critical periods of life. Emde and Sorce (1983), Massie (1977), Massie and Campbell (1983), Ruttenberg and colleagues (1983), Sander (1983), and Stern (1971, 1983), for example, have shown that during the first few months of life there is a special need for adequate and specific environmental stimulation, a period during which there is extensive organisation of infant behaviour. This patterning may well be one of the crucial determinants for later cognitive as well as social aspects of development.

Finally, Mahler's work (1963, 1968; Mahler, Pine & Bergman, 1982), beginning with her study of childhood psychosis and continuing with her research outlining the normal separation–individuation process, has consistently pointed out the importance of transactions between mother and infant as the keystone for any cogent understanding of either normal or disordered psychological development.

Theoretical and conceptual approach

The accumulating evidence from the field of infant research and the less than encouraging therapeutic results in older children with serious psychological disturbances (where therapeutic intervention has been initiated after the preschool era has been left behind) left no doubt as to the advisability and, in fact, the necessity of very early diagnosis and intervention, no matter what nosological or aetiological factors are implicated.

Our approach was based upon Mahler's theoretical premise that the onset of childhood psychosis takes place during the first year of life, in connection with the infant's failure to experience regular and predictable gratification of his affect hunger. The subsequent symptomatology ranges along a spectrum from almost complete withdrawal from the human environment, the autistic psychotic defence, to attempts at reinforcing a delusional fusion with the mother, the symbiotic psychotic defence; it is doubtful whether autism in pure form ever occurs.

Within a remarkably short time, the normal infant, through a myriad of sensory experiences, primarily with his mother, comes to be able to localise some sensations within his own body boundaries. Thus, by the end of the first year, the baby is investigating his own body, as well as his mother's, and making comparisons, and this awareness of his own body has, in fact, major implications for his successful passage through the separation–individuation process and his eventual development of social relations and an autonomous ego. The average mother facilitates this process almost entirely unconsciously, by her own emotional investment of her infant's body, his varied states, and his emotional responsiveness. She responds by numerous large and small gestures, intonations, and visual, tactile, and kinaesthetic interactions.

Our treatment methods of these young children were essentially based upon and guided by the knowledge of these normative mother–child interactions as they were accumulated over many years' time, during a parallel eleven-year direct-observational research study of our own (Galenson, 1971; Galenson & Roiphe, 1971, 1976, 1979, 1980; Roiphe, 1968, 1973a; Roiphe & Galenson, 1972, 1973, 1975), as well as those landmarks established by Mahler and her colleagues (Mahler, 1963, 1966, 1968; Mahler & Furer, 1972; Mahler & Gosliner, 1955; Mahler, Pine, & Bergman, 1975) in their separation–individuation research.

By the time even the youngest of the psychotic children I will describe was referred to our therapeutic nursery, a mutually destructive interaction between mother and child had already been established, and the rest of the family was already seriously affected by the presence of the psychotic child. Thus both our experience with normal infants, as well as our initial impressions of the psychotic infants, indicated that both the child and his immediate family should be included in the diagnostic as well as the therapeutic process. We assumed that all the parents of these seriously disturbed children would show an important degree of psychopathology themselves, so that our treatment design required the greatest flexibility to adapt to the needs of the particular family. Furthermore, as we expected, deviations in all areas of development were already present in the children, even in the five psychotic children who were not yet two years old at the time of their referral to our nursery. This paper will deal with the evaluation of developmental deviations in the infants, the influence of that assessment on the evaluation of parental psychopathology, and the consequent choice of an appropriate treatment design.

Although it is now appreciated that the events of the first year provide the matrix for future development, developmental disturbances during this early period are rarely brought to the attention of the psychiatrist. Emotional disturbances during the first and second year are so frequently manifested as disordered physiological functioning and somatic problems that these emotionally disturbed infants usually come to the paediatrician, who is rarely in a position to fully appreciate the nature of the infant's psychopathology. The stressful atmosphere of the paediatric examining room does not provide an opportunity for the detection of such early deviations as an unusual lack of vocalisation, an inert baby, or one with unusually intense stranger or separation anxiety. These very early deviant patterns are rarely seen by the psychiatrist.

However, by the second year of life, behavioural disturbances that indicate developmental deviations are often gross enough to alarm parents and paediatricians alike, for it is during this second year that enormous developmental steps are likely to occur. Mahler and her colleagues have demonstrated that the second year is crucial in terms of the infant's capacity to begin to function separately from the mother. It is also the year of psychosexual advance, encompassing the anal and urethral phases and early genital phase development, and the emergence of such ego capacities as the symbolic function in its many aspects—gesture, play, other non-verbal forms of symbolisation, and speech. This very rapid pace of development increases the infant's vulnerability to disturbances in development.

The events of the pre-oedipal period remained relatively obscure until the direct observational research of Mahler and her co-workers cited above. Mahler has described the separation–individuation process, beginning in normal autism and eventuating, under normal circumstances, in the establishment of relatively stable mental representations of self and object, a process taking place simultaneously with libidinal phase progression and along with increasingly complex ego structuralisation.

While there has not been a systematic attempt to correlate the development of object relationships and psychosexual development, this matter has been seriously considered by many clinicians and theoreticians. For example, Furer (1964) commented,

> There may well be a relationship . . . between awareness of bowel functioning, increasing differentiation of aggressive drive and differentiation of the self, which explains the narcissistic investment of the faeces in psychosis. . . . The anal sphere seems highly important in the process of self and object differentiation.

And Nagera (1964), in discussing the problem of the connection between the drives and ego, but how, when, where, and why the drives make their contribution to ego development is still a rather obscure area. He points out that we assume that development on the drive side acts as a trigger to the ego and vice versa.

The interrelationship among psychosexual, object relations, and ego development has been of particular interest for our therapy with disturbed infants. However, this cannot easily be identified, particularly if the landmarks indicating progressive development in all three areas are not systematically classified. For example, it is essential to be able to identify that anal zone awareness (the psychic representation of anal zone experience) is indicated by a relatively invariant behavioural sequence and that yet another behavioural sequence is the result of the derivative influence of anal experience.

We have reported on the emergence of anal, urinary, and genital schematisation and of various aspects of symbolic functioning during the second year of life. Furthermore, it was possible to specify and categorise those behaviours that appeared to be directly connected with oral, anal, and genital zonal events and those that were more distantly connected with and derivative of these zones. As illustrative of this approach, direct anal zone behaviour, according to our observational data, included exploration of the anal area and the stool, signals of the awareness of defecation, tugging at the soiled diaper, hiding during defecation, resisting soiled diaper changes, and naming the stool itself. Anal derivative behaviour, in contrast, includes interest in the toilet and toilet area, interest in the toileting and diapering of others, crouching in enclosures, hiding or collecting and piling objects, and using toys that have a resemblance to the anal function in their structural and other aspects (Galenson, 1971). These derivative sequences were observed to occur regularly in the seventy children studied, in conjunction with their anal phase development. Similar sequences have been identified in connection with the urinary and genial zones as well.

While the normal sequence in relation to libidinal development has been delineated fairly clearly, the situation in regard to aggression remains the subject of considerable unclarity and disagreement. Anna Freud (1972) pointed out that there is a fusion of aggression with libido in infancy and that this interrelationship leads to the "borrowing of various tools for aggressive discharge"—the teeth for biting, excrement for dirtying, the penis for aggressive display. She remarked, however, that it has not yet been shown how the aggressive drive itself undergoes consecutive transformation, and she noted that observation of "toddlers", with their more primitive and transparent behaviour, would be a very promising field in this regard.

Method: the therapeutic setting and approach

The nursery was housed in a large room, along one wall of which was a one-way vision room. At one end of the nursery was a comfortable seating arrangement for the mothers, and the remaining portion was supplied with toys, chairs, and tables appropriate for infants and toddlers. A bathroom and kitchen that communicated directly with the main room were important adjunctive therapeutic areas.

Each therapeutic group consisted of about eight children, mostly below three years of age, who were involved in treatment with their mothers at any one time. (Only three psychotic children were in the therapeutic nursery at one time.) They attended three or four sessions each week, each session lasting two hours. Most families remained with us for at least two years, and many were in treatment for three years or longer. Their mothers, in the nursery during the session, participated in a mothers' group that took place at one end of the room twice a week for one hour. At other times, the mothers were drawn into the therapeutic work with their child; on occasion they were asked to leave the nursery briefly if the child was thought to be ready for a brief separation experience. Fathers attended once a month, if they could be persuaded to come. Treatment was carried out within the nursery room by the particular staff member assigned to the family. The parents were also seen by the same staff members in individual sessions at least once a week.

Our treatment design, although flexible, was based upon five basic principles:

1. No matter what the aetiology, we considered that the parents, particularly the mothers, were already an integral part of the pathological situation and therefore required treatment themselves, along with their children.
2. We were convinced that maternal identification with the therapist and his therapeutic attitudes could be accomplished most effectively through non-verbal channels, particularly in relation to this early developmental phase.
3. Therapeutic work at this relatively primitive level of largely non-verbal communication with the infant strains the resources of even the most experienced staff; therefore, constant support and "refuelling" of staff is necessary to prevent "burnout".
4. Planning for long-term treatment is essential, if the therapeutic gains are to be consolidated. When children were ready for it, some began individual treatment in our Outpatient Child Psychiatry Clinic while they attended a modified school situation, until ready for regular school classes.
5. Although our major goal was to offer therapy to the disturbed infant, research and training were major components in the work of the nursery. This diversified focus led to constant re-evaluation of methods and results and comparison with data from other sources.

Clinical aspects

Demographic data

Twenty-nine children were seen in all over a six-year period, of which eighteen were boys and eleven girls. At the time of initial referral, nine were under two years of age, eight were between two and two-and-a-half years, eleven between two-and-a-half and three-and-a-half years, and one was five-and-a-half years old.

Sixteen were white (nine male and seven female), ten were Puerto Rican (six male and four female), and three were black (one male and two female). This racial distribution is interesting in view of the fact that our hospital district included a large black population.

The youngest group was referred in the main by paediatricians and social workers. Speech and hearing clinics and neurologists referred some others, and there were a few self-referrals.

Ten children who were evaluated did not remain for long-term treatment because of the parents' refusal. Three were withdrawn immediately upon diagnosis, while seven were withdrawn by their parents after a period of time ranging from three months to one year. In most of these instances, the child's improvement had apparently been too rapid, and the mother had not been prepared for her child's psychological separation and individuation from her.

The psychotic group

Of the total who remained in treatment beyond one year, ten were diagnosed as psychotic—all boys. Their diagnosis could be established rather easily at the initial interview, even in the youngest, who was fifteen-and-a-half months old, on the basis of their characteristic visual aversion and their deviant social interaction, which indicated varying degrees of decathexis of the human environment. The initial parental complaint in nearly all instances was deviant speech development or absence of speech. Several of these children had spent many months or even years (in some cases) undergoing diagnostic procedures elsewhere in connection with suspected auditory or neurological disturbances.

Three boys under two years of age showed excessive quietness, visual avoidance, head banging, and preference for inanimate objects. One of these boys, fifteen-and-a-half months of age at the time of the initial referral, began to emerge from his withdrawal and developed communicative language very rapidly, convincing evidence of the urgency of early detection and treatment.

Maternal attitudes and early history of the psychotic children

Every mother in our group showed serious deviance in her relationship with her psychotic child by the time the family was referred to us. In several instances, it could be established that the mother had indeed avoided certain close contacts with her child dating from the child's earliest months, although this information did not come from the mother herself. For example, a series of home movies of one child (Massie, 1977) and his mother showed that the boy had apparently been developing normally and had repeatedly attempted to establish visual fixation with his mother up to his fifth month; his mother, however, consistently avoided visual confrontation, turning the child away from her. She herself, however, was unaware of the behaviour. This case resembles the two patients reported by Franknoi and Ruttenberg (1971) and Massie's (1977) case reports as well, where home movies showed a similar visual avoidance by the mother. In two other mothers, we noted in our nursery that they, too, avoided visual regard, not only with their child but with other people as well.

Another important finding of our nursery population was the history of a degree of serious maternal depression that had been present during the first year of several of our psychotic young patients.

Psychosexual development and self–object differentiation in the psychotic group

To summarise the nature of psychopathology in comparing the deviant infants in our therapeutic nursery with their normally developing peers in our research nursery, some of the deviant infants had not been able to establish even a partially gratifying symbolic relationship with the mother; others had achieved this, but then had failed to move beyond it. This distortion of the separation–individuation process had given rise to a proliferation of defensive reactions, including the use of extensive denial, displacement, condensation, and perceptual de-differentiation in which the inanimate was animated and the human dehumanised. In the deviant group, ego development, including use of the symbolic function; reality testing; time, place, and person orientation; secondary process thinking; and visual, auditory, and tactile perception were all seriously compromised.

The progression of drive development in these deviant children was also disordered: phasic primacy, with an orderly sequential progression from one instinctual phase to another, did not occur. Intense hostile aggressive impulses tended to be discharged through somatic routes on the child's own body or might find random expression toward the outside world rather than in focused aggressive acts directed at others or in phase-appropriate motor or other types of activity.

In short, the disturbance of early childhood psychosis appeared to involve all areas of psychic functioning; failure in adequate differentiation of self from object, inadequate drive differentiation, with a predominance of aggressive impulses, which are then body bound or indiscriminately discharged, and distortions in all areas of ego functioning.

Thus, all ten psychotic children showed many behaviours that expressed drive impulses from three levels of psychosexual development: anal, oral, and genital, such as excessive sucking, indiscriminate defecation and urination, and excessive genital handling. Furthermore, there was little if any of the type of derivative behaviour that we noted in our normal infants during their second year. We regard this derivative behaviour, or play, as a fundamental foundation for the developing symbolic function and therefore a necessary precursor of language development.

In regard to object relations, their sexuality was autoerotic and there was no evidence of object-related fantasy life (Nagera, 1964) at an age when such fantasy has normally emerged. Self-object differentiation was delayed, not only in its libidinal but in its aggressive expression as well. Neither aggression nor affection was object-directed; bodily pain was hardly noticed or reacted to, and the mother had not yet emerged as a special person for these children.

Ego functioning in the psychotic group

None of the children was testable according to standard testing requirements. However, by utilising many brief sessions, often as many as ten in all, it was possible to obtain a baseline of performance. While secondary process development was markedly delayed in all, there was beginning structuralisation in some sectors of the seven older children:

1. a kind of categorisation activity, such as piling inanimate objects according to some shared attribute (all crayons, all books, etc.)
2. a definition of objects by their use, for example, running a car along a table, opening a book
3. early representational play with dolls before words were available.

Motoric development was intact in all but the three youngest boys, who showed a lack of vigour and periods of deterioration in both gross and fine coordination. Apparently the motor apparatus achieves relative autonomy sometime during the third year and proceeds in its development in spite of gross psychopathology.

In regard to perception, all the psychotic children avoided visual eye-to-eye encounter and tended to screen out the human voice to such a degree that almost all had been suspected of deafness and several had been tested for this repeatedly before they were referred to us. As the children improved in their human relatedness, visual and auditory perception improved also, and these sensory modalities were now utilised in the service of increasing self–object differentiation. Then the child began to make contact with the mother for the first time through the distance receptors of visual or auditory contact, rather than the more primitive tactile kinaesthetic modes.

As alluded to above, symbolic functioning was disturbed in all these psychotic children. Although several of them had developed what appeared to be transitional objects, these were not used for the usual comforting but to achieve complete autistic withdrawal; these inanimate objects had become the sole object of their libidinal attachment, rather than a partial substitute for the mother. The autistic children showed no interest in picture books and little if any creative language; some were entirely echolalic. (In most, there had been a history of excessive quietness during their early months of life, with little babbling thereafter, and the few words that did emerge during the second year had disappeared after a short while.)

In keeping with this disturbance in language symbolisation, they had failed to develop derivative behaviour or semi-symbolic play with toys. Some had become attached to a piece of string, a telephone book, a favourite recording or the TV, the so-called "psychotic fetish", that appeared to serve for screening out the animate world. They were clutched in desperation rather than being used either "playfully" or creatively.

Treatment of the psychotic group

We assumed that the psychopathology of the psychotic child resulted from a disruption of the mothering relationship, and we aimed at restoring and enhancing this interaction. Our approach, modelled after Mahler's (1968), utilised the mother as part of the therapeutic team. However, we worked within the setting of a group where each psychotic child had his own therapist but could also join with the other children, whenever he was ready for such contact. We fondled, held, rocked, and fed the child, using the tactile, kinaesthetic, and oral routes primarily, along with some verbal interpretation. The mother was similarly fed and catered to and gently and gradually involved in interaction with her child. Ours was a relatively structured environment—predictable, too—that was essential for treatment of these children, since they tend to disorganise under the impact of any intense or unpredictable stimuli.

Illustration of successful treatment

Although the early history available in this case was scanty, the affective climate for potential disruption in the mother–child pair was established well before the baby's birth. The child was conceived as the result of a pathological relationship between the parents; pressure by the father caused the mother to acceded to his wishes and become pregnant. Hence the child was a specific gift for the father and *a priori* an object viewed at the very least with ambivalence by the mother. The pregnancy and delivery were normal.

During the first two months B was breast-fed and was carried in a body-sling by his mother for many hours at a time as she went about her housework. Both nursing and prolonged body contact were abruptly terminated when he was eight months old. About this, the mother stated simply, "He turned me off; I turned him off." Thenceforth his bottles were propped and he was left in his crib without maternal input for hours on end. The mother became pregnant again when B was five months old. She had planned this new baby for herself. B responded to his mother's further withdrawal into her new pregnancy by head banging and shrieking for prolonged periods as he lay in his crib.

At seven-and-a-half months, he sat without support and at eight months he began walking without having crawled first. At eight-and-a-half months, to complicate an already deteriorating situation, B was suddenly removed from his parental bedroom to a bedroom of his own, and he was hit by his father for his screeching. Following this, B became mute, his head banging increased in duration and intensity, and at nine months he was examined because of his forehead bruising by the family paediatrician, who counselled the parents to spend more time with B. The birth of this sister when B was thirteen months old, his father's subsequent two-week absence from home, and four days spent at his grandparents' without preparation for any of these events precipitated such a severe regression in B that at the paediatrician's insistence he was brought for treatment to our therapeutic nursery.

At fifteen months, B was a devastated child with severe disturbance in almost all areas of his development. The outstanding symptoms of head banging, lack of speech development, avoidance of the mother and other human contact, screeching, fleeting eye contact, indifference to beatings, unresponsiveness to pain, rejection of solid foods, and a serious sleep disturbance all attested to the seriousness of his regression.

Shortly after treatment was initiated, the head banging ceased. However, at the end of one year of treatment, B (now aged twenty-six months) remained poorly related and essentially mute. At home, the eating and sleeping disturbances continued unabated, while his play in the nursery was diffuse and impoverished and his sole attachment was to a red fire engine that produced a whirring noise when it was rolled.

On his first psychological test, B at age twenty-four months achieved a score of eighty, corresponding to the lowest end of the normal range.

During his second year of treatment, as a new therapist slowly began to develop a therapeutic relationship with B, his mother's depression deepened because of circumstances in her own life and her attendance at the nursery dropped precipitously. Contact was maintained through a series of lengthy telephone calls. Finally, a home visit was made in which a new type of therapeutic contract was drawn up. B's father agreed to bring B to our nursery sessions himself, to work directly with the therapist and B. The mother similarly agreed to assume a more active role; she, too was to be drawn into the work whenever an appropriate opportunity presented itself. Thus both parents became an integral part of the therapeutic work with B during ongoing nursery sessions in what was to be a crucial turning point for the treatment.

The family's attendance at the nursery improved dramatically. The therapist's prior work over many months, providing B with a stable person for attachment, began to take hold, and the constrictions that had marked his previous behaviour began to dissipate. Anal and urethral concerns, developmental themes appropriate to the second year of life, along with their derivative play behaviours, emerged at age thirty-two months. B's play behaviour slowly became more focused and was increasingly characterised by a marked increase in object-directed aggression. Simultaneously, B became attached to his first transitional object, that he hugged and kissed. This flowering expression of aggression and subsequent libidinal behaviour was accompanied by the development of semi-symbolic doll play that coalesced around themes of eating, sleeping, and bathing. At age thirty-four months, B began to use three-word sentences and could utilise this new capacity to verbalise his feelings toward his parents and his therapist.

In retrospect, it was apparent that the initial period of treatment between fifteen and twenty-five months of age had permitted B to express toward the outside world much of the rage he had formerly turned against himself. As the aggression emerged, at first diffusely and then in a focused object-related manner, the impaired ego functions began to improve, culminating in the beginning of communicative speech and the advent of symbolic play. These gains were confirmed by the findings on the psychological testing done at the end of his second year of treatment when he was three years old; of thirty points within the year. Although some evidence of his former pathology remained, the overall clinical picture resembled that of a neurotic rather than a psychotic illness.

When B was thirty-seven months old, the family moved from our area, and B was treated thereafter by a particularly empathic speech therapist who continued to provide B with a special one-to-one relationship. B was also enrolled in a neighbourhood cooperative nursery.

The family returned for follow-up when B was almost four years old. He was then attached to his speech therapist and had utilised the normal nursery situation appropriately. He was now well related and clearly remembered and responded to important people appropriately and to playthings in the nursery, and the harsh, bark like quality that had characterised his speech had faded. He now spoke fluently but with some mild stammering and stuttering. The quality of the mother–child interaction was strikingly improved in that the mother appeared to derive great pleasure from her newly acquired ability to recognise and respond to B's needs. The brief psychological testing during the follow-up visit showed that B had maintained the gains achieved during the previous year. There had been major strides in his symbolic play and language, and the traces of his former ego deviance were at a minimum.

This was a successful outcome, in contrast to other children in whom the improvement was painfully slow and far less dramatic. However, this illustrates that illness can be dramatically modified, particularly if treatment begins early enough, and if the parents are involved in the treatment process.

Treatment results

The prognosis was enormously enhanced if the child was below three years of age on admission and if the mother was included from the very start, not only as part of our therapeutic team approach, but also in individual treatment. With her participation, although it was a long struggle, the outlook was far more favourable. The nursery setting was appropriate for the treatment of psychotic children, provided each child was assigned to an individual therapist as well as participating in the group and provided there were no more than three psychotic children in the total group of eight children at any one time.

Discussion

The vital importance of the early coenesthetic experience during the first six months of life, that is, the combination of sensory inputs involved in close physical contact with the mother, has long been stressed by Mahler (1963, 1965, 1968, etc.), Spitz (1945), and others. This seems to provide the basis for the establishment of a *core sense of self* and probably must be available during a certain critical period if normal development is to proceed at all.

Beginning at about five or six months, the visual–motor apparatus gradually takes over, providing the principal modality for self–object differentiation. Apparently this can occur only when the earlier core body-self has already developed. Without this, adequate hand–eye–mouth integration does not take place, and sequential psychosexual organisation, progressive self–object differentiation, and adequate ego development, particularly in the symbolic function, do not take place.

We are increasingly impressed by the balance that must be maintained between a sufficient maternal libidinal investment on the one hand, and an excessively strong libidinal and aggressive tie by which some mothers bind themselves to their children in a crippling, disharmonious union. Perhaps the most vivid and beautiful illustration of the optimal kind of tie between mother and child has been captured by Daniel Stern (1973) in his analysis of gazing patterns between mother and infant. A mother who can engage her child in visual play and yet allow him to withdraw and return again when his inner state of arousal requires the presence of further stimulation is likely to be able to facilitate his total development in a manner that is optimal for him.

The mothers of our psychotic children, for reasons of their own pathology or pathology within their children, were unable to engage them in a strong enough libidinal tie. This interfered with the normal emergence of oral, anal, and genital phase dominance and drive modulation; inadequate self–object differentiation; and delay in ego functioning, particularly in regard to the development of secondary process thinking; and the autonomous functioning of visual perception, completing the psychopathological picture.

There seems to be good evidence for our work with these psychotic children that the three developmental lines are interrelated; self–object differentiation is delayed, the orderly sequence of psychosexual development is disturbed, phase dominance is not achieved, and ego development in every sector is delayed from the earliest months on.

Summary

While the psychopathological entity known as early childhood psychosis has been recognised as a clinical disorder for many years, considerable disagreement remains regarding its aetiology, the details of its symptomatology, and optimal treatment methods. A body of data is available to us from a ten-year project with ten psychotic children, ranging in age from thirteen months to three-and-three-quarter years when treatment was begun with them and their parents. Analysis of these data some five years after the termination of the project provides insights into the nature of the illness and effectiveness of treatment methods.

References

Bender, L., & Farretta, G. (1973). The relationship between childhood schizophrenia and adult schizophrenia. In: A. Kaplan & H. Morton (Eds.), *Genetic Factors in Schizophrenia*. Springfield, IL: Charles C. Thomas.

Bettelheim, B. (1967). *The Empty Fortress*. New York: Free Press.

Bomberg, D., Szurek, S., & Etemad, J. (1973). A statistical study of a group of psychotic children. In: S. Szurek & I. Berlin (Eds.), *Clinical Studies in Childhood Psychoses*. New York: Brunner/Mazel.

Call, J. (1983). Toward a nosology of psychiatric disorders in infancy. In: J. Call, E. Galenson, & R. L. Tyson (Eds.), *Frontiers in Infant Psychiatry, Vol. I* (pp. 117–128). New York: Basic Books.

DeMeyer, M., Norton, J., Allen, J., Steel, R., & Brown, S. (1973). Prognosis in autism. *Journal Autism Childhood Schizophrenia, 3*: 199.

Emde, R. N., & Sorce, J. F. (1983). The rewards of infancy: emotional availability and maternal referencing. In: J. Call, E. Galenson, & R. L. Tyson (Eds.), *Frontiers in Infant Psychiatry, Vol. I* (pp. 17–30). New York: Basic Books.

Frank, G. (1965). The role of the family in the development of psychopathology. *Psychological Bulletin, 64*: 191.

Franknoi, J., & Ruttenberg, C. (1971). Formulation of the dynamic factors underlying infantile autism. *Journal American Academy of Child Psychology, 10*: 713.

Freud, A. (1972). Comment on aggression. *International Journal of Psychoanalysis, 55*: 163–171.

Furer, M. (1964). The development of a pre-school symbiotic boy. *The Psychoanalytic Study of the Child, 29*: 448–469.

Galenson, E. (1971). A consideration of the nature of thought in childhood play. In: J. B. McDevitt & C. F. Settlage (Eds.), *Separation–Individuation: Essays in Honor of Margaret Mahler* (pp. 41–74). Madison, CT: International Universities Press.

Galenson, E., & Roiphe, H. (1976). Some suggested revisions concerning early female development. *Journal of the American Psychoanalytic Association, 24S*: 29–57.

Galenson, E., & Roiphe, H. (1979). Development of sexual identity: discoveries and implications. In: T. B. Karasu & C. W. Socarides (Eds.), *On Sexuality: Psychoanalytic Implications* (pp. 1–17). New York: International Universities Press.

Galenson, E., & Roiphe, H. (1980). The preoedipal development of the boy. *Journal of the American Psychoanalytic Association, 28*: 805–827.

Mahler, M. (1963). Thoughts about development and individuation. *The Psychoanalytic Study of the Child, 18*: 307–324.

Mahler, M. (1965). On early infantile psychosis: the symbiotic and autistic syndromes. *Journal of the American Academy of Child Psychiatry, 4*: 554–568.

Mahler, M. (1966). Notes on the development of basic moods: the depressive affect. In: R. M. Loewenstein, L. M. Newman, M. Schur, & A. J. Solnit (Eds.), *Psychoanalysis—A General Psychology: Essays in Honor of Heinz Hartmann* (pp. 152–168). New York: International Universities Press.

Mahler, M. (1968). *On Human Symbiosis and the Vicissitudes of Individuation, Vol. 1: Infantile Psychosis*. New York: International Universities Press.

Mahler, M., & Furer, M. (1960). Observations on research regarding the "symbiotic syndrome" of infantile psychosis. *The Psychoanalytic Quarterly, 29*: 317–327.

Mahler, M., & Gosliner, B. J. (1955). On symbiotic child psychosis. Genetic, dynamic and restitutive aspects. *Psychoanalytic Study of the Child, 18*: 325–342.

Mahler, M., Pine, F., & Bergman, A. (1975). *The Psychological Birth of the Human Infant*. New York: Basic Books.

Massie, H. (1977). Patterns of mother–infant behavior and subsequent Childhood psychosis. *Child Psychiatry and Human Development, 7*: 211–230.

Massie, H., & Campbell, B. K. (1983). The Massie–Campbell Scale of mother–infant attachment indicators during stress (AIDS Scale). In: J. D. Call, E. Galenson, & R. Tyson (Eds.), *Frontiers in Infant Psychiatry* (pp. 394–412). New York: Basic Books.

Mykelbust, H., Killen, J., & Bannochie, M. (1972). Emotional characteristics of learning disability. *Journal of Autism Childhood Schizophrenia, 2*: 151.

Nagera, H. (1964). On arrest in development, fixation and regression. *The Psychoanalytic Study of the Child, 19*: 222–239.

Ornitz, E., & Ritvo, S. (1976). The syndrome of autism. *American Journal of Psychiatry, 135*: 1371–1374.

Pollin, W., Strabenau, J., Mosher, L., & Tupin, J. (1966). Life history differences in identical twins discordant for schizophrenia. *American Journal of Orthopsychiatry, 36*: 492.

Rimland, B. (1964). *Infantile Autism*. New York: Appleton-Century Crofts.

Roiphe, H. (1968). On an early genital phase: with an addendum on genesis. *The Psychoanalytic Study of the Child, 23*: 348–365.

Roiphe, H. (1973a). Some thoughts on childhood psychosis. *The Psychoanalytic Study of the Child*, 28: 131–145.

Roiphe, H. (1973b). The infantile fetish. *The Psychoanalytic Quarterly*, 28: 147–166.

Roiphe, H., & Galenson, E. (1972). Early genital activity and the castration complex. *The Psychoanalytic Quarterly*, 41: 334–347.

Roiphe, H., & Galenson, E. (1973). Object loss and early sexual development. *The Psychoanalytic Quarterly*, 42: 73–90.

Roiphe, H., & Galenson, E. (1975). Some observations on the transitional object and infantile fetish. *The Psychoanalytic Quarterly*, 44: 206–231.

Ruttenberg, C., Kalish, B. I., Fiese, B. H., & D'Orazio, A. (1983). Early infant assessment using the Behavior-Rating Instrument for Autistic and Atypical Children (BRIAAC). In: J. D. Call, E. Galenson, & R. Tyson (Eds.), *Frontiers in Infant Psychiatry* (pp. 413–424). New York: Basic Books.

Rutter, M. (1967). Psychotic disorders in early childhood. *British Journal of Psychiatry*, 110: 133.

Rutter, M. (1972). Childhood schizophrenia reconsidered. *Journal of Autism Childhood Schizophrenia*, 2: 315.

Sander, L. W. (1983). Polarity, paradox and the organizing process in Development. In: J. D. Call, E. Galenson, & R. Tyson (Eds.), *Frontiers in Infant Psychiatry* (pp. 333–346). New York: Basic Books.

Spitz, R. A. (1945). Diacritic and coanesthetic organization. The psychiatric significance of a functional division of the nervous system into a sensory and emotive part. *Psychoanalytic Review*, 32: 146–162.

Stern, D. (1971). A micro-analysis of mother-infant interaction. *Journal American Academy of Child Psychiatry*, 10: 501.

Stern, D. (1973). Mother and infant at play: the dyadic interaction Involving facial, vocal and gaze behaviors. In: M. Lewis & L. Rosenblum (Eds.), *The Origins of Behavior, Vol. I*. New York: Wiley.

Stern, D. (1983). Early transmission of affect: Some research issues. In: J. D. Call, E. Galenson, & R. Tyson (Eds.), *Frontiers in Infant Psychiatry* (pp. 117–128). New York: Basic Books.

Szurek, S., & Berlin, I. (Eds.) (1973). *Clinical Studies in Childhood Psychosis*. New York: Brunner/Mazel.

Treffert, D. A. (1970). Epidemiology of infantile autism. *Archives of General Psychiatry*, 22: 431.

Wing, L., & Wing, J. (1971). Multiple impairments in early childhood autism. *Journal Autism Childhood Schizophrenia*, 1: 311.

INDEX

Abraham, K., 104
Academy of Child Psychiatry, xlviii
Academy of Pediatrics, xlviii
acting out, xxx, 17, 28, 31, 35, 43, 51, 120, 188 *see also*: sexual
   behaviour, xxxiii, 16, 26, 28–29, 32
Adelson, E., 162–163
Albert Einstein College of Medicine, xviii–xix, xxxiv, xlix, liii, 32, 47, 95, 108
Albert Einstein Sensory-Motor Scales, xxxviii
Allen, J., 191–192
anal, xliv, lvii, 28–29, 56, 63, 75, 77–78, 85, 118, 131, 134, 137, 139–141, 152, 154, 170, 196, 201, 204
   area, 56–57, 131–132, 196
   awareness, xlv, liv, lvii, 83, 131–132, 140
   function, 56–57, 62, 64, 78, 196
   phase, xlv, lvi, 74–75, 77–78, 131, 136–137, 170, 178, 195–196, 207
   zone, xlv, 56, 58, 131, 134, 154, 196
anger, 61, 65, 72, 85, 101, 110–111, 113, 127, 165, 170–173, 183, 185, 188
   with mother, lviii, 10, 48, 64, 102, 118, 170, 172, 183, 185
Anthony, E. J., xlv–xlvi
anxiety, lv, lviii, 10, 30, 49, 53, 55, 58, 63, 65, 69–70, 75, 77–78, 86, 99, 104, 108–109, 111, 114–120, 124, 127, 132, 134, 136–137, 139, 149, 162, 171, 173, 181–182, 185
   see also: castration
   acute, lii, lv
   extreme/severe, 9, 146, 183, 187
   genital, 86
   pre-oedipal, lv, 87, 139, 141

212 INDEX

separation, lv, lviii, 54, 57, 63, 75, 77, 87, 103, 109, 115, 139, 146, 183, 186–187, 195
stranger, 29, 53–54, 56, 58, 63–64, 68–69, 168, 195
unresolved, xxii
Arlow, J., liii
Association of Child Psychoanalysis, xlvi
attachment, lviii, 56, 114, 138–139, 165, 168–169, 173, 183, 204
infant, lviii
libidinal, 138, 202
maternal, lviii
oedipal, 136, 165
autistic/autism, xxxii, xlvi–xlvii, 162, 192–195, 202

Bannochie, M., 192
Barnard College, xvii
Barnett, H., xxvii, xxxiv–xxxvi
Bass, M., xxv
Baumgartner, L., xxvi–xxvii
Bell, A., 98, 117
Bellvue Hospital, xvii, xxv
Bender, L., xxxii, 192
Berenberg, S., xxvi
Bergman, A., xlvi, 88, 162, 178, 192–194
Berlin, I., 191
Bettelheim, B., 192
Bibring, G. L., 163
Birksted-Breen, D., 88
bladder
control, 101, 117, 123–124
function, 93, 107, 123
Blau, S., 130, 178
Blos, P., Jr., 163
Bomberg, D., 192
Bornstein, B., xxxiii
bowel, 29, 101, 124, 131, 154
control, 101, 123
function, 93, 107, 123, 196
movement, 96–100, 118

Brazelton, B., xlvi–xlvii
Brown, S., 191–192
Bruner, J., 3

Call, J., xix–xx, xlv, xlviii, lvi, 192
Campbell, B. K., 193
case studies/clinical illustrations
Ann, 28
B, 203–206
Ben, 179–188
Billy, 108–120, 124–127
Jake, 4–7
Janet, 167–174
Julie, 75–77
Malcolm, 146
Martha (mother of Janet), 168–171, 173
Ruth, 9–10, 29–30, 47, 52–65, 68–69, 72
Sandy, 30
Suzy, 95–102
castration, 86–87, 94, 101, 118–119, 139, 149–150, 187
anxiety, lv, 10, 31, 65, 86–87, 101–102, 104, 118–119, 130, 137, 139, 141, 146, 149, 187
complex, 85, 103–104, 141, 150
pre-oedipal, 138–141, 144
reaction(s), xl–xli, liii, lvi, 9, 48, 64, 81–84, 86–88, 93–94, 100, 102–103, 107, 118, 136–138, 140–141, 144, 149
Child Development Project, xix, 163
child/children *see also*: deaf, mother, observation(al)
analysis/analyst, xxviii, xxxiii, xlv–xlvii, xlix, 89
development, xxxv, xl, xlii–xliii, 70
–parent relationship, 11, 82, 166, 182, 192
psychiatrist(s)/psychiatry, xviii, xxvii–xxix, xxxiv–xxxvi, xxxviii–xl, xlii–xliii, xlvi, xlviii–xlix, 52
psychosis, 191–193, 201, 207

Chodorow, N., 86
Cinderella, 180
Columbia Psychoanalytic Group, xxxv
Columbia University's College of Physicians and Surgeons, xvii
Commonwealth Fellowship, xvii, xxv–xxvi, li
communication, xviii, xx, lx, 3, 8, 17–18, 35–37, 39, 41–43, 73–76, 78, 138, 166, 168, 174, 197–199, 205
conscious(ness), lix, 17, 23–24, 64, 70, 82, 129, 146, 155, 172 *see also*: preconscious(ness), thought, unconscious(ness)
  awareness, xix, 4, 143
Coornand, A., xxxiv
Corman, H., xxxiv–xxxv
Cornell University Medical College, xlix

deaf, 21, 202
  children, lvi–lvii
  infants, xxxix
  mothers, lvi–lvii
  subjects, 21
defecation, liv, 30, 62–63, 77, 131, 154, 196, 201
deHirsch, K., xxx
DeMeyer, M., 191–192
depression/depressive, xli, xlviii, lix, 49, 94, 103, 108, 153, 169–171, 181, 184–185, 200, 204
  moods, 48, 102, 138
  reaction, 10, 48, 64
Diethelm, O., xxvi, xlix
doll(s), xvii, lv–lvi, 20, 28–29, 51, 54, 57, 60–63, 65, 77, 99, 101, 132, 135–136, 138, 148, 156, 172, 179–182, 184, 187, 201, 205
  see also: toy(s)
Donne, J., 127
D'Orazio, A., 192–193
Dore, J., 3

dream, xxi, 23, 70–71, 125, 186
Dupkin, C., 177–178

ego, 5, 17, 48, 77, 84, 110, 116, 124, 131, 136, 163, 194–196, 206
  body, 5
  -centric, 18
  development, 11, 68, 82, 84, 137, 141, 184, 196, 200, 206–207
  early, xx, 9, 68, 74, 193
  function(s), xx, 9–10, 15–16, 54, 57–58, 65, 74, 81, 102, 116, 140–141, 201, 205, 207
  super-, 85
Elise, D., 86
Elkisch, P., 15, 24
Emde, R. N., 193
envy, 85, 153
  breast, 154
  penis, 85, 94–95, 177
  pregnancy, 154
Erhardt, A., 129, 178
Erikson, E., xliv, xlix, 15, 26, 148–149, 153
Escalona, S., xix, xxxiv–xxxvi, xxxviii–xli, xlix, 6
Etemad, J., 192

faeces, 30, 56, 62–63, 68, 76, 100, 117, 123, 131–132, 134, 154, 158, 187, 196 *see also*: bowel
Farretta, G., 192
Fields, B., 182
Fiese, B. H., 192–193
Fraad, L., xxvi, xxxiv–xxxvi
Fraiberg, S., 162–163
Frank, G., 192
Franknoi, J., 200
Fraser, A. C., 112
Freud, A., xxviii, 94–95, 197
Freud, S., xviii–xix, xxvi, 5, 15–17, 83–85, 95, 125, 130–131, 140–141, 151–153, 155–157

214   INDEX

Furer, M., 51, 95, 120, 194, 196
Furth, H. G., 21, 23

Galenson, E. (*passim*)
    cited works, xvi, xviii–xxii, xli, xlv,
        xlix, 9–10, 35, 49, 75, 81–83, 85,
        93–94, 104, 113, 130, 143, 145,
        148, 161, 163, 178–179, 182,
        188, 194, 196
Garlock, J., lvi
Geleerd, E., xxviii
gender, xxi, xxii, 86, 129, 151–152,
        155, 157–158, 178, 181
    choice, xxi
    definition, 87, 155
    development, 151, 155, 157
    differences/differentiation, xlix,
        152, 155, 158
    disorder, lvii, lix, 178
    disturbance, xvi, lvii, lix, 152,
        177–179, 183, 188
    identity, xxii, 129–130, 178–179, 183
    specific, xix, 143
genital(s) (*passim*) *see also*: anxiety,
    play, sensation(s), stimulation
    area, 29, 57, 60, 69–70, 96, 98–99,
        119, 134–135, 137, 148, 154–155
    arousal, 59–60, 118–119, 123, 126,
        146, 149
    awareness, xli, 49, 57, 83, 140, 145,
        147–148
    curiosity, 10, 57, 62, 132
    development, 47, 130
    difference, xxi, xli, liv, 9–10, 29, 47,
        57, 59–61, 83–88, 100, 136, 139,
        147–148, 152–153, 158, 183
    discovery, 48, 54, 131
    interest, 57, 107, 119
    outline, 93, 107, 120
    phase, xlv, 70, 83, 85, 118, 123–124,
        134–135, 139–140, 144–145,
        147–149, 152, 154, 158,
        172–173, 178–179, 195, 207
    zone, 58, 60, 136, 140

Gosliner, B. J., 117, 194
Green, R., 178
Greenacre, P., xvi, xviii, xxvi, xlvii,
    li–liii, 8, 12, 17, 27, 31, 40, 44,
    47–48, 59, 74–75, 87–88, 94, 100,
    117, 135, 148, 153, 156
Greenson, R., 178
Groos, K., 37
Grossman, W., 85

Hampson, J. G., 178
Hampson, J. L., 178
Hartmann, H., xxiv
Heider, G. M., xlix
Heksch, B., li–lii
Himmelstein, A., xviii
Himmelstein, P., xviii

image/imagery, 15, 21–22, 65, 89, 113
    see also: mental, object, self
    auditory, 27
    body, xli, xliii, 15, 41, 68, 103, 133,
        136, 141, 149, 152, 155, 182
    development, xliii
    disturbance, xli
    inner/internal, 23, 25, 38, 41
    maternal, 61, 64–65
    mental, 21
    mother, 48, 102, 111, 113, 116
    thought, 27
imagination/imaginative, 23, 27, 38,
    89–90, 156 *see also*: play
impairment, lvii, 205 *see also*:
    language
    hearing, lvi–lvii, 167
instinctual
    development, 58, 82, 143
    drives, 51
    modes, 26
    phase(s), xliv–xlv, 82, 143, 200
    pressures, 49
    zones, 88
International Psycho-Analytical
    Congress, Stockholm, xix

Jacobson, E., 85
Johns Hopkins's Henry Phipps
    Clinic, xlix

Kalish, B. I., 192–193
Kaplan, B., 7, 26, 50
Kaufmann, M. R., xxvii–xxix
Kestenberg, J., xlvi
Khan, M., xix
Killen, J., 192
Kleeman, J. A., 126, 130
Kramer, J., xl, xlii
Kris, E., xxxiv, 126
Kris, M., xxxiii
Kubie, L., xxi–xxii
Kulish, N., 86, 88

LaFarge, L., xv–xvi, 89
Lamar, N., xxv
Langer, S. K., xvi, xliv, 3–4, 7–8, 12,
    18–21, 24–26, 28, 38
language, xv–xvi, xlix, liv, lvii, 5, 8,
    11, 16–23, 25–27, 42, 73, 77–78, 98,
    157, 167–168, 173, 199, 202, 206
  acquisition, 73, 157
  development, liii–liv, lvi–lvii,
    23–24, 42, 76, 78, 125, 170, 184,
    199, 201
  discursive, 8, 19
  expressive, 11, 73, 75–76, 168, 170
  impairment, 21, 43
Lebovici, S., xx
Lenox Hill Hospital, xxvi, xxxii
Levine, M., xxv
Lewis, M. M., 36
Lexington School for the Deaf, xviii
libidinal/libido, 7, 44, 82, 138, 171,
    197, 201–202, 205–207
  aggressive, 11, 73–75, 78, 207
  phase, 5, 42, 44, 67, 195
Lipton, R., 130
Loewenstein, R., xxviii, xxxiv
Long Island University Hospital,
    xxvii–xxviii

Mahler, M., xvi, xl–xli, xliv–xlvii,
    liii–liv, 7, 15–16, 24, 39, 47–48, 51,
    83, 88, 95, 102–103, 117–118, 120,
    123, 138, 144, 152, 155, 162, 178,
    192–195, 202, 206
Massie, H., 193, 200
Masters Children's Center, 95, 120,
    123
masturbation, liv, 49, 59, 87, 93, 96,
    99–100, 103, 107, 119–120, 123,
    130, 134–138, 141, 153, 172, 179
  see also: stimulation
Maxwell, G., 38
Mayer, E. L., xvii, 83–84, 86
mechanism
  defence, 48, 102
  introjective-projective, 40, 60, 116
memory, xxix, 17, 23, 40, 70, 110, 116,
    125–126, 135, 162–163, 170, 172,
    188
Menninger Foundation, xxviii, xlix
mental
  activity, 23, 125
  combination, 22
  experimentation, 22
  function, 21
  health, xxv
  image/imagery, 21
  imitation, 23
  life, 12
  organisation, 7, 15, 21, 24, 35
  problem solving, 23
  processes, 16, 31, 124
  representation, 10–11, 22, 48, 50,
    54, 56–57, 62, 64–65, 71,
    148–149, 168, 172, 195
  self, 55, 62
Meyer, A., xlix
Meyer, J. K., 88, 177–178
Michels, R., 89
Miller, R., 130
Money, J., 129, 178
Mosher, L., 192
Moss, D., 86

mother (*passim*) *see also*: anger, deaf, image/imagery
  and child, xxxvi, xxxviii, xlvii, 78, 111, 114, 165, 169, 171–172, 194, 207
  bad, 48, 102, 113
  body, 40, 50, 53, 134
  –child, xlii–xliii
    interaction, xxxviii, xli, 7, 194, 205
    pair, 52, 95, 108, 203
    relationship, lvi–lvii, 7, 10–11, 30, 48–49, 61, 64, 74, 78, 139, 164, 168
  good, 48, 102, 183
  –infant
    interaction, xxxix, xlvi, 74–75
    relationship, 162
  urination, 133
Mount Sinai Hospital, xvii, xxv, xxvii–xxix, xxxiv, lvi
Muller, F. M., 35
Mykelbust, H., 192

Nachman, P., xvi
Nagera, H., 196, 201
National Institute of Mental Health (NIMH), xxxviii
New York Psychoanalytic Institute, xviii, xxxiii, xlv
New York Psychoanalytic Society, xvi
Newman, L., 178
normal development, xxxiv, xxxviii, xli, 9, 24, 48, 52, 162, 193, 206
Norton, J., 191–192
nursery, xl–xliv, xlvi, liii, lix, 51–53, 56–60, 69, 71, 94–96, 99, 101, 108–109, 111, 113–115, 117, 119, 144–145, 152, 195, 197–198, 200, 204–206
  research, xlvi, liii, lvi, 28, 47, 83, 95, 108, 123, 144, 200
  school, 68, 72, 169, 180

session, 52, 61, 111, 114, 204
therapeutic, xv, xviii, xlvi, 161, 194, 197, 200, 204

object (*passim*) *see also*: self
  bad, 62, 114
  developing, 16, 47, 53–54, 102–103, 120, 137
  directed aggression, 55, 205
  external, 71, 81, 156
  good, 114
  image, 114
  internal, 81
  loss, 30–31, 62, 75, 78, 85, 87, 104, 116, 118–120, 124, 136–137, 140–141, 144
  love, 124, 127, 138
  new, 25
  phallic-shaped, 58, 135, 148–149
  primary, 43, 156–157, 184
  relations, xlv, lvii–lviii, 10, 16, 31, 42, 47, 53–54, 57, 65, 81–82, 84, 87–88, 102, 120, 129, 136, 138, 140, 144, 152, 155, 177, 195–196, 201, 205
  transitional, 11, 44, 56, 61, 63, 76, 135, 139, 144, 156, 186, 202, 205
observation(al)
  child, lii, 81–82, 88–89
  direct, 28, 31, 49–51, 67, 74, 108, 123, 125, 145, 147, 152, 157–158, 194–195
  infant, 49–51, 67, 73–74, 86, 89, 130, 132, 161, 163
  material, 28, 31
  psychoanalytic, 125–126
oedipal, xl, 85, 93, 103, 107, 130, 138, 140, 152, 154–155, 157–158, 167, 177 *see also*: anxiety, attachment
  dynamics, 83, 87
  period/phase, 65, 83–84, 86–88, 130, 140, 147, 152, 167
  pre-, lv, 11, 87, 119, 130, 136–141, 144, 162, 166–167, 188, 195

Olesker, W., 86
O'Neil Hawkins, M., xxxiii
oral, 39, 50, 56, 70, 74–75, 78, 85, 133, 137, 140, 170, 188, 196, 201, 203, 207
    aggression, lviii, 74–75, 77–78
    behaviour, 53, 55, 126
    rage, 74, 188
Oremland, J., xvii, 89
Ornitz, E., 192

paediatric/paediatrician, xv, xvii–xviii, xxv–xxvii, xxix–xxx, xxxiv–xxxvii, xlvi, xlviii–xlix, li, 53, 69, 195, 199, 203–204
Payne Whitney Clinic, xvii–xviii, xxvi, xxviii, xlix, li
Peller, L. E., xliv, xlix, 15
penis, 4–6, 48–49, 61, 70, 83–85, 96–100, 117–119, 130–133, 135, 148–150, 156–157, 185–187, 197 *see also*: envy
phallic/phallus, lv, lviii, 7, 62–63, 70–71, 83–84, 87, 94, 120, 133, 135, 141, 146, 148–150, 154, 172, 178–179, 183, 185 *see also*: object
    phase, xlv, 84, 86–88, 94, 118, 178
    shape, 58, 62
Piaget, J., xvi, xxxviii–xxxix, xliv, 3, 7, 18, 21–25
Piaget Object Permanence Developmental Scales, 6
Pine, F., xlvi, 51, 88, 95, 120, 162, 178, 192–194
play (*passim*) *see also*: doll(s), symbolic, toy(s)
    activity, 10, 36–37, 41–42, 56
    behaviour, 16, 23–24, 26, 31–32, 47, 65, 205
    childhood/children's, xliv, xlix, liv, 5, 7–8, 16, 21, 35, 49, 67, 70
    derivative, xliv, lvii, 51, 131, 170, 185, 205
    genital, xliv, 148, 150
    distorted, 27
    early, 36, 49–50, 62
    experience, 25
    fantasy, 136
    -ful(ness), 37, 41–43, 55, 110, 187, 202
    functional, 23–24
    genital, 131
    -ground, xli–xlii, 52, 95, 108
    imagination/imaginative, 138, 178
    infantile, 44, 50–51
    non-verbal, 16, 20, 35
    normal, 27
    obsessional, 76
    -room, 168, 181–183, 187
    silent, 16
    therapy, xxxi
    -things, 37, 205
    visual, 37, 207
Pollin, W., 192
Potter, H., xxvii, xxix
preconscious(ness), 16–17 *see also*: conscious(ness), unconscious(ness)
Provence, S., 130
psychological
    complaints, 181
    development, xix, xlvi, 11, 143, 145, 193
    disorders, 161, 182
    disturbances, 163–164, 193
    entity, 191
    organisation, 131
    problems, xxxvi, 161, 181
    processes, 191
    structure, 165
psychosexual
    development, liv, 9, 81–86, 88, 90, 126–127, 140, 147, 149, 170, 195, 200–201, 207
    organisation, 10, 206
    phase, xix, liv, 143
    sphere, 138
    zone, 5
Pumpian-Mindlin, E., li

rage, lviii–lix, 30–31, 74, 110, 181, 183, 187–188, 205
Rand School of Social Science, xvii
Rapaport, D., xlix
repression, xix, lix, 60, 133, 156, 172, 179, 184
Rimland, B., 192
Ritvo, S., 84, 192
Roiphe, H. (*passim*)
    cited works, xvi, xix, xli, xlv, liii, 9, 48, 54, 81–82, 93–94, 104, 107, 118, 123, 130, 143–145, 148, 161, 163, 178–179, 194
Rosen, V., liii
Rosenbaum, M., xxxiv, xl
Rothenberg, M., xxxvii
Ruosso Therapeutic Nursery, xviii
Ruttenberg, C., 192–193, 200
Rutter, M., 191–192

Sachs, L. J., xl, 94
Sander, L. W., xlv, xlvii, 193
Schafer, R., 85
Schechter, D., xxxv
schizophrenia, 116, 192
self, lvii–lviii, 10, 28, 31, 48, 50, 54–55, 86–88, 93, 102, 107, 112, 116, 118–119, 124–125, 129, 140, 151, 154–156, 178–179, 195–196, 201, 206 *see also*: mental, stimulation
    -absorbed, 131, 135
    -aware(ness), xxi
    -biting, 29, 55
    body, 41, 59, 103, 157, 206
    -definition, 113, 152, 158
    -directed aggression, 55, 60
    -disintegration, 136
    -esteem, 10, 64–65, 102–103
    exploration, 28, 50
    -identity, 65, 87
    -image, 42, 62, 74
    -object differentiation, 59, 82, 134, 143, 200–202, 206–207
    -observation, 110
    -part, 156–157
    -representation, lviii, 62, 119–120, 127, 164, 171, 173, 183
    -sufficiency, 53
    -supporting, xxxii
Senn, M. J. E., xv, xix, xxv, xxvii
sensation(s), 5–6, 8–9, 30, 57, 59, 64, 70, 107, 112, 124, 194
    bodily/body, 24, 28–31, 50, 74
    genital, 29, 59–60, 85, 93, 107, 118, 123, 133, 140, 144, 148, 183
    sexual, 64
    somatic, 70
sensorimotor, 21–24, 26, 37–39, 43, 50, 191
sexual (*passim*) *see also*:
    psychosexual
    acting out, 30
    activity, 48–49, 93–94, 98–99, 101, 107, 151
    arousal, 59, 93, 102–103, 107, 120, 145
    behaviour, xl, 97–99, 126
    bi-, 86, 177
    curiosity, 59, 97–98, 101–103
    development, xl, xliv, liii, 48, 81, 93, 95, 103, 107–108, 124, 126, 141, 151, 161
    difference(s), xv, 9, 48, 58, 64–65, 85, 102, 123–124, 135–137, 139–140, 147, 158, 172
    excitement, 72, 83
    hetero-, 165
    homo-, 181, 188
    identity, xvi–xvii, xix, 129–130, 133, 140–141, 143, 146
    interest, 9, 48–49, 93, 99, 101, 107
sexuality, liii–liv, 86, 139, 151, 155, 183, 201
    bi-, 178
    early, xix, 81
    homo-, 188
    infantile, xix, liv, 81, 130

Shapiro, V., 162–163
Sheera, 182
shower(ing), 63, 96–97, 99, 133, 135, 186
Sleeping Beauty, 180
Snow White, 180
Socarides, C., 87
Solnit, A., xvi, 89
Sorce, J. F., 193
speech, 17–18, 35–36, 40–43, 50, 54–55, 58, 65, 73–75, 77–78, 157, 162, 195, 199, 204–205
  external, 18
  infant's, 42, 74
  inner, 18
  outer, 18
  pathology, xxx
  vocal, 17–18
Sperling, M., 178
sphincter, 42, 74–75, 77–78, 94, 98, 124, 152, 154
Spitz, R. A., 130, 153, 206
splitting, 65, 102, 113–114, 164, 168, 171, 173–174, 183, 188
Steel, R., 191–192
Stern, D., xlvi–xlvii, 193, 207
Stewart, W., 85
stimulation, 38–41, 44, 67, 70, 75, 97, 120, 126, 131, 134, 136, 178, 182, 188, 193, 207
  external, 37–38, 43
  genital(s), 152, 179
  self-, 130–131, 134–135, 179
stimuli, xx, 37–38, 40, 42, 203
Stoller, R., 129, 148, 177–178
Stone, L., 74
stool *see*: bowel, faeces
Strabenau, J., 192
subjectivity, 12, 73, 151
  inter-, 89
symbol, lvii, 4, 20–21, 23, 25, 28, 50, 58–59, 68, 157
  formation, 5, 11–12, 27, 50, 67–68, 71, 154

symbolic, 5–7, 11–12, 22–25, 28, 31, 41–42, 44, 51, 54, 58, 60, 62, 70, 103, 135, 158, 200
  development, xliv, 6, 10, 64, 75–76, 182
  element, 19–20
  fantasy, 153
  function, xliv, 4, 7, 11–12, 15, 23, 25, 31–32, 35, 55, 75, 78, 138, 144, 149, 195–196, 200–202, 206
  games, 24, 26
  play, xliv, 10, 23–25, 27, 31, 51, 54–55, 63–64, 76–78, 113, 202, 205–206
  representation, 3–4, 7–9, 11, 31
  substitution, 156, 182, 186
  thought, 3–4, 8, 10, 23–25, 153
symbolisation, xv–xvi, 4–7, 10–11, 21, 28, 31, 47, 58, 63, 65, 195, 202
symbolism, 8, 18–20, 24, 27, 42, 49–51
  development of, xliv, 3, 8, 18
  discursive, 19–20
  musical, 8, 18–20, 24, 26, 50
  pre-representational, 8
  presentational, 19–21, 26, 28
  primitive, 9, 49
  verbal, 25
Szurek, S., 191–192

temper tantrums, 54, 61, 76, 124, 168, 170, 185–186
therapeutic model, 162–163, 166
  psycho-, 165
  tripartite, xvi, 161
Thompson, N. L., xxi, xlix
Thomson, J. A., 37–38
thought *see also*: image/imagery, symbolic
  conscious, 16–17
  non-verbal, 16–17, 23, 27, 31–32
  pre-linguistic, 4, 8
  preverbal, 12, 17
  process(es), 12, 16–17, 19, 21, 35, 41–42

unconscious, 17
verbal, 16, 18
toilet(ing), 31, 54, 56–57, 61–63, 70, 76, 96–100, 109, 114, 117, 132–133, 135, 144, 196 *see also*: toy
   flush(ing), 54, 57, 62–63, 99–100, 104, 114, 132
   handle, 10, 57–58, 62
   paper, 61, 117
   training, 48–49, 56, 65, 68, 76, 93, 97, 101, 107, 123, 131–132, 139, 180
Topeka, xxviii, xxxvi, xlix
toy(s), xliv, lvii, 4–5, 10, 28–29, 37, 51, 54, 56, 58, 62–63, 65, 108, 110, 119, 135 *see also*: doll(s), play
   animal, 132, 148, 168, 170, 180–182, 187, 196–197, 202
   bear, 25, 29, 61
   bed, 20
   broken, 10, 58, 61, 63, 137
   broom, 4
   car, 7, 135
   dog, 29, 61–62
   horses, 63
   toilet, 29
transference, 163–164, 166
Treffert, D. A., 192
Tupin, J., 192
Tyson, P., 86
Tyson, R., xx

unconscious(ness), 5, 11, 24, 129, 146, 155, 163, 194 *see also*: conscious(ness), preconscious(ness), thought
   fantasy, 27, 82

urinary, xliv, liv, lvi–lvii, 28–29, 56–57, 61–64, 72, 83, 100, 132–134, 136–137, 140, 154, 196–197
urination, 56, 59, 62, 72, 76, 77, 96–101, 132–133, 139, 154, 185, 201 *see also*: mother
urine, 76, 123, 132, 134, 137, 154
   stream, 5, 154

Vernon, M., 21
Vogel, S., 130, 178
Vygotsky, L. S., 3, 7, 17–19

Waelder, R., 15, 23
walking, 36, 40–42, 53, 56, 68, 71, 95, 109, 124, 165, 203
Werner, H., 3, 7, 26, 50
Wilder, J., xlii
William Alanson White Group, xxxv
Wing, J., 192
Wing, L., 192
Winnicott, D. W., xlix, 44, 113, 116
witch(es), 180–181, 183, 186, 188
Wolf, M., 130
Wolff, P. H., 21, 26
Woodward, K., xxvi, xxxii
world
   external, 27
   inner, 76
   outer, 76, 112
   outside, liv, 127, 200, 205
World Association for Infant Mental Health, The, xx